131

D0897978

WEALTH FOR ALL

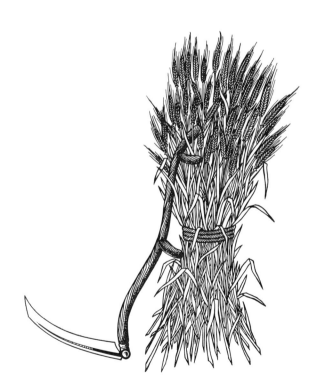

Books by R. E. McMaster, Jr.—

Cycles of War, The Next Six Years, 1977
The Trader's Notebook, 1978
The Trader's Notebook, 1979
The Trader's Notebook, 1980

Wealth for All, 1982
(Book 1—Religion, Politics and War)

Wealth for All, 1982
(Book 2—Economics)

WEALTH FOR ALL

Economics

R. E. McMaster, Jr.

A. N., Inc.
P. O. Box 67
Whitefish, Montana 59937
1982

Published by
A. N., Inc.
P. O. Box 67
Whitefish, Montana 59937

This book is dedicated to
Bob Thieme, Kurt Koch, Mickey Fouts, Richard Russell, Stuart Crane, R. J. Rushdoony and Gary North,
who provided me with both the insight and
the encouragement to pursue economic truth.

TABLE OF CONTENTS

OVERVIEW

The way the world really works is a far cry removed from the way the American public perceives it operates. Pleasant illusions are far more popular than painful facts. The normal state of affairs for each of us individually should be increasing wealth through time, natural tragedies and wars aside. Inheritance, free solar energy and cumulative technology in a *"fair play"* economic system should, in just one generation, provide each of us with such a substantial base of economic wealth, that we should then be free to pursue the development of our individual talents, which are not only in our own best self-interest but also in the best interest of society-at-large.

Cooperation should be the norm in our society, not conflict. Conflict and class warfare are harmful social mutations, stemming from a political and economic system that benefits a few special interests and exploits the masses. The age-old question of whose rights are superior, those of the individual or those of the group, is easily resolved to the benefit of both when a long-term perspective is enacted within the framework of a truly free market where individual men develop their talents, are responsible, and commodities are monetized on the local level.

Beyond question, the economic, political, social and environmental evils that exist today are a result of, and will disappear as soon as, each of us personally becomes responsible in every area of life. In truth, human misery today can be directly tracked to the failure of each of us, individually, to assume all of our personal responsibilities. Freedom, happiness, prosperity and security are all bound up in our willingness to assume our individual responsibilities. For example, the man who starts a business assumes responsibility for that business. He has accordingly also assumed risk. But he receives commensurate rewards with the assumption of responsibility and risk. He reaps the fruits of prosperity and maximizes his security also. After all, if the business fails, the owner of the business is the last one to lose his job. Thus the owner, the risk taker, has the greatest job security. So, assumption of risk and the security which Americans so desire today are one and the same. We are most vulnerable, by contrast, when we strive for security alone, as is overwhelmingly the case today.

The tremendous number of controls and programs which governments at all levels impose upon us today are an arrogant and proud attempt to stop time, the underlying assumption being that we *"know it all,"* that we can thus achieve security in an ever-changing world, and that further change and growth is unnecessary. Such pride goes before a fall. This is exactly what we should expect at the end of a 200-year national cycle and at the end of a 510-year civilization cycle.

The Great American Dream of *"rags to riches"* is a myth! The economic system is so constructed with booby traps, regulations, and incentives to assume debt, to be wasteful and short-term oriented, that it is next to impossible to succeed long-term. For the most part, those who have become wealthy today are either wealthy on paper, or have become prosperous through debt which, as articles in this *"Wealth for All"* series of books will show, not only contributes to inflation, but is directly harmful to society. They have promoted conflict and class warfare in the process. The system is so designed.

The present economic and political system is effectively, by design or negligent accident, bankrupting, enslaving and impoverishing us all, spiritually and materially. Americans live with the illusion of a high standard of living. The harsh reality, however, is that when debt obligations are considered, many, if not most of us, are in the red—technically bankrupt. With little or no understanding of economics and the financial curse of compound interest, Americans merrily skip along the road to slavery, calling it all the while the road to freedom. Unconcerned about a tax system which demands more of them than the Vietcong does of its slaves or feudal lords did of their serfs, each generation of Americans burdens the next with more debt as the productivity fleecing process continues ad infinitum.

There is no reason for enduring the economic burden we bear today. The economic and political logic of the Founding Fathers who built this great country is still applicable today. Human nature has not changed. Cause and effect still rules supreme. It is no accident that the United States of America became the most prosperous country on the face of the earth. It is a by-product of the economic and political rules under which our society operated. Those rules could just as easily be restored today, quickly returning us to *"Wealth for All."*

Wealth is seldom destroyed. Rather, it is transferred. There is a great deal of information in these two *"Wealth for All"* volumes about why very few are so rich and many are so very poor. It all boils down to special interests filling the vacuum of our personal irresponsibility, and violation of the principle that theft is wrong at all levels, including theft by government. This moral *"theft"* issue is a religious one.

The greatest resistance you personally will face to understanding *"Wealth for All"* and applying it in your own best self-interest **and** the best interest of society long-term will come from within you. You will be your own worst enemy. All of us like to feel secure in what we have learned, that what we have been taught is true. None of us likes to feel that we have been deceived. But Machiavelli warned us, *"One who deceives will always find those who allow themselves to be deceived."* Thus, the greatest psychological hurdle that you will face in overcoming your aversion to what follows is your natural resistance to change, and pride.

None of us likes to feel that we have been played for a sucker. The truth of the matter is, however, we all have been fooled. While our educational systems have been excellent when it comes to teaching us technical material and how to function in the factual world, by contrast, education today is a dismal failure when it comes to teaching us how to think, and in providing us with guiding abstract models about how the world really works. It is the conclusion of many who have watched the accuracy of the *"Wealth for All"* analysis through the years that too many Americans today are empty-headed, robot-like, nonthinking humanoids. Sadly, most Americans consistently act contrary to their own best interests long-term.

Why should you believe me? In addition to my track record and credibility established professionally, you need also to know that I have moved about in powerful circles. I have worked with the richest men in this country. I have interacted at the highest levels of government, all the way from the Shah of Iran to the White House. I have been able to call up and talk to any congressman or senator in the Republican Party. I've worked within the system. Sad to say, the system stinks, unless you are a willing bureaucrat or a manipulator at the top. What we suffer with today is a bad case of *"institutional constipation."* I was not able to unclog the system, working alone, within the system. But all of us, as individual plumbers, can free things up in no time at all.

Each article in each *"Wealth for All"* book is dated so that you will be able to discern the original date of publication as it appeared in THE REAPER, a newsletter. Very little editing has been done to the *"original"* piece. This is important. Why? There is an old proverb that states, *"Those who live close to the truth are seldom surprised by the future."* By leaving the *"original"* essay basically untouched and dated, you will see that the analyses and projections made have, in most applicable cases, come substantially true. There is your proof! Cling to it. You will know that what you are reading is true because the analyses and projections made at the time of *"original"* publication are, for the most part, now history. *"Those who live close to the truth are seldom surprised by the future!"*

Next, it is important that you understand my motivation behind producing this *"Wealth for All"* series of books. First of all, I'm fed up with seeing the trusting American people so totally and consistently deceived. Secondly, I want to help move our country back onto a constructive course. My intentions are in keeping with the understanding and discernment of some of the great minds who have built this country. Consider the following quotes:

> *"The minority, the ruling class at present, has the schools and press, usually the church as well, under its thumb. This enables it to organize and sway the emotions of the masses, and make its tool of them."*
> Albert Einstein

> *"I really look with commiseration over the great body of my fellow citizens, who, reading newspapers, live and die in the belief that they have known something of what has been passing in the world in their time."*
> Thomas Jefferson

> *"The press of this country is now, and always has been, so thoroughly dominated by the wealthy few of the country that it cannot be depended upon to give the great mass of the people that correct information concerning political, economic and social subjects which is necessary that they shall have in order that they shall vote and then act in the best way to protect themselves from the brutal force and chicanery of the ruling and employing class."*

Edward W. Scripps, founder of Scripps-Howard Newspapers.

At this point, you may well recall the timeless words of Abraham Lincoln:

> *"It is true that you may fool all the people some of the time; you can even fool some of the people all the time; but you can't fool all the people all the time."*

There has been enough foolishness in American society for too long.

Finally, these *"Wealth for All"* books are an attempt to head off a violent revolution in this country, the growing probability of which is almost beyond question at this point, the culmination of which would be the fulfillment of a long-ago, patiently laid plan. When economists tell us that the only effective way to fight inflation is to throw millions of people out of work, as economists admitted in the BUSINESS WEEK of February 22, 1982, we know the economic system is bankrupt. Inflation and/or unemployment lead to revolution. When respected political analysts tell us, *"The way the country is constituted now, the road to political authority and influence is less open to those of political genius. Opportunities to move up are somehow clogged by institutions,"* as William W. Abbot did in the U.S. NEWS of February 22, 1982, we know the political system is likewise bankrupt. The American public is increasingly politically frustrated and alienated. Alienation in a democracy leads to revolution. A bankrupt economic and political system is a revolution waiting to happen! But revolutions always lead to tyranny. So, to put it quite bluntly, our personal peace and prosperity in the remaining years of our lives and our children's lives depend directly upon our individual willingness to get involved and become responsible in all areas of our lives. Misery always eventually fills the vacuum of irresponsibility. There is no other way. There never has been. There never will be. Human nature has not changed.

The answer, ultimately, is spiritual. Correct religious assumptions precede accurate principles; these lead to clear thoughts and ideas, both written and verbal. These, in turn, result in productive and constructive deeds, leading to good habits, and a prosperous destiny for all of us. As Abraham Lincoln said, *"It is difficult to make a man miserable when he feels he is worthy of himself and claims kindred to the great God who made him."* In terms of our American Christian heritage, God himself solved the problem of eternal salvation for man through Jesus Christ. In terms of solutions in time, as heirs with Christ, we are responsible, and thus must be free to pursue and develop our God-given talents, not only so that His will for our lives will be fulfilled, but so that we will maximize our own best self-interest long-term. The will of God, and each of our own best self-interests, properly understood, are one and the same. Organized religion today, sad to say, has missed this basic point.

Again, under the principles of *"Wealth for All,"* increasing inheritance from generation to generation, free solar energy leading to increasing material abundance, and cumulative technology mean that economic welfare should not even be a consideration for us. Each of us, in a properly ordered economic and political system, should be so rich and secure that we're literally freed from nearly all basic economic considerations so that we can pursue the development of our individual talents from which all men will benefit. Such an encouraging economic system is practically possible today, promoting cooperation rather than conflict. Just as each snowflake is unique, so, too, are each of us uniquely created individuals who have a special contribution to make to our fellow man, promoting cooperation, harmony and peace in time.

"Wealth for All," the essay which appears at the beginning of each of these two volumes, is the summary statement. The two volumes under this *"Wealth for All"* umbrella are:

1. RELIGION, POLITICS AND WAR
2. ECONOMICS

Each book stands on its own. Yet each volume is also an integral part of *"Wealth for All."*

It is my deepest hope that the little time and effort you spend in working through both of these volumes will give you not only a clear understanding of how the world works, but also provide you with the factual and abstract basis upon which you will be able to personally prosper and make decisions that will again restore our country to the greatness which it once had, and as our ancestors intended, it deserves today.

R. E. McMaster, Jr.
August 2, 1982

WEALTH FOR ALL
(An Economic Manifesto)

10/16/81

Economics all boils down to two basic ingredients—land and labor. A well-watered, nutrient and mineral rich, humus-filled earth in a temperate climatic zone, populated by healthy, hard-working, future-oriented, free and creative individuals brings forth the best of all economic worlds.

The commodity futures market, overall, is one of the best lead indicators of future economic activity. Commodities, being the sensitive and volatile *urchins* they are, are like the tip of a whip. Their backlash carries all the way down to the whip's handle. The rural country (tip of the whip/commodities) eventually speaks to the cities (handle of the whip/mature, developed economic centers).

The laws of physics teach us that *energy* and *matter* are interchangeable, basically one and the same. As such, the *abstract* and *concrete* are one and the same in the real world in a never ending flow. This perspective is pregnant with economic truth. Economic exchange, thus, when you boil it all down, is nothing more than the exchange of goods and services, the swapping of *matter* (goods) for *energy* (services and labor) and vice versa. Money, in the sense of classical economic exchange (barter), is a real good, a commodity, *matter*, whether in the form of gold, silver, tobacco leaves, salt, barley, sea shells, wheat—all of which have historically served as money. Money is subsequently also **potential**, stored, inactive *energy*, ready to spring forth **kinetically** as the catalyst for the production of additional goods (*matter*) and services, the end product of the mixture of land and labor. Quickly, we, too, see that all honest money is ultimately a product of the land, a good, a resource, a commodity, *matter*, if you will. This viewpoint is consistent with the laws of thermodynamics, the basis of physics and the concrete application of theological truth. The first and second laws of thermodynamics state simply that *energy* is neither created nor destroyed (first law), but that when *energy* is transferred or used, useful *energy* is lost in the transition process (second law). The second law is referred to as entropy—that all things move toward a state of decay.

The first and second laws of thermodynamics hold true in a **closed**

1

system. While we appear to live in a closed system on this earth, we constantly are blessed with a new shot of *energy* each and every day, courtesy of the sun. So, in fact, we live in an **open** system. Because the sun provides us with new, real, useable *energy* each and every day, we have the opportunity to make real economic progress and create real new wealth by using working man's productive efforts to groom the earth and prevent the natural disorder which automatically occurs as the sun's *energy* creates new *matter*. The sun creates *matter* (real new wealth) on its own. But this newly created *matter* (real new wealth) will become disorderly and far less useful unless man takes dominion over it.

Real new wealth (*matter*) is created as new *energy* (solar) comes into the system. Grass, trees, and ocean vegetation grow freely. Cows, horses, sheep and fish eat the grass, leaves and algae and subsequently produce calves, foals, lambs and more fish. New *energy* creates new *matter*. Real new wealth is thus created. *Energy* in and *matter* out as the system goes. (*Matter* subsequently produces *energy*, too—wood, oil.) Solar *energy*, mixed with man's efforts, brings to harvest the fields of wheat, corn, oats, barley and soybeans—all of which are real new wealth. These grains grow randomly, utilizing just the *energy* of the sun. When hardworking productive man is added to the equation, aided by the blessing of favorable weather, production of grain protein explodes, as does meat protein. Man's dominion over animals short-circuits the *"law of the jungle."* It's a miracle. And it's ultimately free. The sun shines and also out pops the oranges, grapefruit, walnuts and pecans. Pineapples and bananas join the *"natural hit parade"* which feed man, providing him with the physical *energy* necessary to increase the bounty of new free wealth (greater agricultural production) or, for example, in the case of mining, harvest other natural resources which then create a virtual supermarket of economic goods (*matter*) for mankind.

After a lifetime of productivity, a man, if he has planned wisely, practiced deferred gratification and sexual restraint, gained wisdom and looked to the long-term, can leave a boatload of material goods to his lineage. So, ever-increasing wealth should be a normal state of affairs for mankind if he will only act consistent with his long-term self-interest. Man's long-term spiritual instincts must thus rule over his short-term animalistic desires if this wealth inheritance is to occur. So, multigenerational families are crucial for individual man's, and thus collective man's, increase in wealth.

Reward is also commensurate with responsibility. Parents take care of children. When the children grow up, they take care of their elderly parents with the family's resources. Turn about is fair play. Men have the incentive to work and save for their own future (old age), as well as for their children's. The incentive to raise secure, loved, happy, productive children is apparent. As a result, there is less crime, less taxes for police forces and less welfare, and so the entire society benefits psychologically, socially and materially. The destructive inheritance and property taxes are abolished. Women are important as mothers. (The hand that rocks the cradle rules the world.) Minorities are no longer displaced by women in the work force. Social Security is unnecessary. The *"throw-away"* society disappears, as do drugs, abortion and illegitimacy. Property rights are thus seen as necessary for human rights.

Finally, a culture's technological advancement is cumulative. Technological advancement in a free society finds higher, better and more efficient ways to utilize natural and human resources at less cost in less time. Technology, thus, is an additional creator of new wealth. The free market has given us the technology we enjoy today. Technology creates a shortage of labor, making people more valuable and necessary. Some day technology will provide us with a machine that creates excess energy. De Palma's, Jefimenko's or Maglich's prototypes refined?

In summary, natural catastrophes and personal tragedies aside, **wealth from the sun,** particularly when combined with man's efforts, **wealth from inheritance,** and **wealth from technology are all cumulative. Thus, the normal state of affairs for mankind collectively is increasing WEALTH FOR ALL through time.**

Given this perspective, doesn't it stand to reason that real money should be tied to real new wealth in order to prevent the curse of inflation, which the masses never recognize, due to their economic ignorance, until it's too late and the system is about to self-destruct (hyper-inflation) or crater into a depression (deflation). Money should be spent, not borrowed into existence, at the local level, equal to the amount of new wealth created and demanded by the market. (Monetarist theory is thus satisfied.) Free market money, commodity money, should be allowed to co-exist with government money as a check against government and to allow for freedom of choice. It is an unethical and immoral banking and economic system, as well as a destructive one long-term, that allows a few to become filthy rich at the expense of the masses, particularly when the few become filthy rich not due to any real productive increase of goods and services on their part which would benefit all of mankind, but rather due to speculation in *"zero sum games,"* use of other people's money without their direct approval or participation, and the paying of outrageous interest to a nonproductive middleman (banker). Isn't it logical that *"real"* money should only be created consistent with the creation of real new wealth as demanded? Wouldn't such a system provide a sound economic framework, a set of *"fair rules"* for the economic game, which would still stress incentive, reward the most productive, and encourage the most capable to prosper, but only when they served the best interest of the masses long-term, consistent with their own long-term self-interest? Doesn't it make sense that debt should only be short-term (less than seven years), that debt should be utilized for productive purposes only, such as for producing new goods and services, that debt should never be for consumption (short-term gratification) (supply side economics satisfied), and that debt should be free of the abstract, compounding rate of interest? When monetary interest is involved in an economic system, those who put up the money (bank deposits) for the economic activity are intellectually, and often geographically, removed from the economic venture. Thus, the natural check against misuse of investment funds is removed. The feedback loop, responsibility and accountability, is reduced. More economic boondoggles, embezzlements and other marginal, fraudulent economic activities are able to occur, all of which are contrary to *"the greatest good for the greatest number"* long-term. Also, *"interest"* does no work. Neither does it show mercy on *"trial and error"* man. It grinds on and on. It compounds. Eventually it consumes economic man. Such is the case today.

Economic reality is that the production of goods nearly always precedes the production of services. Goods first, services second is the natural order of things. How can it be otherwise? Unless there are basic goods provided to meet man's basic needs, such as food and shelter, which provide the necessary energy and protection for mankind, no services are produced. Furthermore, without goods (*matter*) produced in excess of that needed to sustain basic life, there would be no excess potential *energy* floating around in the economic system to produce the additional goods (*matter*) and services which make life so much more enjoyable. It is these enjoyable things, these things that make life more pleasant, which is what real wealth is all about.

Again, recall that all real new goods, all real new wealth, and, therefore, all real new money originates in the rural country. This is concrete reality. Wealth ultimately comes from the natural environment. Even great ideas (abstract) and energy require some matter (concrete) to come to economic fruition. But, while real new wealth (raw materials) ultimately comes from the rural country (natural environment), the highest and best use of labor through the division and specialization of labor, as well as the best abstract ideas that creatively find a way to utilize the earth's resources, are usually spawned in the cities' intellectual centers. The rural country is the resource pipeline to the city where the finished goods are usually created, where the resources are transformed for the higher satisfaction of man. Services follow. Goods and services proliferate as a result of the rural country's excess and the city's creativity and productivity combined with capital.

The city can (and usually does) become a parasite living off of the rural country, if it fails to stimulate new and better productivity within the voluntary division of labor. When the economic system gets out of balance, and there is no longer parity, no economic equality (fair play) between the rural country and the city, and when the city has devoured its country host (bankrupted the rural country through city welfare and the creation of money), the city then dies, too. This happens at the end of a civilization cycle. **This is why world cities are historically both the highest achievement, as well as the culmination, of a mature civilization.** It's *"truth in tension"* realized. We are now at the end of a 510-year cycle for Western civilization. We have some critical choices which must be made. It's either radical change for Western civilization or revolution and poverty. Take your pick. It will be one or the other. And, it will come within the next 20 years.

It's easy for the city to dominate the rural country. But it is in the city's self-interest **short-term only** to dominate the country. Intellectual power gravitates to, and expands synergistically in, the metropolitan complexes. Because thoughts precede action, because the pen is mightier than the sword, because the abstract in an ultimate sense rules the concrete, and because all these activities usually originate and take place primarily in the city, so the city rules over the rural country. On a day-to-day level, in our developed culture, we see this reality very clearly. Men in the cities, for the most part, work with their minds, getting rich, while their brothers in the country, toiling with their hands, become poor. The short-term, misguided, but historical rule of a civilization's progression is that men in the city get increasingly richer while those in the country decline into poverty, sustained only by loans, speculation and part-time jobs in the cities. This unfavorable skewing of economic wealth (a city becoming richer and richer while the country becomes poorer and poorer) is suicidal, because ultimately the country is the resource lifeline to the city. When the country, in its economic death throes, is forced to cut the resource lifeline to the city, the city dies and the entire civilization crumbles. This is where we are now in our civilization, at the end of the 510-year Western civilization cycle. So, events and time are *"square."*

The city's short-term perspective, that of raping the rural country, of ruthlessly gobbling up its resources at bargain prices and under-compensating its labor via the creating of money out of nothing (inflation) for short-term benefits, is a knife to the city's own jugular long-term. Long-term, the city cannot afford to bite the hand that feeds it, literally. Consistent with the laws of physical and economic reality, the city, in its own best interest **long-term**, should allow the country to be the original source of money. After all, the country produces money's true equivalent, real new wealth, which leads to real new goods and services. The sun, for now, is still the ultimate source of physical life and material wealth which is created in the rural country. Money is first and foremost a commodity, and only later a commodity substitute.

This economic subordination by the city to the country is difficult for the following reasons: Men in the city are, by and large, smarter, more intellectual than their brothers in the country. Thus, they are more fit to lead, plan and dictate to their country brothers. Marx called farmers effectively the *"rural idiocy."* So, it is difficult for city men to become subordinate to their intellectual inferiors, country folk. It is contrary to man's pride. But pride, long-term, always leads to destruction. When men are proud, they do not/cannot listen, and thus do not learn, change, adapt or grow. They suffer and die in an everchanging world. Established institutions, like government, are the ultimate manifestations of pride, terribly slow to listen or change. Pride is short-term, and men today, just like throughout history, are predominantly proud and thus short-term oriented. They are just more so today, as one would expect to be the case, at the end of a 510-year civilization cycle. A short-term orientation is an animalistic character trait. Animals are short-term, fact oriented, non-thinking creatures which **react** to concrete reality, with no ability to contemplate the long-term, abstract realm. This is man's tendency, too. Greed is also a short-term orientation, in violation of the wealth-creating, long-term, economic law that *"self-interest is best served by service long-term."* (Classical economics is satisfied—the *"unseen hand."*) Greed is now pervasive in the cities. Cities are the home ground of the *"rat race,"* where men scramble greedily to get rich quick at all costs.

It flies in the face of human nature to believe that the cities will automatically humble themselves economically, in accordance with economic law, before their basic country brothers. After all, through the thinking genius of the cities come the abstract ideas which lead to patents, technology **and weapons**, produced from country resources, which can and do have the ability to overpower the rural country in the twinkling of an eye. Perhaps city men should earn more. Thinking, creative men are always the bosses of labor. But, city men should not, in their own short-term self-interest, be allowed to fraudulently create money. They have not created new wealth. Thus, to prevent this natural tendency toward self-destruction, a **moral** framework must be socially established (abstract separation of church and state is impossible) for the economic system to allow all members of society to prosper long-term, their individual economic achievement consistent with their individual temperaments, talents, convictions, abilities and production. In the marketplace, whoever meets the public's needs best, profits most. Race is never a significant factor.

In a way, the commodity futures market is the ultimate slap in the face to the rural country. Thinking men get rich in the cities trading paper commodities which represent real commodities produced in the country. Meanwhile, the real producers of commodities in the country go broke working with their hands. Country folks slowly, but surely, slide into poverty. Country folks are forced to buy everything they need at retail, while selling all they produce at wholesale. Thus, country people can only become increasingly impoverished, particularly as long as favorable weather for crop production exists and farm revolts do not occur. (Bad weather hastens poverty.) Eventually, the resource lifeline to the city (country excess) is effectively cut, the city disintegrates, and the whole civilization falls.

Decentralization of city industries, mixing them in with the country's real new wealth production, would provide a practical, healthy balance for an economy long-term. It also should be obvious now that the creation of money out of thin air (inflation), whether by using the printing press, the Federal Reserve's monetizing of the federal deficit, credit cards, or through the creation of credit via the fractional reserve banking system—all of these economic heresies are creations of the cities. These money-creating shenanigans are foreign and antagonistic to sound, long-term, progressive economic reality.

It should come as no surprise that these economic heresies are all spawned in the cities. Cities are historically the production centers of heresies. It should be evident why banks have the nicest buildings and structures downtown, too. Bankers get rich, short-term, until economic reality comes knocking at their doors. The miracle of compound interest, while a windfall blessing for the banker short-term, is a curse for all of mankind long-term. The love of money is the root of all evil. Banks and bankers, OPM-types and governments love money. But, bankers cut their own throats with their fractional reserve banking system because, while they prosper for awhile, the system itself is ultimately inflationary. And so, in the terminal stages of inflation, bankers usually lose big as the rates they charge for money can no longer keep up with the rate of inflation, or they get whipsawed in booms or busts, or make bad loans and investments, or are subject to a bank *"run."* Finally, the piper is paid, and the bankers are strung up from the lamp post, right along-side their cohorts, the OPM-types and the politicians. What we are talking about is a revolution. This happens in a small way at the end of every 50-year economic cycle, and in a major way at the end of the 510-year civilization cycle. We are at the end of both. Avoid harm's way. Being a banker, an entrepreneural OPM-type who has become undeservedly enriched (thanks to inflation) via the use of the economic assets of ignorant others, or a cooperating politician are the most high-risk occupations going at this late stage of our civilization.

It almost goes without saying that for men to be creative, productive and responsible, they must be free, subject only to natural and moral law. And this means free of government. When government is the central planner, it is looked to, to be responsible for the welfare of all the people, to plan creatively for their futures, and direct productive enterprises. But, we see that experientially government fails miserably in the Soviet Union and its satellites such as Poland. Government is a parasite, an overhead expense. It can only take from some first and then redistribute to others. The larger the government, the bigger the parasite. The bigger the parasite, the closer the civilization is to its demise. If government bureaucrats were creative and could correctly anticipate the future (plan), they would be risk-oriented entrepreneurs. Government is an overhead expense, which, once it has redistributed all of society's wealth, with an ever-increasing take for itself, breaks the economic back of the society.

A strong central government effectively enslaves its citizens through bureaucratic regulations. Slaves, like children, react and are short-term oriented. Therefore slaves and children are pretty much one and the same, both uncreative, both unthinking, and neither free. And, they are neither productive nor responsible. So government, particularly the federal government, must be minimized, not only so that the free division of labor will be enhanced, consistent with each individual man's unique talents, but so that man will also be free to become creative, productive and responsible, to succeed, **or** to suffer the pain of failure which negatively reinforces a lack of initiative, which negatively reinforces a lack of creativity, and which negatively reinforces laziness and irresponsibility. Without government support, without a federal government *"safety net,"* men are forced to grow up, to accept the responsibility of freedom. They can no longer be children or slaves. They have to think and grow. This is particularly enhanced in a decentralized environment. Man and men, individually and collectively, are always better off when they accept responsibility in all areas of their lives. For example, welfare payments (taxes) to Washington are out-of-sight and out-of-mind. A man who is forced, however, to give his hard-earned money to a lazy neighbor is liable to revolt, to put him to work mowing his lawn. This is why decentralized government provides *"the greatest good for the greatest number"* **long-term.** The waste, fraud, laziness and overhead of the government bureaucracy is cut in a decentralized system. Furthermore, the federal government can then concentrate on its sole priorities—national defense and internal peace and justice maintenance.

We are so blind. The same advice we give to the underdeveloped Third World countries, which, if they apply it, brings them prosperity, applies equally to us. In Third World countries, even in the cities, the jobless rate is very low. If people don't work, they starve. Unemployment is voluntary. Folks become responsible in a hurry. Minimum food amounts to an effective check on population growth. They are, thus, very much in touch with economic reality. They work. And the whole economy benefits. *"The greatest good for the greatest number"* kicks in. This theological truth, that if a man doesn't work, he doesn't eat, has been violated historically by mature cities, which not surprisingly, were/are, the center of religious heresies (Alexandria, Babylon, Rome, London and New York). Yes, consistent with the economic laws, truths and realities that we have discussed above, is the perspective, from the labor side of the equation, that simply, if a man doesn't work, he doesn't eat (local, decentralized charity excluded in cases of real need). It takes work, both mental and physical work, the sweat of men's brows, to prosper economically and maximize real wealth for the *"greatest good for the greatest number"* long-term.

The earth is cursed in a sense. It is miserly (disorderly) in that it does not readily produce all the wheat, oats, barley, sheep, cattle, fish, bananas, pineapples or coconuts we want on its own without our effort (our expended physical energy). So, abstract theological truth must be used in harmony with concrete economic reality for real wealth to increase for all of mankind. Cities, the highest and best source of abstract ideas, try to play God. That is why cities are also the centers of government. Government is a parasite which attempts to play the role of God as it creates something (money) (laws) out of nothing. Government also says that if a man doesn't work, he can still eat (food stamps). Cities are the source of these short-term, unrealistic, abstract, social welfare ideas that create social friction. The warped, abstract, short-term, theological heresies of the city produce a distorted economic fantasy land that cannot survive long-term. The laws of cause and effect, of equal and opposite action and reaction, come into play long-term. For, during tough economic times, the people in the cities suffer the most. They receive, in kind, economic retribution for their easy, parasitic, good times. For, city folks can't produce the basics of life. When the economic chickens come home to roost long-term, the people in the city suffer miserably. They can't feed themselves.

Michael Lipton, in his book, WHY POOR PEOPLE STAY POOR, observed that in the poor Third World developing countries **investment in the agricultural sector of the economy brings investment returns (real new wealth) three times higher than those in other parts of the developing economy.** Is this scientific observation consistent with the principles we have delineated previously? Of course. Reality rules long-term in all cultures. Folly can only last for a short while. The cities of mature Western civilization are growing folly centers, and unnecessarily so. When resources in Third World countries are poured into the cities (the potential parasite) rather than into the host (the rural areas), this misallocation of resources leads to overcrowding in the cities, rural stagnation and poverty, followed by general poverty in the entire nation. Isn't this exactly what we are witnessing in our own nation now? Can't we learn from the Third World's example? Can't we learn from our own history? A healthy civilization develops its rural, raw material resources, and then, next, its cities. The cities pump out productive ideas, products and services in a low-cost, efficient division of labor way, which benefits the rural country. But the city, even though it is able to economically and intellectually dominate the rural country, refuses to do so. It also refuses to be the creator of money. Instead, it returns to its roots, the rural country, and establishes its industries there in the country, thereby promoting decentralization, responsibility and freedom. Decentralization, responsibility and freedom are all linked in the vital long-term chain and perspective which promotes *"Wealth for All."*

Now let's turn and attempt to grasp the economic importance of the recent devastating decline in commodity prices. The late Carl H. Wilken, an American farm economist, proved that a definite link exists between the value of farm products and national income. Wilken's evidence suggested that **real new wealth created in the economy multiplied itself seven times as it worked its way through the economy.** (There is that *"magic"* number *"seven"* again.) Put simply, $1.00 of farm income generates $7.00 of other income. Also, a 1% increase in unemployment results from a 1% drop in farm income, according to Wilken's studies. Wilken stated that the only factor that remains consistent with the earned profits and savings of a nation as a whole is the total price paid for all the raw material production. Agriculture is the largest source of this new wealth. And, as discussed previously, this new wealth is renewable and additional thanks to the sun. When combined with the savings, creative thoughts and hard work of free men, it generates increased wealth year after year. What we are dealing with here is the multiplier effect which works for the benefit of all mankind. What a folly it is for man to chain himself to the lazy, uncreative, multiplier effect of compound interest, which enriches only a parasitic few, unjustly so for awhile, but which causes rampant instability, encourages short-term ill-advised speculation, leads to moral corruption and the destruction of governments, and impoverishes the masses long-term.

When the price of raw materials drops, there is an exact ratio decline in terms of national income. There is also a commensurate increase in debt expansion and unemployment according to Wilken. Economic good times are multipled by abundant production of real new wealth. Economic bad times are magnified by declining raw material production and debt assumption. Again, Wilken purported that the total national income is five to seven times the annual price paid for all raw material production. Thus, real new wealth, economic parity, ties real money directly into its production as demanded. Stability and prosperity result long-term. Then, there is no need for banks in their present sense, for the purpose they exist today, to loan money.

It is well documented that multinational banks today are contrary to the best interests of mankind long-term. Multinational banks provide the capital, through loans, which finance the multinational corporation ventures in communist countries (the USSR, China and Angola for examples), that allows and encourages communism to survive. Furthermore, multinational banks provide loans directly to the communists so the communists can build the capital facilities necessary to produce the weapons to not only enslave their people, but also the masses of the earth, eventually destroying us. Finally, adding insult to injury, multinational banks, by providing the capital for the industrial plants built in the communist countries, eliminate American jobs. The slave labor which works in industrial plants in communist countries (or countries reconstructed after a war) can produce cheaper goods and services than those produced on the free market by free men in Western civilization. So, the deposits the free working man makes in a multinational bank go to finance his own economic self-destruction, if not political destruction, long-term. And where are these multinational banks located? In the big cities!

Banks should be transformed into decentralized warehouses, joint venture, partnership and stock centers, where men with land, labor, ideas and capital of all types meet in order to structure productive economic enterprises, exclusive of (void of) monetary *"interest."* If monetary capital, money, is poorly invested in a joint venture, partnership or a stock, its unproductive use is limited to this misguided venture. No monetary *"interest"* hangover remains to curse man in future time. In other words, the budget is balanced. The laws of thermodynamics control. An economic check and balance is created by limiting the poor use of labor, capital, money, land, etc. to a unique venture or organization on a *"pay as you go"* basis. This economic isolation, thus, keeps men from being cursed by the mistakes of their forefathers in generations down the line. It is no accident that it has been historically proven that debt is long-term detrimental to any enterprise. It's clear cause and effect. Furthermore, because money earns no *"interest,"* men are forced to carefully look for productive economic ventures in which to invest their money in order to increase their wealth. This, too, benefits all mankind because better decision-making occurs. Men become individually responsible and thus accountable for the investment of their excess funds. No devious, indifferent, dishonest, uninformed, incompetent, undiscerning or corrupt banker or OPM-type is left to make the decision as to what economic ventures do or do not deserve an infusion of capital.

Money is power. Power corrupts. Politics is power. Power corrupts. Money and politics combined is absolute power corrupting absolutely in a ruthless, evolutionary *"king of the hill,"* *"law of the jungle"* way. This is why the connection between banking, business and politics in an evolutionary-biased culture such as ours is so apparent, and also so corrupt. Absolute power corrupts absolutely. Is this in the interest of *"the greatest good for the greatest number"* long-term? No. In the best interest of the individual? No way.

Finally, a man can save his money if he wishes, to spend, for his children, or until a good investment comes along. The pressure to *"earn interest,"* which leads to poor investments via deposits in banks, is thus absent. Patience, a virtue, is instead practiced. While such saving is penalized in the sense that wealth-creating opportunities are bypassed, this is a short-term perspective. Saving, and effectively stopping time in this way, allows man the time to research, reflect, and then decide upon the very best economic investments. Because man, with a stable monetary system, is able to *"stop time,"* he is not moving backward short-term, financially, as a result of his failure to *"earn interest."* Again, the pressure to *"earn interest"* short-term leads to the pressure to invest money short-term. And short-term decision making is nearly always against the best interest of man long-term.

Interest on money borrowed is a treadmill working against error-prone man. Booms and busts are brought about by the expansion and contraction of credit. Most men miss the turning points. Debt is a form of slavery. An interest/debt-free economic system provides for the *"greatest good for the greatest number"* long-term. The all too popular OPM method (Other People's Money), which has mush-roomed as never before in these inflationary times, leading to booms and busts, is strictly limited under a *"non-interest"*-oriented financial system. Instead, real economic return is more closely tied to an individual's real productivity, involvement, assumption of responsibility and accountability. The tendency for a few to become very, very rich because they are clever, due to currency speculation, at the expense of the economically ignorant masses, by borrowing to purchase or create assets particularly during inflationary times, is thus checkmated. Thus, the probability of revolution is sharply reduced.

Revolution is spawned when there are a very few rich and many poor in a society. Such income disparity always occurs in inflationary times. This is the breeding ground of communism, too. But, we have already seen that communism is government, an overhead expense, a parasite, playing the role of God. Communism leads to mass misery and economic poverty everywhere. It has been conclusively shown that communism can only survive as long as a free market and free economy exists to support it. This is why Russia depends upon Western loans, technology and grain. If communism ever became the world's government, there would be no way of determining the value of anything, either. Price (reflecting value) is only determined in a free market between buyers and sellers. Under communism, men, with no incentive to get ahead, maximize their self-interest by being lazy and moonlighting. Furthermore, because communism, if it became the worldwide government, is a parasite, civilization would self-destruct. The parasite would have totally devoured the host. At best, a massive slave state would exist.

Entrepreneurs get rich using other people's money (OPM). They do this with money borrowed from banks on which they pay interest. They are, thus, not accountable directly to the providers of the capital (money). It is a far better system, more just and equitable, as well as conducive to individual growth and responsibility, for entrepreneurs to deal directly, by way of joint ventures, partnerships, or stock issues, with those who have the capital. This is why the raising of money for projects through these methods, not by borrowing, is far more economically prudent and fair. There is more accountability, more checks and balances against abuses which may be the modus operandi of greedy, unethical, short-term oriented entrepreneurs. Entrepreneurs still have the incentive to be productive. They can structure the deal any way they wish. Banks are thus cut out, save maybe a service or finder's fee, and are not allowed to be pyramiding parasites, particularly via the fractional reserve banking system. The productive efforts of small men are thus rewarded in this way, as opposed to being penalized through the OPM system. Labor, thus, has a stake and sees a common self-interest with management and entrepreneurs. Labor unions, which fight management and discriminate against other workers, disappear. (Marx is satisfied.) Jobs are created by men with foresight, entrepreneurs, who start businesses to meet consumers' needs. Entrepreneurs cannot be *"educated,"* because education teaches about the present and the past. Entrepreneurs deal with the future, and so are key. Entrepreneurs must be protected and encouraged.

Geographic proximity is desirable to enhance the checks and balance system. With geographic distance comes greater economic foolishness. The way that money is spent at the local and state level, as opposed to the federal level, is a good example of this.

With decentralized government, and money spent, not borrowed into existence consistent with the demanded production of real new wealth, taxes all but disappear. A *"head tax,"* encouraging family fidelity and sexual restraint, and/or a *"flat tax"* on income encouraging saving and production (long-term benefits), are best. The non-productive efforts of all the tax CPAs and attorneys, as well as the IRS, are eliminated. Local men, women, local churches, schools and local civic groups meet the health, education and welfare needs of the local people. Thus, the human condition, psychologically, socially and economically, is enhanced. Real meaning in life comes from relationships with people who assume responsibility. And, the health, education and welfare needs are met more efficiently, with all the concomitant local checks and balances, on the local level. Taxes, then, on the federal level are only needed for defense against all enemies, foreign and domestic. Taxes are also for a well-run court system that settles disputes and brings criminals to justice, preferably on the local level, with equality under law.

With the decentralized, constitutional, local militia concept, foreign wars cannot be fought, young men cannot be butchered, a world empire cannot be built, the federal government is held in check, and there is no incentive for multinational banks and corporations to finance and promote wars for the purpose of the economic destruction of a foreign power, so they can then finance the reconstruction effort and make tremendous profits, by lending money, earning interest and rebuilding industry. Nor is there the waste and all the expense of the outdated, expensive, unnecessary military/industrial defense systems. The military item works or it is not purchased. Esprit de corps is also enhanced when a locally-manned militia elects its own qualified officers. A dangerous professional military, which is always a coup threat, is eliminated. Wars have difficulty getting off the ground where there is free trade in open markets. Men have no reason to fight with other men who enrich them through the exchange of goods and services. Wars destroy wealth. Wars are inflationary.

At the end of 1945, banks were only lending about 17¢ of every dollar deposited. Bankers used their political clout in Washington to change this general public prosperity. A few years later, at the end of 1952, banks were lending out only approximately 37¢ of every dollar deposited. They again protested to the politicians and used their political influence to gain *"most favored status."* In 1952, when the Farm Act of 1952 was enacted, the Steagall Amendment was effectively eliminated. The Steagall Amendment had provided 90% parity for farmers. Its purpose was primarily to ensure a stable dollar, **not** to benefit basic agricultural producers. (Farmers are always behind the economic curveball because they buy at retail and sell at wholesale.) The November, 1980 issue of ACRES, U.S.A. reported:

> *"The cumulative loss to realized net farm income, small business income, rental income and corporate income from 1952 to 1979 is an incredible $2,428.8 billion with the largest loss—$977.4 billion—attributed to realized net farm income alone.*
> *"The dollar loss to the private sector was off-set by the increase in the public debt of the nation, from $500 billion in 1950 to an estimated $4.8 trillion in 1979. The difference between the loss of $2,428.8 billion and the public debt of $4.8 trillion can be largely accounted for in 28 years of accumulated interest." [Emphasis added]* [1]

What does all this mean to us? It means that real new wealth and money can only be created first in the rural country where the real new *energy* (solar energy) is converted into *matter* and harvested, and then transferred to the city where creative, abstract ideas can be applied to transform this new *matter* into its highest and best use with a minimum of labor under the free division of labor. The illusion under which we suffer today is the false *"wealth"* created primarily by the fractional reserve banking system in the cities through debt and compound interest. Debt and compound interest is to economics what abortion is to life. Compound interest, an abstract concept, which, theoretically, can increase to infinity, is an ever-heavy anchor which pulls down and impoverishes finite, limited, economically ignorant, error-prone, common man. *" 'It may take 20 years, but we're going to see the emergence of a national banking system.' "* (THE WALL STREET JOURNAL 10/7/81) If so, we're approaching the end of the age of the financial dinosaur. Wealth and money, first created in the rural country, are true and honest on both an abstract and concrete level. Wealth and money, first created in the city, are illusions and shams which cannot last long. Reality comes home to roost for us, here and now. The 1981 net farm income, in uninflated dollars, was the lowest since The Great Depression.

The reality of life is that few men perceive, much less act, in their own best self-interest long-term (enlightened Christians, libertarians and conservatives aside). Acting in one's long-term interest in all areas is rare. Collectively, men are undisciplined. Thus, collectively, men, by acting in their own self-interest short-term (selfishness), act contrary to the best interest of those they affect and interact with long-term, as well as often short-term, in addition to acting against their own self-interest long-term. The rise and fall of nation after nation, civilization after civilization, attests to this pitiful fact. Governments always gleefully fill this destructive vacuum, created by a short-term orientation which is usually joined by irresponsibility. Governments always fill the vacuum of irresponsibility. Men who lust for power over other men are drawn to government like moths to a flame. Government power feeds their insecurities. Politicians and bureaucrats are seldom strong enough individually, much less collectively, to realize that they lead best from behind, that they lead best by serving, and that the public will adore them and give them endless power if they don't need or abuse it, and, instead, return it (power) by way of freedom and service to the people. A necessary check against power-lusting politicians is to allow only those who pay taxes and receive no government benefits to vote. Privilege is then commensurate with responsibility, and social conflict brought about by envy, brought about by wealth redistribution programs, legislated by politicians elected by the nonproductive members of society, is alleviated.

Government power fills the vacuum and assumes the responsibility of personal, and then collective, irresponsibility. Yet government is an overhead expense, a parasite, which lives off the host of productive, responsible free men until it devours them and the system comes unglued. ATLAS SHRUGGED.

What we have done in this manifesto is present a structural, moral framework whereby men are positively reinforced for acting in their own self-interest long-term and negatively reinforced for acting in their own self-interest short-term. When men collectively follow their natural, animalistic tendencies to secure the satisfaction of their own self-interests short-term, like animals, they exercise the *"law of the jungle"* and the *"survival of the fittest."* Man is pitted against man in cut-throat competition. The weak fall by the wayside. This is why neither communism (socialism) or debt capitalism works. Neither meets the criteria of providing for *"the greatest good for the greatest number"* long-term, nor for the individual. Every man is important. Every man has something to contribute. The miracle of the long-term view, and in fact the greatest achievements of civilization are made through the voluntary cooperation by free men in the free market's division of labor, where each man does what he does best, whatever he so chooses to do, for which he is rewarded by profits if the people value his service or buy his product. The marketplace does not discriminate racially. Production is what counts. A man is rewarded because, consistent with the long-term view, a man sees that his own *"self-interest is best served by service to others."* Thus, with the long run perspective, both collective human good and self-interest are not only served, but both are maximized. The *"greatest good for the greatest number"* is resolved to the benefit of the individual, too. The individual and the group both benefit because the individual, by meeting the economic requirements of the group, profits, and thus serves his own self-interest. Competition to serve others in the marketplace thus becomes, in the long-term, cooperation within the framework of the division of labor in the free market. Monopolies, always created by government, corrupt this natural perfection. All the destructive side effects, all the regulatory, physical, psychological and sociological damage done to mankind, individually and collectively, disappear when the short-run perspective is abandoned. **Evil is men doing what they consider right in their own eyes, short-term. Good is men acting in their own self-interest long-term.** The long-term view results in a full cup overflowing, self-actualization as Maslow would call it, resulting in *"the greatest good for the greatest number"* and the maximum achievement for the individual, as wealth for *"one"* becomes a by-product of *"Wealth for All."*

*   *   *

"He shall lend to thee, and thou shalt not lend to him: he shall be the head, and thou shalt be the tail." Deuteronomy 28:44

Wealth for All: Added Confirmation
11/6/81

One of the critical threads of truth running throughout *"Wealth for All"* is that the economic viability of the rural country is critical for the entire civilization's economic health. Enlightened bank-dominated governments realize this and so they subsidize (enslave/feudalize) the farmers to ensure that enough food is produced to feed those in the cities. Romania and Poland are not so blessed with such *"enlightened"* governments. In September, Romanian farmers were ordered, in no uncertain terms, to increase their food production for people in the cities. Now, a few months later, an AP release from Bucharest, Romania is head-lined with the title, *"Threat of Imprisonment Calms*

Panic Buying by Romanians.'' (typical for a tyrannical state) The AP
release read,

> *"An anti-hoarding edict that threatens greedy shoppers with
> five years in prison is restoring calm to markets plagued by short-
> ages and bad food, the government says . . .*
>
> *"The government restricted sales of sugar, cooking oil and butter
> last Friday, and warned that anyone caught with more than a
> month's supply of basic foodstuffs could be jailed for five years.''*[2]

Two quick observations:

1. When the economic free market of a nation deteriorates,
particularly agriculture, the city dies. We are seeing the proof of
this pudding in Romania and Poland now. And, since the communist bloc countries are economically dependent upon Western
civilization, we would expect such trouble and economic chaos in
the communist parasites first, a preview of coming attractions for
Western civilization.

2. The conservative, constitutionally oriented western United
States are heavily populated by Mormons. Can anyone imagine
the Mormons, who are asked by their religion to store up a year's
supply of food, giving up their foodstuffs in an economic crisis if
such an edict is issued by our federal government (ex post facto
aside)? Not likely, particularly as well organized and well armed
as the Mormons are.

On October 16th, Poland's government agreed to freeze food
prices. The food price freeze was a result of strike alerts and wildcat
strikes over food shortages in eight provinces.

Since then, there have been strikes or strike threats in 28 of Poland's
49 provinces over food shortages. A general strike was staged on October 28th over the lack of food. Poland has gone back to real money—
barter with the likes of tobacco and alcohol. From the THE WALL
STREET JOURNAL, quoting a Pole, *"Money no longer matters."*

Warsaw, Poland is not so pretty these days. It's disturbing to contemplate the fact that the only thing that successfully distracts hungry
men and women from their biological distress, is a greater biological
threat, that of death in war. Recent civil unrest in Romania and
Poland is a catalyst for war.

Now, let's turn to our own country. Farmers have been sustained in
recent years by loans collateralized by farmland which has been increasing in value. Now that farmland values are only rising slowly,
and declining in many locations, lenders are increasingly unwilling or
unable to finance or refinance farmers'. operating capital. Expect
agricultural bankruptcies to soar, or increasing government control.

Agricultural prices, adjusted for inflation, are at Great Depression
levels. A farmer receives $2.30 for a bushel of corn which costs him

$3.10 to grow; he receives $3.60 a bushel for wheat which costs him $5.30 a bushel to raise. Agriculture is a bankruptcy waiting to happen. The farmer has only been able to hang on the past few years thanks to increased credit lines supported by ever-inflating agricultural land prices. But this land strength has now run out, too.

Is the government likely to act? No, not until the crisis is as bad as it has become in Romania and Poland, when the city folks scream bloody murder, figuratively and literally, at the politicians. Governments, parasites that they are, seldom anticipate. They only react when the crisis is upon them.

Those of us who are future oriented cannot get a hearing. We're not powerful like the industrial, establishment religion, labor, education and government leaders. But these powerful folks are primarily concerned with the here and now, and so they seldom anticipate the future. Nearly all our institutions are geared toward a day-to-day, short-term view. Antagonistic to the free market, which historically is the best anticipator of future demands, and which is by nature long-term oriented, these establishment giants, by contrast, seek to effectively stop time, promote the maintenance and status quo of the organization, promote bureaucracy, false security, government subsidies and monopolies, limit *"competition,"* and minimize risk. An early awakening by the general population to this problem is unlikely because, as a result of Machiavellian planning decades ago, the masses, too, are brain-washed, possessed of a short-term view.

Are food shortages on the horizon? Will there be riots in the cities? Count on it. Purchases of bulk wheat and a wheat grinding mill are highly recommended, as is food storage, the development of a garden, a greenhouse and the purchase of milk goats and chickens, both of which are very efficient protein producers and require a limited amount of space.

Wealth for All: City vs. Country Breakdown
11/6/81

*"Food is rotting in **rural Ghana** while an estimated 4 of every 5 children in the capital, are suffering from malnutrition, according to one of the country's leading doctors.*

"Herman Odoi, head pediatrician at the Princess Marie-Louis Children's Hospital, said the mortality rate for the cases of nutritional deficiencies that reach the hospital had doubled since 1977.

*"Dr. Odoi says a **major reason for the deterioration is the acute food shortage and rapidly rising food prices brought about by Ghana's general economic decline. Food is abundant in rural areas,***

with frequent reports of produce rotting on farms rendered inaccessible by washed-out bridges and impassable roads." [Emphasis added]

Source—Daily News Digest, Box 39850, Phoenix, Arizona 85069,
from Reuters

This breakdown in the Third World may be a preview of what is coming our way. Our interstate highway distribution system is deteriorating rapidly. Now, 9% of our interstate system is in *"poor"* shape; over 50% of the pavement will need replacing by the end of the 1980s; only 63% of the roads are in *"good"* condition now; 40% of the bridges are *"functionally obsolete"* or *"structurally deficient"* at the present time. Where is the money going to come from to finance these billions of dollars of repairs when the federal government, the states, the cities and the corporations are all battling for the same limited capital supply? The money simply won't be available unless *"Wealth for All"*-type changes are made. Otherwise, we will duplicate the same downhill spiral as Ghana, with starving cities isolated from the food producing country.

Wealth for All: The Ultimate Fallout
6/18/82

Today, the only real new free wealth we have still comes from the sun. Thanks to the sun, energy is translated into real new matter, which is real new wealth (money). Thus, the supply of money can ever be increased in society because real new wealth is continuously being created through solar energy. Commodities, monetized at the local level by the free market, on demand, should be a source of new money. This new real money, created at the local level, will lead to political decentralization, a dispersion of population from the cities, and more freedom for man. (Freedom and a free market in money go hand in hand.)

The finer, important things in society are only realized when there is excess capital (wealth) available. For example, primitive societies do not have the capital (wealth) to attempt to solve water and air pollution problems or finance such things as medical research and development. Western civilization, by contrast, has been able to attack these issues, which greatly impact the quality of life, because the capital surplus in Western civilization has made such *"quality of life"* advancements possible. That the financing of such important areas has been cut back in recent years is not so much a result of political action, as it is a consequence of present economic necessity. We have squandered our capital base through wasteful bureaucracies, centralization, loaning (giving) of our wealth abroad, financing our enemies, and wealth redistribution programs.

The long-term solution to the *"quality of life"* desires of man is ultimately bound up with the *"Wealth for All"* concept. With the abolition of debt capitalism, and the resultant demise of alienating compound interest, the balance between *"quality of life"* priorities and the economic realities of free enterprise will be more easily met. When *"the people,"* through stock ownership, partnerships and joint ventures (not debt), directly own and thus are directly involved with all capital intensive economic projects in this country, then economic self-interest, environmental and social issues will become one and the same for society. The free enterprise owners of factories and power plants (the people), for example, will decide more equitably the economic trade-offs between such things as air pollution and rate of return. Both of their interests will be vitally at stake. A sane, reasonable solution will be found.

Finally, by having real new wealth monetized at the local level, the inefficiencies, not to mention the corruption (inflation) of debt created out of thin air, will disappear. Excess capital will accumulate due to greater human efficiencies brought about by cooperation in the free market, stored real new wealth generated each year from solar energy, cumulative technology in the civilization, and the increased wealth generated through inheritance. This will allow man the extensive capital base necessary to more freely spend on the *"marginal"* economic areas of life, the *"quality of life"* items. Put more simply, once this wealth base is more greatly created and distributed freely throughout all of society, and the basic economic and recreational needs of man are met, man will look for some place else to spend (invest) his money (the Third World). This will make capital (money) available to finance the *"quality of life"* projects to an extent never before seen in human history.

The ultimate fallout should be in the development of human potential. Under the *"Wealth for All"* system, since man's basic economic needs will be met, man will be free as never before to develop his talents, which will in turn benefit society. Cooperation will be enhanced as free men exchange the *"fruits"* of their developed talents. With the welcome death of international debt capitalism, and a return to political decentralization, international economic free trade will again be able to rapidly expand, leading to enhanced world-wide cooperation and harmony. The Third World will follow our example. They still look to us to lead. The communist systems will fail, by economic default.

THE WHEAT RESERVE
by
Dr. Stuart Crane

5/29/81

I own a wheat elevator (bank). Farmers store wheat (gold) in my elevator. A farmer puts 100,000 bushels of wheat in my elevator. I issue him a wheat receipt (gold receipt) for 100,000 bushels. Other farmers store 20,000, 10,000, 15,000 or 18,000 bushels of wheat in my elevator. I issue all of them receipts for wheat. Some farmers take their wheat out of my elevator and sell it or use it. Others sell their wheat, but the wheat remains in my elevator. They actually sell their wheat receipts. Most farmers find they can take their elevator receipts, their wheat receipts, and buy things with them. They may exchange them also. Are these farmers buying and selling wheat? No, they are buying and selling receipts **for** wheat.

Now, since I run my own elevator I notice something about it. Farmers bring wheat in and take wheat out. Sometimes I have one million bushels of wheat in storage, sometimes 800,000 bushels, sometimes 600,000 bushels, but I **never** have less than 300,000 bushels of wheat in my elevator. Farmers are coming and going all the time, but there are always 300,000 bushels of wheat in my elevator. One day I want to make a large purchase. The wife wants a new fur coat. I start to go down to the bank and take out a loan. But then I think to myself, "Wait a minute. I don't really need to pay interest. I can do something else. What if I write up a receipt for 10,000 bushels of wheat and sell it? If the person I sell the receipt to wants the wheat, I've got 300,000 bushels of wheat minimum in reserve. No one would know the difference. Wheat looks all the same. So I'll sell the wheat receipt. Later, I'll buy the 10,000 bushels when I have the money. Then I'll buy back the wheat receipt for 10,000 bushels and tear it up. We'll all be even then, and I won't have to pay any interest to the bank. Boy, am I smart."

So, I issue a wheat receipt for 10,000 bushels and sell it. Now, what happens? I know I never really have to buy that wheat receipt back because I am never down to 10,000 bushels in my elevator. Inflation in wheat receipts has just begun. I have issued more wheat receipts than

22

there is wheat in my elevator.

Pretty soon, the wife wants to live in a bigger house. So, I write another receipt for 20,000 more bushels of wheat. Next, the church needs a little money. I give them a wheat receipt for 5,000 bushels. And so it goes. (Prices start to rise in the valley. Inflation, you know.) Before too long, I'm a big shot. The mayor places me on the city council. I'm on all the corporation boards. Everybody knows that I'm a successful businessman. I've got the biggest car in town. My family is respected. I'm quoted in prestigious business magazines. I am "Mr. Nice." But back in my office, when I close the door, I sit and worry. Why? I've written so many receipts that I only have 400,000-500,000 bushels of wheat in the elevator. There are 2,000,000-4,000,000 bushels of wheat receipts going around. If too many people come in and ask for their wheat all at once, they will find out I am a cheat. I am really worried. Sure, I'm a big shot to the outside world. I can kid the world. But here in the back room, I sit biting my nails. What happens if they ask for more wheat than I've got? I become really concerned. Then I have a bright idea. I scurry down the road to see old Joe. Joe runs a wheat elevator, too, you see. I say to Joe, "Joe, you and I are in trouble." "What do you mean we are in trouble?" asks Joe. "I've got a successful business." "Now look, Joe, you're doing the same thing I'm doing. You've written more wheat receipts than you have wheat." "I wouldn't do a thing like that," says Joe. "Come on, Joe, don't you kid me. We're in trouble." "Yeah, we sure are," says Joe.

"Now, if people find out I have written wheat receipts without having the wheat to back it up, they're going to suspect you, too. And, if everyone comes in and asks for their wheat all at once, you can't back up your wheat receipts any better than I can back up mine. If they catch me, they're going to come after you.

"You know who the dirty people are? They are the people who would run us and ask for their wheat. They are the bad guys. See what would happen? If those bad guys come and ask for **their** wheat, and we can give them their wheat, all those **other** people who hold wheat receipts will lose out. Sure, we'll be ruined, but good folks will be ruined, too. They bought our wheat receipts in good faith. They're going to find out that their wheat receipts are no good. It will be disastrous. Everybody will lose. Therefore, it is our civic duty to see that folks don't find out we wrote phony wheat receipts. You see, as long as they don't know our wheat receipts are phony, they are just as good as real wheat receipts. People buy and sell them and think they have value. As long as folks think they are worth something, what difference does it make?

"OK, here's the way out of this dilemma. We'll hold a little convention of all the wheat elevator operators in the valley. We'll get them all together and say, 'Gentlemen, we've all been writing some phony wheat receipts. There are a lot more wheat receipts floating around than there is wheat. And everyone of you is still in business because you've been doing the same thing we've been doing.

" 'Now, you know how terrible it would be if people found out we all have been writing bad wheat receipts. It would wipe out the thousands of innocent people who hold our phony wheat receipts right now. We've got to protect these innocent people from finding out we are crooks. So, let's face facts. We can't buy the wheat receipts back. We can't make things straight. We simply haven't got the wheat. The only practical thing to do is to keep the people from finding out that their wheat receipts are no good. So here's what we're going to do. Each of us is going to put 50,000 bushels of wheat into one central elevator, so that if any one of us gets too low, he can draw down wheat to cover his wheat receipts. That way, nobody finds out we've been cheating. We'll call the operation The Wheat Reserve (The Federal Reserve).

" 'Now, we're going to have to do some other things. We will have a nice new wheat insurance corporation (Federal Deposit Insurance Corporation) which will guarantee that you are not going to be in default. Some of you will think you are so protected that you will write even more phony wheat receipts. What else we're going to do is have an agreement among us that we will work and pull together. Each of us will belong to a super organization, a super trust. This super trust will control how many phony receipts we can each write. That way, we will all cheat equally. Otherwise, some of you will cheat more than others.

" 'Also, we're going to have to stabilize the price of wheat receipts so that some wheat receipts don't sell for less in the market. That would highlight the biggest cheaters.

" 'Now, see Bill over there? Bill is looking for a job. If we elect Bill governor, Bill promises to pass a law saying that we can set up a monopoly—our control trust—to guarantee we will regulate wheat receipt writing, and that all our wheat receipt writings are official wheat receipts. Wheat receipts will have to be accepted by people as real wheat receipts, whether they are or not. Legal tender wheat receipts is what we'll have. People cannot question the legitimacy of the wheat receipt. And, folks will have to recognize our monopoly on wheat receipt writing so no new cheats can come in and write wheat receipts and pass them off as our wheat receipts. Bill also promises to pass a law that anybody who makes a copy of our phony wheat receipts will go to jail as a counterfeiter. Only members of our monopoly can write phony wheat receipts. This is all for the good of the people because if there are too many phony wheat receipts around, people will get suspicious. We've got to keep new phony wheat receipt writers out of the business. Also, down the road, we've got to make sure that people cannot call for their wheat receipts all at once. After a few years, as this thing goes along, people will get used to our system.' ''

(Now, remember who the bad guys are in bank runs. Why, they are the people who come in and ask for their money back. The people who run a bank are the people who are bad, aren't they? They are causing a lack of faith in the banking system and the subsequent crash that hurt everybody. Our textbooks tell us that the bad guys are the people who ask for their money back that they deposited in good faith. Why are they the bad guys? The bank doesn't have their deposited money. It's interesting, isn't it?)

" 'Let's take a hard look at a run on wheat receipts. After a few years, people become accustomed to these nice, new official-looking wheat receipts. They can't get wheat (gold, silver) for them, but they don't think about it anymore. We next pass a law saying that it's illegal to have wheat for the wheat receipts. Look! What would happen if people, for some strange reason, asked for their wheat from all of us at once? Sure, we have this central wheat pool, and transfer wheat back and forth to keep any one of us from getting caught. But, what if everybody asked for wheat all at once? We wouldn't be able to deliver. So here's what we are going to do. Old Bill is still up there as governor. It costs each of us only a small amount to finance a good political campaign to make sure that the right guy makes the right laws. So, we'll have Bill make us a new law. It will be illegal for people to have wheat for their wheat receipts. Now, there are official wheat receipts and there is some wheat there. But folks can't have any wheat. We'll make it illegal for anybody to hold wheat unless they are a member of our association. Now, members of our association can hold and own wheat, but no one else can. You understand that this is for the good of the people. It keeps those bad guys from asking for more wheat than there is. They couldn't ask for more wheat than there is if we had wheat behind every wheat receipt. But we have issued more wheat receipts than there is wheat. And this creates the potential of a run on our wheat elevators. So, to protect us against the run, we've got to make sure that people can't have the wheat. But, we have to be honorable about this whole thing. We've got to give wheat to other members of our own association. You see, we're going to have to pay off our fellow club members in real wheat. But, you don't have to pay off to non-club members. What a fine operation, our Wheat Reserve

(Federal Reserve) and Community Wheat Insurance Corporation (Federal Deposit Insurance Corporation).

" 'After a few years more, people won't even think of not getting wheat for their wheat receipts. Then we will make yet another new law. It will say that we won't be required to have any wheat behind our wheat receipts. We'll tell the people that a wheat receipt is the same thing as wheat, and there is no need to have wheat anymore. We can take all the wheat. We will guarantee to redeem every wheat receipt with another wheat receipt.' "

(This is like going into a parking lot, taking a parking ticket, and getting a receipt for your parked car. Later you go in and say to the attendant that you want your car back. You give him the receipt. He says, "Oh, sorry, we sold your car. But, we'll be happy to give you another car receipt. You can have a blue parking ticket or a green parking ticket. What color of ticket do you want?" You say, "I want my car back!" He tells you again, "We sold your car. You had a Chevrolet. We'll give you a Buick parking ticket, how's that?")

(Here's another example. You go down to the green stamp redemption center. They tell you, for your green stamps, that they will give you a nice, new book of green stamps for your old book. You say, "Well, I would like a prize." They reply, "Well, sir, we're not giving any prizes, but we will redeem your green stamps in green stamps." Isn't that nice?)

" 'While we have this little club going, we've got yet another problem. We have to make sure that the insiders in other associations in other valleys cooperate with us in order for our wheat receipts to appear good. The deal we'll cut with people in other associations in other valleys is that we will promise to give them wheat for our wheat receipts that they hold. In turn, they will give us wheat for their wheat receipts that we hold. In other words, among monopoly clubs, we will play it straight and redeem wheat. But we will not redeem wheat for people in our club area who aren't members of our association. Nor will we redeem wheat for ordinary people outside of our club area who obtain our wheat receipts. If they get paid in our wheat, our wheat supply gets lower and lower. So, we are going to establish a dual market. Other monopoly club members can get wheat, but no one else can get any wheat, whether they are in our club area or outside of it. Who knows. The day may come when we will close the wheat window to other monopoly clubs, too.

" 'There is still one problem left. Some of the other monopoly wheat areas are giving wheat for their wheat receipts. Our wheat receipts won't exchange for the same value as theirs. People prefer their wheat receipts to ours. These are bad people. They are upsetting the inter-community wheat market. And then there are other people in other valleys who have monopoly wheat associations, but won't redeem their wheat receipts for us even when we hold them. That is, they have soft wheat receipts. They want repayment only to the monopoly association. How are we going to handle this? We're going to have to merge all the monopolies into one big monopoly. We're going to have to have one worldwide wheat reserve. We'll call it the International Wheat Fund (International Monetary Fund). Then, all wheat receipts will be equally phony. And the wheat market will be stabilized. There can never be a run on wheat anywhere anymore. The only way we will have ultimate protection is for everyone in all monopolies worldwide to agree to join our International Wheat Fund.' "

*   *   *

Daniel Webster on The Central Bank

"What sort of institution, Sir, is this? It looks less like a bank than a department of government. It will be properly the paper-money department. Its capital is government debts; the amount of its issues will depend on government necessities; government, in effect, absolves itself from its own debts to the bank, and, by way of compensation, absolves the bank from its own contracts with others. This is, indeed, a wonderful scheme of finance. The government is to grow rich, because it is to borrow without the obligation of repaying, and is to borrow of a bank which issues paper without liability to redeem it. If this bank, like other institutions which dull and plodding common sense has erected, were to pay its debts, it must have some limits to its issues of paper, and therefore there would be a point beyond which it could not make loans to government. This would fall short of the wishes of the contrivers of this system. They provide for an unlimited issues of paper in an entire exemption from payment. They found their bank, in the first place, on the discredit of government, and then hope to enrich government out of the insolvency of their bank. With them, poverty itself is the main source of supply, and bankruptcy a mine of inexhaustible treasure. They trust not in the ability of the bank, but in its beggary, not in gold and silver collected in its vaults, to pay its debts, and fulfill its promises, but in its locks and bars, provided by statute, to fasten its doors against the solicitations and clamors of importunate creditors. Such an institution, they flatter themselves, will not only be able to sustain itself, but to buoy up the sinking credit of the government. A bank which does not pay is to guarantee the engagements of a government which does not pay! John Doe is to become security for Richard Roe. Thus the empty vaults of

the treasury are to be filled from the equally empty vaults of the bank, and the ingenious invention of a partnership between insolvents is to restore and reestablish the credit of both.

"Sir, I can view this only as a system of rank speculation and enormous mischief."

Source: *Hard Money News, Winter 1980-81*
170 North Robertson Blvd., Beverly Hills, CA 90211

FUNNY MONEY
by
Don Bell

Once upon a time there was discovered a new and pleasant land, one that was oceans apart from the old and intrigue-infested lands in other areas of the earth. This new and pleasant land was in time occupied by industrious and, for the greater part, God-fearing men and women. They severed their old world political and economic, and sometimes their religious ties, battled and won their independence, wrote a new and unique compact called a Constitution, formed a government according to its provisions, and the people prospered as no people had ever prospered since the dawn of history. However, as always seems inevitable in the course of the rise and decline of civilizations, a strange kind of evil began to infest the land. It grew slowly, step by step, Act by Act, so gradual that even today few people realize what has happened to them and their land. It began when a small group of New York gnomes began to take control of the Government in Washington. The dictionary defines gnomes as a race of creatures who live underground and guard treasure hoards. Hence the phrase gnomes of Zurich in reference to International Bankers. Such gnome-like creatures are indigenous to the Empire of the City of London, to Wall Street in New York, to the privately controlled Reichsbank in West Germany, the Banque de France, the Bank of Italy, and other tax havens where international banking activities prosper.

With government authorization the people of this new and pleasant land were deceived into giving their real money, which consisted of minted pieces of gold and silver, in exchange for little rectangular pieces of greenish paper purporting to be of certain values, but actually worth nothing more than the cost of printing. The year 1913 was the year of the great betrayal. The Federal Reserve Act was passed on the twenty-third of December and signed by President Wilson that same night. The Sixteenth Amendment was ratified and became a part of the Constitution. The Seventeenth Amendment was ratified and the States lost their right to appoint Senators to represent them in Washington and had to have them popularly elected instead, which unbalanced the whole federal system so carefully laid out in the original Constitution. Also in that year tax-exempt foundations and other

29

tax shelters became prevalent among the gnomes and their associates, so that David Rockefeller could testify before a Congressional committee: *"You know, gentlemen, that I do not owe any personal income tax. But nevertheless, I send a small check, now and then, to the Internal Revenue Service out of the kindness of my heart."*

But the one act that was perhaps the most monstrous of all was the turning over of the Nation's gold to the gnomes of New York, now in charge of the Federal Reserve System. Dr. Martin Larson, probably the foremost authority on the Federal Reserve System (outside of its members, who seldom talk about it), recently told those attending a Freeman Institute Century Club Banquet: *"When Franklin D. Roosevelt went into office in 1933 he followed the desires of the bankers, just as Woodrow Wilson had done before him back in 1913 when he promised in his campaign speech to get the Federal Reserve Act passed. One of the first things that Roosevelt did . . . was to close all the banks. Then he got the Gold Reserve Act passed in 1934 under which the United States government gave the Federal Reserve System all the gold that was in Fort Knox. They gave it to them as an outright gift. They didn't even ask for a receipt in return for the gold. This was at a time when gold could be produced for about $12 an ounce. Americans who owned gold were told, under penalty of felony, that they had to turn in all their gold coins to the United States government or to the Federal Reserve System. As of 1954, the Federal Reserve System owned about 28,000 tons of gold in Fort Knox—worth something like $30 billion at $35 an ounce. Now between 1955 and 1972 this gold was sold to foreign investors at $35 an ounce. Today it is worth several hundred billion dollars. As it was sold, the gold was taken out of Fort Knox and placed in the vaults of the New York Branch of the Federal Reserve System. So far as I know, it lies there at this date and is stored there for foreign owners at the expense of the American taxpayers."*

In this connection, there has always been much speculation about who owns the Federal Reserve System. We don't mean the managers of the twelve Federal Reserve Banks who run them for the owners, or the members of the Federal Reserve Board who make decisions in favor of the owners, or those who sit in the Open Market Committee which operates only through the New York Branch of the Federal Reserve. We mean the *owners* of the Federal Reserve. This has been one of the best kept secrets of this century, because the Federal Reserve Act of 1913 provided the names of the owner banks must be kept secret.

To continue with our story, from the adminstrations of FDR through the administrations of Nixon, the Federal Reserve gradually managed to have the Federal Government sever all monetary connections with gold. In a less complicated way, the same thing happened to silver in 1965. Even the present copper-based penny is due to be discontinued because of its value in copper. So, what we actually are using in place of any money of real value are these Federal Reserve notes—notes which are not redeemable and must be accepted as legal tender for all debts, public and private. There is also checkbook money, computer-entry money, and credit card money, none of which represent money of real value. All they have is the peoples' confidence in them.

Now, when the Federal Reserve System began to slowly deprive American taxpayers of all their money of real value, there also began a whole system of economic theories and national planning schemes which would slowly convert our Constitutional Republic into a Social Welfare State, even though there wasn't enough tax revenue to sustain any such programs. That's when unbalanced budgets began and the national debt started mounting into monetary infinity. So that, at a time when the National debt had legally topped a trillion alleged dollars, and when the annual interest on that debt had become $100 billion, unemployment was dangerously high and inflation had become a double-digit affair, up stepped Candidate Ronald Reagan with a plan that was supposed to solve all these problems, slowly, yes, but surely, definitely. The people elected him because they were sure he had something better to offer than Jimmy Carter.

Source: Don Bell Reports, P. O. Box 2223, Palm Beach, Florida 33480

*   *   *

"I believe that banking institutions are more dangerous to our liberties than standing armies."

Thomas Jefferson

A FRACTURED FINANCIAL FAIRY TALE

8/14/81

Once upon a time, on a planet far, far away, lived a rich man. Now this was no ordinary rich man. This rich man had accumulated, through trusts, foundations and his family's clandestine business operations down through the generations, about all the wealth and power any sane man could want. When heads of state came to visit the president of his country, who he helped install in office, they always took time to drop by and visit, recognizing the true power behind the throne. Being hated by the few little people who took the time to review his activities, who couldn't appreciate his right to use and abuse wealth and power, this rich man desired to multiply his wealth many times. It was a greedy game for him. It was the love of money. He already owned and controlled one of the biggest banks in the country. And his family was notorious for their ruthlessness in the early development, monopolizing, and continuing control of the oil business. The problem came with the attempt to expand his banking empire. The 50 states in his country all had separate banking rules and regulations which made it difficult, if not impossible, for him to set up interstate banking. It made this rich man very, very sad that the people who ran the 50 states thought he should not control all the money in the country. So, he devised a brilliant scheme to increase and combine his oil and banking empires.

Now, in a separate part of the world, a historically unstable people had stumbled onto a literal ocean of oil reserves. In fact, the reserves of these unruly groups were the largest in the world. Knowing a great deal about the oil business, this rich man surveyed his world's situation and saw that if the 13 unstable countries which produced this tremendous amount of oil would simply get together, they could form an oil cartel. Then they could raise the price of oil significantly to their financial benefit. Of course, this new cartel would have to deal with our rich man's oil enterprises, since he already had significant control of oil companies, refineries and tankers which would bring the oil from these underdeveloped countries to world markets. So, he set out to execute his plan.

In one of these wild and woolly oil-rich countries, he found a

32

monarch, somewhat of a proud peacock, who our rich man thought could be established as the military power in the area who would bring all the other unstable tribesmen into line. With his tremendous political power in his own country, this banker/oil magnate convinced high-level officials to sell this peacock puppet all the military equipment needed to stabilize the rowdy oil-rich area. After a period of time, thanks to the peacock, the *"wild and woollies"* settled down, and then were educated regarding their *"common"* economic self-interest. Greed being what it is in other worlds as in this world, the leaders of all these oil-rich countries agreed to form a cartel and jack up the price of their oil. Who knows? From under $2.00 a barrel, the price of oil could double to $4.00, and then double again to $8.00, rise to $16.00 or maybe even to the staggering sum of $32.00 a barrel. Who knows? The sky's the limit. In any case, with any oil price increases, our rich man knew he would profit tremendously. After all, then he could raise the price of his own oil, too, which he owned in vast quantities at locations all over the globe. The value of his oil companies, tankers, refineries and service stations would likewise appreciate. It was a win-win deal for our rich man. But there was an added bonus, a real plus, that made his master plan one gem of a deal. In one fast sweep, he effectively established 50-state branch banking. All the people in all 50 states now made their deposits in his new branch bank—the new oil cartel. So clean, so neat. No fuss. No mess. And, of course, as he had previously arranged, his big branch bank, the oil cartel, agreed to make all their financial deposits derived from oil income in overseas branches of our rich man's bank or even directly to the home bank, located in his nation's financial center.

Being always one step ahead of the crowd, our financial mastermind knew exactly what he would do with all the money. He would loan it to the poor countries of his world, those nations headed by aspiring political leaders who fretted every day, with sweaty palms, about whether or not their leadership and nation would hold together. The loans to these deadbeat countries allowed our banking and oil financier to call the shots not only in the political and economic arenas of these poor countries, but also in world commodity markets. Our rich man rejoiced, as he contemplated the tremendous profits he would reap from inside information about the world's commodity markets, which he now had the power to effectively manipulate and control. He already knew how to control the *"powers"* in the poor countries. All he had to do was to finance some guerrillas out in the bush to overthrow the newly established, green political leaders in these underdeveloped countries if they got out of line. So, effectively, his financial power assured a balance of power (terror), whereby he could pull the political puppet strings in these backward countries. A little financial clout goes a long way when it comes to intimidation of the *"world's weakies."*

The only problem that remained was how to ensure the repayment of these loans from these young struggling countries. Our rich man needed some type of insurance. Thankfully, again, through his manipulative efforts, and the efforts of some of his fellow bankers, he had the political leaders of his country establish international development banks, subsidized by his country's ordinary taxpayers. These international development banks, as they were called, effectively guaranteed our rich man's loans and cashed him out of any deals which went sour. It was a no-risk, win-win situation again. This was truly the lazy man's way to riches. And, as an important back up, he saw to it that the political leaders in the Third World countries moved toward socialism. This ensured a centralized concentration of power and the maintenance of his world financial empire.

Through a complex maze of international corporations, offshore trusts and foundations, our rich man never worried about paying any taxes either. He had seen to it, in the meantime, that laws were passed, preventing the ordinary folks from getting rich. This way no one could challenge his empire. If an ordinary person was talented, worked hard and did well in business, without accumulating any debt, he was still prevented from getting rich because the graduated income tax swept away the majority of the fruits of his labor each and every year. And after a few years, business failure, setbacks or discouragement would set in, as it always does, and this talented common man would fall back into the masses where he belonged. So clean, so neat. No mess or fuss. And other ordinary men who aspired to become wealthy by using debt, not realizing that throughout history debt is long-term detrimental to all business enterprises, would fall into a different snare. Sure, these debt-heavy folks could avoid the tax trap for awhile and appear to get rich. However, they were always on a debt treadmill, with payments coming due month after month. Every now and then the piper came by, when they didn't have enough to pay. And, all it took to wipe these debt dudes out was for our rich man to exercise his political clout and have the central bank keep money tight so that these aspiring common folks' cash flow would dry up. Then they would go belly up. To our rich man, these recessions or depressions ever so often were great. It provided him with a tremendous opportunity to buy up for a song land, resources, plants and equipment created by the sweat of the brows of other men who had slaved long hours.

Was our financial and oil magnate concerned about the word getting out to the common folk, triggering a revolution, that would result in him being hung from a lamp post? Not at all. He knew his history too well, that human nature was a constant. He knew that the masses were first and foremost concerned with security, that they would not brave the risk and responsibility necessary for freedom. Thus, all he had to do was promote the development of social programs in government that provided for cradle-to-grave security, to not only keep the masses happy and his competitors paying outrageous taxes, but also to guarantee that the politicians who supported his programs would be elected and reelected to office by those on the dole. He even financed a revolution in a distant foreign country, about which the common folk knew very little, so that a militaristic enemy could arise. This way the little people would always be preoccupied with and overly concerned about their safety. This foreign military concern not only did his dirty work around the globe; it also helped consolidate his political influence in a strong central government in his own country where key government officials did his bidding. The little people were grateful for the military protection.

He was able to finance the military expenditures and wars, too. Oh, the money he made from financing those glorious wars. Knowing that the general public would never go to war if they knew how much it cost and had to pay for it at the time of the war, our rich man always conveniently arranged for the central government to borrow money from his bank to finance the military escapades. Sure, there was inconvenient inflation for the masses, but for the most part, it was lost in the fervor of war. He had learned long ago that it was important for nations to be constantly at odds with each other, not only so that he could finance military expenditures on both sides, but also so that the common people would always have enemies. After all, if people all over this world got to know each other too well and traded among themselves freely, without any government restrictions or hostilities, then he would be out of a job. Who would need to borrow money from his bank? He wouldn't be able to loan nearly as much, and his profits would drop off sharply.

Our rich man also made a real financial killing from financing post-war reconstruction. There are few financial endeavors more profitable than the after-war reconstruction effort, and banks get in on the ground floor.

Our rich man had even taken out additional insurance against a public backlash. Long ago, his father and grandfather had established, at the highest political levels, an educational game plan whereby the public would be educated in the public schools and taught to do his bidding. He rejoiced in the brilliance of his family's foresight. It's a lot more difficult to convince a man to work against his own self-interest when he realizes where his own best interest really lies. But when you can take children while they are young and educate them to be technically proficient, but brainwash them to act contrary to their own self-interest in the areas of economics, politics, religion, morals, ethics and history, well, now, how much better can you have it? People do your bidding to their own detriment and smile.

By being rich and powerful, our rich man also was able to establish a monopoly in the media and effectively control what the *"big gun"* newspapers, radio and television networks had to say. This reinforced the educational propaganda put out according to his master plan in the public schools. He also established a stranglehold on religion. By having religious leaders teach the people to spend all their time worrying about the *"sweet by and by,"* our rich man was left to run wild in the *"here and now."*

Finally, knowing that the common folk liked naturally to be entertained, rather than be responsible, our rich man sponsored all types of entertainment and sporting events to capture their interest. Being consistently enthralled and occupied with having a good time, the common folk, thus, never saw any reason and never had any time to think about what was really important, what was really going on in their world controlled by our rich man, even though day in and day out he slowly but surely accumulated the assets of the common folk as they whistled and laughed on their way to the economic graveyard.

*   *   *

There are two theories of history: 1) History is evolutionary, that is to say it happens by chance; and 2) History is planned; it is a deliberate outworking of men's ideas.

The public school system with its evolutionary theology conditions the American public to think of *"history as chance."* This precludes the perceptual framework necessary to think of history as being the result of planning, even though recent history testifies to this fact. We have government and private think tanks which plan for the future. They plan history. The so-called Russian Revolution was the result of planning. It is a serious cogitative error to believe that the events which occur in today's world are random in nature.

*   *   *

"Free education for all children in public schools."

THE COMMUNIST MANIFESTO

* * *

"A heavy progressive or graduated income tax."
THE COMMUNIST MANIFESTO

* * *

"I Chase Manhattan to its branch office at 1 Karl Marx Square in Moscow, . . ."

GLOBESCAN
September 10, 1982

* * *

"One way of insuring a 'fantastic recovery,'. . . would be to 'raze our industry' the way German and Japanese industry were devastated by World War II."

Albert M. Wojnilower,
chief economist at First Boston Corp.
in THE WALL STREET JOURNAL,
September 22, 1982. Reprinted by permission
of THE WALL STREET JOURNAL, Copyright
Dow Jones & Company, Inc., 1982, All Rights Reserved.

IF I WERE A RICH MAN

9/10/82

If I were a rich man, long ago I would have established a central bank to help me consolidate financial and following political power in the country; many years ago I would have established a graduated income tax to make it difficult for other men to obtain my elevated position of wealth and power; long ago I would have had abolished the states' selection of senators so that I could better consolidate power at the federal/empire level through their "popular" election; many years ago I would have seen to it that there were convenient world wars to destroy the wealth of hardworking and productive people, so that I could finance not only the war effort, but also the reconstruction effort and further increase and concentrate my wealth and power internationally; long ago I would have established a boom/bust inflationary and deflationary cycle triggered by my central bank, whereby I could profit from the extremes of inflation and deflation, further increasing my wealth and power; many years ago I would have seen to it that democracy was established, allowing people to vote for their own economic self-interest out of the federal treasury through spineless politicians, so that not only could the people be controlled, which is the case with all democracies, but so that also it would be easy for me to buy political power by making poor politicians rich; long ago, in my scheme to establish a one-world empire and condition that last free country on earth to slavery and poverty, I would have established the public school system, to brainwash the youth to do my will willingly, fought two no-win wars to demoralize the youth of the country, financed the drug trade to blow the minds of the nation's youth so that my socialistic one-world empire could be established, and make leisure time and entertainment the focus of common folks' activities.

Now, my master plan is almost complete. My boys over at the central bank engineered an inflation in the 1970s that hooked nearly everyone in private sector, both businesses and consumers, into excessive debt. Then my cronies at the central bank changed the game and brought about the devasting money crunch that crippled all the borrowers in the 1980s. And now, finally, when it's becoming obvious to all of us that we are headed for a tremendous crash and depression, the soothsayers of the day are pointing to me and my fellow cronies with financial and oil empires, saying that we are about to collapse. Sure, they know that there were two problems with my bank: 1. A devastated bond portfolio, and 2. Disastrous Third World loans. However, I'm not stupid. I've already solved my bond portfolio problem. Thanks to my friends over at the central bank and cooperating economists, I loaded up on bonds (bought long) at the beginning of this year and made a killing as the price of bonds rose. Furthermore, I was able to unload the losers that I had in my bond portfolio on this rally. So much for that problem. Now, all I have to be concerned about is the loans that I have made to the Third World deadbeats. Approximately $200 billion of them are in trouble. Does this bother me? Not at all. Sure, I knew these loans would eventually be deadbeats long before I made them. But, the Third World is stupid. And by making loans to these Third World low lifes, I was able to make a killing in profits establishing my banks there, not to mention the tremendous increase in my wealth acquired by financing the development of these Third World countries which, in turn, gave me control over their hack political leaders. To back me up, I had my political cronies establish laws which forced the American taxpayers to use their hard-earned productivity to make contributions to the world development banks that I established, that both guaranteed my loans, bailed out my bad loans, and subsidized my investments.

Frankly, I hope these Third World losers default. It will help me complete my plan. The tulip mania panic upside in gold has convinced almost everyone that this engineered, worldwide depression will bankrupt my international financial network, that my banks will fail, that there will be a run on the dollar, that the system will collapse, and we will have a revolution. Hogwash! I have already hedged against such a loss and a default on these loans. The American consumer will again pick up the tab. Boy am I glad that he was educated years ago in the public school to turn over all his hard-earned productivity, his money, to me and my banking cronies. By so doing, the American consumer has allowed us to wheel and deal with a ruthlessness seldom seen in human history. Little does the American taxpayer understand the price he has paid for being irresponsible with something as basic as his productivity, his earnings. But, that's another story.

I have now gone short a fortune's worth of stocks and bonds. My boys over at the central bank are about to tighten up the money supply again and jack up interest rates, their excuse being that it is necessary to prevent a run on the dollar, as evidenced from the panic that is taking place now in the gold market. And, we can always use the excuse of Treasury financing. When bonds and stocks crash, my short positions will not only offset my losses from these Third World loans, furthermore, I will make a profit, all at the expense of the American investor. He will literally transfer his wealth to me.

Don't these suckers know that the scarcest commodity around today is cash, that no one is liquid. Everyone still must pay their bills in cash or cash equivalents. After I bust gold back down to $100-$300 an ounce, then I'll buy it all up again, have my politicians make the dollar again gold convertible at some high price, further raking in profits for me, and then we'll start the money game all over again. The American consumer and investor, of course, by this time will be broke. The ignorant masses in this democracy then will call for more federal control, further allowing me to centralize my influence and power in this empire. I will be able to eliminate what little competition remains. I'll probably have the government declare a moratorium on all home mortgages, and then have the government assume the liability for those mortgages, moving us quickly, through financial means, into a socialistic state, where nearly everyone effectively lives in government-owned housing, just like in the Soviet Union. The people will cheer as they become slaves. The mortgage holders will be busted.

You would think that these people would get smart enough, after awhile, to look around and see that all of the signs of a depression are apparent. All the other great nations of the world are in depression —Canada, Argentina, Mexico, Japan, Singapore, South Africa, Switzerland, The Netherlands, Italy, France, Great Britain and West Germany.

A quick aside. Mexico was a real coup. I loaned them billions of dollars, bought off their corrupt politicians, saw to it that the country with its reckless spending and incompetence went bankrupt, so Mexico would default on its loans. Now, Mexico, my largest oil supplier, is forever in debt to me, providing me with oil effectively well below the world market price of $32 a barrel. Pretty slick, eh? And, for icing on the cake, we'll have a socialist revolution in Mexico (Socialist or communist, what's the difference?), leaving only this country as the final plum to be picked. But, back to my discussion on this depression.

One million jobs have vanished permanently since 1978. Dun and Bradstreet now declares that we are experiencing the highest number of bankruptcies in the last 50 years. The F.D.I.C. has 277 banks on its problem list. Office vacancies are the highest since the 1930s. The farmers are in the worst shape since the 1930s. The new tax bill, 60% of which hit business, will further ensure this depression. Effectively 80% of the new tax bill was a tax increase. But, we sold it as tax reform. My man on the Dole did a tremendous job. What suckers the American public are. We even let it out that nine of our largest banks in this country have a debt exposure to developing countries, Eastern Europe and the Soviet Union equal to 220% of our capital. Little do they know how quickly we'll make this up on the downside of this stock and bond market, at their expense, as interest rates soar. Long ago I learned that all it takes is rumors and well-placed bits of information to achieve my desired purposes.

Having 20,000 Mexicans a day cross the southern U.S. border now has ensured social unrest in the independent and wealthy southwestern United States, which will allow us, in time, to further centralize power and control, as hostilities between the races increase in that area of the country. Yes, my boys at Rand, Brookings, the Aspen Institute and at the Hudson Institute have served me well. A cute trick was planting that story in the network evening news that the IRS was about to recall $100 bills. This flushed out all that underground economy and Mafia money, forcing it into precious metals and stocks, before we bust gold and stocks on the downside, thus confiscating that wealth also. It's another version of the same game we played a few years ago with the Hunts in silver.

Yes, anyone should be able to see that this stock and gold move upside is symptomatic of the *"madness of crowds."* Nothing in the economy speaks of hyperinflation. Nothing! None of the other commodity markets are rallying with the precious metals. Anyone should be able to see this is simply a money panic, not a hyperinflation. Don't they understand that the private sector of the economy, which is way overextended due to the pyramiding effect of debt through the fractional reserve banking system, is the main cause of inflation? Can't they see that the contraction of this tremendous debt pyramid in the private sector will more than offset federal government spending and bring about the greatest deflation of all time? Don't they know, that for anything other than that to happen would wreck my multinational banking and oil empire, something I just will not allow? Even the institutions which have loaded up on stocks because they had no place else to run in this money panic will get clipped and clipped hard on the downside, thus busting a lot of pension funds, too. So, I'll get rich during this earthshaking economic contraction on the short side of all these markets. I'll then see to it that my politicians cut all the federal spending programs enough to prevent a government hyperinflation bust. Then, when the general public is crying for relief, we'll see that we put enough people on the dole as slaves, to move us further on the road to my one-world socialistic/humanistic/evolutionary empire. And, then, finally, I can live happily ever after.

Can something go wrong? Well, yes. There are two things that are troublesome. This gold move up has started to get out of hand. Gold has retraced its latest bear leg down by 50%. Gold has rallied to the $500 level of natural resistance. If gold blows fast and hard on through $500 an ounce, it could test the old high of $800 an ounce which, if this happens and is exceeded, could lead to a full blown panic out of the dollar (hyperinflation) and into all tangibles, including commodities, real estate, stocks, etc., in which case, higher interest rates and a belated attempt to salvage the dollar would not work. Then, we'd have to use Executive Orders to seize control of the country, as well as the Monetary Control Act of 1980. So, you can see why I can't cut this coming spike in interest rates too close. The public is almost at the panic stage now, and the defaults by these Third World deadbeats (I loaned them your money.) are forcing me to play my trump card more quickly than I would have liked.

My next problem? This concerns my old friend Israel. Now, you know that a lot of my cronies in these high placed financial circles are of the same religious persuasion as the folks in Israel. And, they have had a bias toward supporting Israel with U.S. taxpayers' money to the tune of $6 million a day. However, just as in the free market, where race and religion are not issues when it comes to money, so is it particularly true in the games we play at this epitome of the humanistic/ evolutionary financial spiral. When it comes to power, control and money, religion be damned. If necessary, we'll cut Israel's throat. And it looks like we may just have to do that. I have already had my boys over at the largest New York daily newspaper turn aggressively against Israel, and thus begin conditioning American opinion to become pro Arab. The Saudi Arabian threat to withdraw $100 billion out of my banks unless my president called off the Israelis from slaughtering the PLO in Lebanon scared the dickens out of me. We put out that fire just in time. The President got on the phone to the Prime Minister of Israel and told him to call off his military dogs, which he did. Whew!

Now, I've heard rumors and, in fact, have some intelligence to back it up, that suggests that Israel may have developed military technology that is superior, not only to that produced by my American military/industrial complex, but also to that of my military surrogate, the Soviet Union, which I have financed industrially and militarily for years and years. This could prove to be a problem. The PLO terrorists that I financed through my Soviet surrogate were causing so much trouble worldwide that my plan for the centralization of power was going along nicely. Terrorism always leads to increased government control. The Israeli move into Lebanon has disrupted that PLO operation significantly, throwing off my timetable to have my Russian surrogate, the Soviet military, move in, take over and control the Middle East, in the process possibly destroying Israel, and then establish iron-fisted control over Middle East oil. Once this is done, once the Soviet Union controls the Middle East and Middle East oil, I can ration the world's oil supply, set the world's oil price, shore up and increase the wealth of my financial empire, and effectively operate a one-world financial slave empire. I'll own everything in sight and bust the Libertarians, Right Wing and Christians, too. This has been the dream of men since the beginning of time. I am just on the verge of accomplishing it. Greedy, you say? *"The love of money is the root of all evil."*

The Arabs can't stand against the Soviets. We financed the Arabs and put them in business in the first place with all our oil technology. The oil cartel we formed for them took the bad press for the skyward streaking oil prices in the 1970s when, in fact, it was me and my oil company sisters who profited the most from that Middle East oil concession. So, to sum it up, my only two worries now are gold and Israel. Gold I hope to take care of in short order. Israel comes next spring, and that could prove to be troublesome. Those boys in Israel put up quite a fight. But, then again, no one ever said you establish a one-world empire easily, and this one has taken nearly two centuries.

* * *

"Centralization of credit in the hands of the State, by means of a national bank with State capital and an exclusive monopoly."
THE COMMUNIST MANIFESTO

* * *

"We cannot expect Americans to jump from capitalism to communism, but we can assist their elected leaders in giving Americans doses of socialism until they suddenly awake to find out they have communism."
Nikita Khrushchev

* * *

"By the end of August, the Federal Reserve had purchased debts of West Germany, Switzerland, Italy, Canada, France, and England, and used those debts as collateral for printing and issuing, on 70 different occasions, about $2 billion worth of Federal Reserve notes from four different Reserve banks.

"There is no legal impediment that would prevent the Federal Reserve from buying the debts of Mexico, Argentina, Bolivia, or Poland and using them for the same purpose."
Congressman Ron Paul, September 10, 1982

THOUGHTS ON ENERGY

3/31/78

A national debate raged over whether the United States had a real live energy crisis. Since we are bombarded daily (or so it seems) with propaganda out of Washington saying we do have an energy shortage, this writer thought it would be interesting to present a few comments from the *"other"* side. One interesting note: There is almost unanimous agreement that a deregulated energy business would solve the problem.

Charles J. DiBona, Executive Vice President of the American Petroleum Institute said, *"I think that much of the problem derives from a widespread, underlying philosophy in the administration that we're running out of oil and gas. There is a fundamental misconception about how soon they will be exhausted—or even more serious, how supplies can be affected by changes in productive incentives."*

THE WALL STREET JOURNAL stated in an editorial that there is *"1,001 years of natural gas"* left in America if only it would be deregulated.

According to THE WASHINGTON POST, if the 100 billion barrels of California *"gunk"* oil were counted in the proven reserves, the U.S. reserves would nearly double.

Dr. William Brown, director of technological studies for the Hudson Institute stated, *"The President said there is no chance of us becoming independent in our oil supplies. That is just wrong. We have at least 100 years of petroleum resources in this country."*

Estimates from the U.S. Geological Survey are that we have a 200-year domestic supply of petroleum, a 300-year supply of natural gas, and a 1,500-year supply of coal.

Well now, what is one to think. Let's ask the PSE (Psychological Stress Evaluator) to test Mr. Jimmy Carter on his honesty concerning the energy question. The PSE is a sophisticated lie detector that measures stress in speech. It is used by 300 law enforcement agencies, and is admissable as evidence in courts in 14 states. The PSE was run on Mr. Carter during his energy speech to the American people and on his address to the Congress. The PSE found stress in Mr. Carter's speech in the following areas (meaning that the chances are good he

44

was at bare minimum, hedging):

"We will not let the oil companies profiteer."

"We do not want to give producers windfall profits."

"No one will gain an advantage through this plan."

"We will monitor the accuracy of data from the oil and natural gas companies for the first time, so that we will always know their true production, supplies, reserves and profits."

"We now believe that early in the 1980's the world will be demanding more oil than it can produce."

"If we wait and do not act, then our factories will not be able to keep our people on the job."

"We will insure that American automobile workers and their families do not bear an unfair share of the burden."

The PSE is suggesting that a President who said he would *"never lie"* to us, is not telling the whole truth.

Edwin C. Barbe, Asst. Professor of Engineering at the U. of W. Virginia has protested loudly about the *"No-Drill program."* He charged, *"Those who ran the American oil and gas industry, and those who ran the American government had . . . reduced the U.S. to an inferior level, by depriving her of her own oil and her own gas . . . and by making American survival 'subservient' to the will of foreign governments."* He noted that from 1956 to 1971, the U.S. had reduced its exploratory drilling by 57%.

HARPER'S editor, Lewis H. Lapham, wrote an article in the August, 1977 issue entitled, *"The Energy Debacle."* He stated that the Carter energy plan was guided by a $4 million Ford Foundation study of 1974 entitled, *"A Time to Choose."* He stated the energy plan *"was brought forth in an atmosphere of secrecy and mistrust,"* and *"a scheme to raise about $40 billion a year in additional tax revenue."* The *"Time to Choose"* plan advocated: heating and cooling standards for all U.S. buildings, the curtailed usage of single family dwellings, new taxes on cars, a federal agency that would award energy on the basis of need and suitability, federal energy stamp programs, a 50% cut in energy, more tax increases and price controls. Lampham notes that the report came under heavy attack from academic circles because it was poor scholarship. HARPER's concluded that the Carter energy plan, *". . . could cost Americans their economic freedom of choice, and inevitably, their political liberties as well."*

OIL: THE WORLD'S KEY COMMODITY

3/5/82

WWWOII—Weather, War, World Trade, Oil, Interest Rates and Inflation are the six key fundamentals which affect commodity prices. None are more important than Oil, which clearly impacts War, World Trade, Interest Rates and Inflation. Oil, like Gold, is a bellwether. As we have been experiencing a worldwide glut of Oil, and thus not surprisingly, slumping commodity prices, it's important that we again gather an overall perspective on World Oil, so that we may correctly anticipate the movement of this key commodity in upcoming years, to better prepare us for the future.

We are presently living at the end of the Oil Age. No, this is not because we are running out of oil. In fact, the world is awash with it, with much left to be discovered in China and the Third World, not to mention technological advancements which allow increased recovery from old oil fields. Of course, Gull Island and California have not been truly developed either, not to mention oil shale. No, oil is becoming a fuel of the past, just as coal and whale oil did before it. Within the next 20 years, providing civilization doesn't fly apart, the technology of the future will provide us with the energy for the future—free and abundant solar energy. Already, the technology is in place to provide us with dollar-a-watt solar energy. A multibillion dollar industry to this end is gearing up even now in Detroit. Solar technology is about to come on stream which will allow the average homeowner to disconnect himself permanently from the public utilities, and even plug his car into his roof's solar energy system, so that he will never again have to drive into a gas station. The total cost? A mere 6-7 years worth of utility bills at today's prices.

Waiting in the wings are the practical applications of DePalma's, Jefimenko's and Maglich's prototypes, technology which will throw off excess energy, above the amount utilized. This potentially opens up to mankind a manual-labor-free lifestyle, undreamed of even ten years ago. Robots hooked into computers are on the horizon, which can potentially quickly move men into an age when most work is mental, rarely physical. Solar energy satellites, which beam energy directly to earth, and coal gasification plants, such as those which are already on stream in South Africa, will provide us with a supermarket of energy technology which will enable us to do such things as warm the oceans, making more parts of the world inhabitable, reclaim water, minerals and land from the seas, rejuvenate the deserts, and who knows, possibly even reestablish a clear water canopy around the entire globe, which will again enable us to live for up to 1,000 years (a result of the reduction in solar radiation which hits the earth, slowing the aging process).

What keeps all this from happening here and now, immediately? Man's general resistance to change, his fear of the unknown, his desire to maintain the status quo, **and the resistance of institutions who have a stake in seeing that things do not change, that oil does not become the fuel of the past.** These institutions, which resist a betterment in the economic condition of all mankind, are the multinational banks and oil companies, the same folks who squelched the synthetic fuel technology developed by the Nazis in World War II. (George C. Scott's movie, THE FORMULA, was a variation of this theme.)

Wealth and power centralized in too few hands leads to corruption, conspiracy and intrigues of all types to the detriment of mankind generally. Such is the black history of *"Big Oil."* (There is nothing quite like decentralization of power and wealth as a checkmate against the propensity for evil in man's nature.)

Going back just to 1938, we find quite a concentration of oil ownership in the hands of just one family.

Holdings of the Rockefeller Family in Equity Securities of Four "Standard" Oil Companies, 1938
(percent of total stock outstanding)

Company	Indi-viduals	Trusts & Estates	Founda-tions	Rockfeller-Dominated Corps.	Total
Exxon	6.45%	2.24%	4.82%	6.69%*	20.20%
Mobil	8.64	7.70			16.34
Standard Oil (Ind.)	2.44	4.39	4.53		11.36
SoCal	7.37	4.49	.46		12.32

* Through Standard Oil Co. (Ind.).
Source: 76th Cong., 3rd Sess., Temporary National Economic Committee, Monograph 29, *The Distribution of Ownership in the 200 Largest Nonfinancial Corporations*, 1940. p. 127.

Source: THE CONTROL OF OIL, John M. Blair, Random House, Inc., NY, 1976

It's too easy for us to forget that years earlier John D. Rockefeller's forefather, Bill Rockefeller, called himself a doctor in Cleveland and peddled *"Nujol"* as a cure for cancer. *"Nujol"* was nothing more than raw petroleum in a fancy bottle. In 1958, *"Nujol"* was still on the market (100 years later), sold as a laxative. It wasn't so long ago either that Rockefeller's Standard Oil and the German company, I. G. Farben, effected a monopoly that controlled important drug/chemical patents. Little wonder that I. G. Farben was one of the few operations that survived unscathed the pinpoint bombing of the Allies in the latter days of World War II.

Recall when Henry Ford invented the automobile. It first ran on alcohol, not gasoline. It was only after the oil companies convinced Henry that gasoline was less expensive, that he converted his world-changing invention to run on gasoline.

Rushing into the present, the two definitive works on the subject of contemporary oil are Dr. John M. Blair's 1976 book, THE CONTROL OF OIL (Random House, 1976) and Joe Stork's work, MIDDLE EAST OIL AND THE ENERGY CRISIS (Monthly Review Press, 1975). Both of these works received excellent reviews. They are both must reading for securing a knowledgeable, in-depth perspective on the oil industry.

Reviews of both of these works were nothing short of spectacular. For example, BUSINESS WEEK had this to say about THE CONTROL OF OIL:

> *"Blair has prepared a devastating case that monopoly—usually with at least tacit government approval—has been the rule, not the exception, in the international oil market for most of this century."*

The ST. LOUIS POST-DISPATCH further commented,

> *"Combining scholarly detachment and a strong commitment to the public interest, Blair has set forth the story of the oil industry's largely successful effort to control the production, distribution and pricing of petroleum."*

Stork's book was just as well received:

> *"Stork's carefully written and documented study of oil development and politics in the Middle East is not a pretty tale. It is a story of unabashed greed, especially on the part of the multinationals, companies without much loyalty to nations or consumers."*
>   THE SEATTLE TIMES.

> *"Stork traces the development of a system in which . . . a small number of multinational corporations have gained oligopolistic control over the world oil market."*   LIBRARY JOURNAL

Anthony Sampson's THE SEVEN SISTERS is also important reading (Bantam, 1975).

The *"biggies"* of the world are

U.S.		International	
"Top Eight"	**"Lesser Majors"**	**"Seven Sisters"**	**Leading "Independents"**
Exxon	Getty	Exxon	Compagnie Française
Mobil	Phillips	Mobil	Pétrole
SoCal	Signal	SoCal	Continental
Stand. (Ind.)	Union	Texaco	Marathon
Texaco	Continental	Gulf	Amerada Hess
Gulf	Sun	Royal Dutch Shell	Occidental
Shell	Amerada Hess	BP	
ARCO	Cities Service		
	Marathon		

Source: *THE CONTROL OF OIL, John M. Blair, Random House, New York, 1976.*

One credible source estimated that these multinational corporations control 40 percent of the world's oil flow. ARAMCO and Exxon monopolize the distribution of oil worldwide. For example, out of the 8.5 million barrels of oil a day produced by Saudi Arabia, the Arabian American Oil Company (ARAMCO) is responsible for marketing 6.5 million barrels. (ARAMCO is made up of Texaco, Exxon, Mobil and Standard Oil of California.) Now we know who really got rich on the skyrocketing price of oil in the 1970s. Back in 1970, the top eight major oil companies controlled 58.1 percent of the refining capacity domestically. Even further back, in 1952, outside the United States, every important pipeline was controlled by the seven principal international oil companies, either individually or jointly. In 1974, in addition to accounting for 50.5 percent of the total domestic crude oil production, the top eight oil companies accounted for 64.5 percent of the output from offshore areas. Nearly half of that offshore amount came from just three of the top eight—Exxon, Standard Oil of California and Shell. Actually things haven't changed much since 1914 when, at the time of the hearings for what became the Clayton Act, House and Senate Committees reported,

> *"The concentration of wealth, money and property in the United States under the control and in the hands of a few individuals or great corporations has grown to such an enormous extent that unless checked it will ultimately threaten the perpetuity of our institutions. The idea that there are only a few men in any of our great corporations and industries who are capable of handling the affairs of the same is contrary to the spirit of our institutions."*

Just like in commodity trading, where the commercials have the inside track on establishing profitable positions and thus reducing risk, so it is now with *"Big Oil."* Today, the majority of the risk is laid off on the independents. Some 80 to 90 percent of all the oil wells drilled in the United States in 1981, including the wildcats, were drilled by independent companies.

What's *"Big Oil"* doing around the rest of the world? Let's take Libya for example, whose oil interests were developed in part by Nelson Bunker Hunt before they were nationalized. (The independent, Bunker Hunt, was nationalized; Mobil and Exxon were not.) Despite all the recent furor over possible assassination teams in the United States, it is noteworthy that the United States purchased about two-thirds of Libya's oil production in 1981. Libya, in fact, was the U.S.' third largest foreign supplier. And Exxon, which in 1981 received much favorable publicity after relinquishing its oil producing interests in Libya, in fact pulled out for political reasons as well as due to employee harrassment, not out of a twang of national conscience.

U.S. multinational oil interests in Angola provide another fascinating study of the confict between national political and international economic interests. In early 1981, thanks primarily to Gulf Oil, the U.S. taxpayer-funded Export-Import Bank, along with the old multinational reliable, Morgan Guaranty Trust, made communist Angola a major loan. The ultimate in hypocrisy and multinational oil company greed was realized when Cuban troops were ordered to protect these American oil interests in communist Angola. *"Big Bucks,"* *"Big Banks"* and *"Big Oil"* are all involved in Angola. That Angola was/is a sanctuary for communist terrorists was/is apparently insignificant. What's important economically was that Gulf negotiated for the right to pump 160,000 barrels of crude oil a day. It has been reported that Gulf was paying the communist government of Angola $6 million a week for petroleum. A Soviet general with Cuban troops under his command is also reported to be part and parcel of the package that protects these American oil interests.

Chase Manhattan and Morgan Guaranty Trust were two of the more notable banks which loaned communist Angola $50 million to purchase oil development equipment. The good old U.S. taxpayer-funded Export-Import Bank loaned communist Angola $85 million for offshore oil development. Gulf Oil, Texaco, Mobil, General Tire, and Boeing have various interests there. Gulf, Texaco and Mobil's political lobbyists convinced the State Department to advise President Reagan to recognize Angola's communist government, too.

In addition to loans made by the Export-Import Bank and the International Development Bank, the World Bank and the IMF have loaned development oil money recently to India. Shell, Occidental, Texaco, Atlantic Richfield and Union Oil are among the beneficiaries of this *"loan."*

In addition to strategic minerals, is there an *"oil"* reason why the U.S. has gotten *"chummy"* with communist China? Of course. Low-priced Chinese oil exports to the U.S. have increased ten times just since 1979. China is now ranked third in world energy output when its oil, gas and coal reserves are considered. THE WALL STREET JOURNAL quoted John T. Emerson, oil analyst for Chase Manhattan,

> *"When adequate exploratory work has been done, particularly in the vast sedimentary basins of western China, the resource base may turn out to be as high as in Saudi Arabia."* [3]

With China possibly becoming the next Saudi Arabia of oil, there is little question why multinational oil and banking interests have taken such an interest in China. China recently invited Western oil companies to bid on the development of offshore oil resources for the first time.

The Caribbean is a *"hot spot"* because most of the oil carried in tankers bound for this country is refined in the Caribbean. This also explains why the Soviet Union in increasing its stranglehold there on various islands. Russia plans eventually to pick off Iran, too, to control the Straits of Hormuz and thus establish a hegemony over Middle East oil. Such a move by the Soviets could come as early as 1983.

In 1980, the Soviet Union was projected to be the world's largest oil producer, with production pegged at 12.2 million barrels a day. Poland, East Germany, Czechoslovakia, Hungary, Romania and Bulgaria are dependent upon the Soviet Union for their oil supply. Aproximately 70 percent of the hard currency the Soviet Union earns is through its oil and gas sales to noncommunist countries. Thus, the world oil glut and resultant falling prices hurt the Soviet Union's oil sales revenue. It is one of the main reasons why Russia has increased her gold sales internationally of late. Being an inefficient bureaucracy, substantial losses of gasoline occur in the Soviet Union each year due to theft, carelessness and other corruptions. Is it surprising to find that three American oil companies were directly involved in negotiations with the Soviet Union in 1981 over the construction of the Soviet natural gas line to Western Europe? The companies which expressed great interest in the Siberian line were headed up by Exxon, Mobil and Texaco.

The following are direct quotes from one of our excellent intelligence sources in Saudi Arabia:

> *". . . increasing censorship in Saudi Arabia. They are running scared . . . The Khomeini-type religious fanatics are increasing rapidly. The Crown Prince's half brother is head of the army, 'Salvation Army.' He is procommunist, with direct lines to Moscow. Fahd did not go to see President Reagan because he was not sure he would be able to return. . . . Russian planes fly over Saudi Arabia constantly to Yemen . . . The whole Middle East*

will eventually fall apart like a mosaic, just like Iran. Nobody will be able to stop it . . . The time bomb is ticking—could go for a year or two, but will explode for sure! The middle class are aware of it. They are living on borrowed time."

Any experienced market trader would have known that in 1980 the top was in the oil market. Every commodity tops out in a similar fashion because people, collectively speaking, act in the same predictable way at market tops. In 1980, U.S. coal was priced at only a third to a half as much as OPEC oil. Thus, the natural corrective pricing adjustment had to be just over the horizon. Also, at that time, the Library of Congress declared, in an infamous study, that oil prices would soar to over $100 a barrel as a result of the war between Iran and Iraq, if all oil exports from the Persian Gulf were halted. It was further claimed, at that time, that by 1985, over half of the United States' productive capacity would belong to OPEC. We were also told that by 1985 OPEC would have such an enormous surplus that it would be able to buy all the FORTUNE 500 companies. Prices are always projected to go to the moon at market tops, and hysterical projections are commonplace.

The bigger they are, the harder they fall. This trickle-down recession, after it hit the most vulnerable segments of the U.S. economy, the automobile industry and single-family housing, was destined to hit the oil industry eventually. Let's review the situation as it unfolded.

For the past 120 years, repeatedly U.S. citizens have been told that crude oil reserves were no more than the equivalent of 10 years' consumption. Thus, the American public has been conditioned to be anxious about oil prices. In late 1980, the price of the United States' imported oil had increased ten times from mid-1973 levels. (In early 1973, a bushel of wheat and a barrel of oil were both selling for about $2.00. Can anyone imagine $34.00 wheat? At $34.00-a-bushel wheat, assuming constant demand, revenues would increase $20 billion.) The soaring price of oil, outdistancing all other commodities, led to a veritable stampede of exploration and employment in the oil, gas and coal mining industries. By late 1980, employment in the oil, gas and coal mining businesses had increased a staggering 90 percent from 1973-74 levels. This was at six times the rate of growth experienced by the rest of the private non-farm economy. It was during 1979 and 1980 that this employment truly exploded, typical of a top. A windfall profit was apparently there for the having, and so everyone jumped in. Investment soared, too. With the year 1979 being nothing to sneeze at, investors put up an additional $9.3 billion for a 34 percent increase in investment funds in the years following, into 1981. Between 1978 and 1980 an amazing 98 percent of the profit increase registered by the top 500 U.S. companies went to the companies involved with the energy industry. In 1981, a record 77,500 wells were drilled.

Meanwhile, while the push was on to increase supply, demand was falling off. In 1980, gasoline consumption in the U.S. declined 7 percent. The demand for OPEC oil by Western Europe, Japan and the United Staes actually peaked in 1978. So, with increasing supply and falling demand, it was only a matter of time until the oil market topped out.

When prices peak out in many markets, they approach the vertical. The 300 percent rise in crude oil prices between 1979 and March of 1980 gave us a *"spike"* top. By August, 1981, some 700,000 barrels a day of refining capacity, 3.7 percent of the nation's total, was put on the shelf, so dramatic had been the decline in demand for oil products. It is estimated that in August, 1981, only 12-13 million barrels of crude oil a day were running through the domestic oil refineries, compared to 18.6 million barrels a day in late 1980. Some oil refineries were said to be operating at only 50-60 percent of capacity. Texaco closed refineries in Wyoming and Oklahoma. In August, 1981, British Petroleum cut its refining capacity in Europe by 25 percent and closed a plant in England. The African members of OPEC held a special meeting to persuade Saudi Arabia to cut back its oil production. Car inventories hit an all-time record high at that time, while car sales dropped to a 30-year low. Utility companies saw a decline in sales. Energy efficiency and conservation became the theme in America. Energy tax credits helped fuel this conservation effort. From first quarter 1980 to first quarter 1981, consumption was down in all categories of energy. Oil inventories were reported to be 60 million barrels above normal supply. The bear market in oil was on.

Investors usually don't see what they don't want to see. When crude oil and petroleum products fell 25.3 percent in July, 1980, the sharpest drop in ten years, the red flag of an oil top was hoisted for all to see who were willing to look.

OPEC was hit hard, too. U.S. oil imports dropped from 32 million barrels a day to 19 million barrels in 18 months, ending October, 1981. As of July, 1981, oil stocks had fallen 40 percent from November, 1980, levels. In January, 1982, small exploratory oil stocks fell some 40 percent. In early 1982, the United Arab Emirates, which is reportedly the third richest member of OPEC, complained that its annual cash surplus was drying up. An early February, 1982 WALL STREET JOURNAL article reported,

> *"Oil traders and analysts in New York, Rome, Paris and London, among the most active oil markets, are watching with astonishment as cargo after cargo of oil goes begging for buyers."*[4]

Spot market oil was selling below official levels. OPEC producers began issuing discounts. Credit payments were lengthened. Refined petroleum products were sold at large discounts.

Plagued by financial trouble, Libya and Algeria pursuaded some Western companies to accept oil as partial payment for merchandise and services. This further pressured oil prices. Non-communist countries' oil consumption fell 10 percent in 1980 and 1981. Henry Wojtyla and Nicles Michas, two excellent oil analysts, declared, *"The oil glut is here to stay. There is nothing temporary about it."* These two gentlemen further forecast current account deficits for OPEC in 1982 and 1983. *"Oil will become a significant deflationary influence over this decade."* (Source: THE WALL STREET JOURNAL)

OPEC exports over imports were projected to yield deficits of $35 billion in 1982 and $20 billion in 1983. International oil prices above $20 a barrel still create an incentive for oil exploration and development of non-OPEC oil, as well as the creation of alternative sources of energy, adding to the problem. The International Energy Agency in Paris is not projecting any petroleum shortages whatsoever until, at earliest, the end of 1984. OPEC itself is projecting an oil glut at least through 1984. In December, 1981, oil stock analysts began discussing the head and shoulders top in the oil stocks.

Focusing stateside, domestic oil well drilling increased 34 percent in 1980 and 36 percent 1981. There were more oil and gas wells drilled in 1981 than any year in history. Some of the small independent oil companies began complaining about a *"Big Oil"* power play which was brought on by the excess supply and by the decline in oil prices. This oil recession might enable multinational oil companies to drive hundreds of small independents out of business. Stripper wells in Ohio, for example, have been effectively shut down due to a glut of oil in the pipeline. Near-term, the temporary glut is a real boon for the major oil companies. Small oil companies, caught in the squeeze between low oil demand and high interest payments, leading to cash-flow problems, could be forced to sell valuable assets to the multinationals. Texaco, for example, is one of the 20 most liquid corporations in America. This is just like the situation presently in protein gold where small, independent farmers are being squeezed out before protein gold (food) prices explode longer-term.

This brings us to some interesting projections concerning the future price of oil. Armand Hammer, the Chairman of Occidental Petroleum, has predicted that we will see $100-a-barrel oil in the next three-five years. (Recall that Armand Hammer has been trading with the Russians for 60 years, going back to the 1920s when he traded

American wheat for Russian caviar and furs.) Interesting also is the fact that throughout 1981, Chase Manhattan began implementing its plan to handle as much worldwide business in petroleum as possible. Also, former Secretary of Energy, James R. Schlesinger, has projected that oil will be priced at $75 a barrel no later than the end of the 1980s.

Before we look into how high the price of oil could be jacked up, let's see who has a stake in soaring oil prices. We'll also observe if these parties have it within their ability to effect a large price increase.

What we find is that *"Big Oil," "Big Banking"* and *"Big Government"* all benefit from high oil prices. There is a potential loss of $5 billion to be absorbed by someone for every dollar drop in the average price of oil. In 1980, every dollar that an oil company shareholder received in dividends was matched by $12.00 in taxes paid to the federal government by the oil company. A 10 percent increase in OPEC oil prices results in a 20 percent increase in revenues to the U.S. Treasury. So, the Treasury has everything to gain from high oil prices. The big multinational banks are dependent on the cash flow generated by deposits from OPEC. Falling oil demand has not only resulted in less bank deposits but withdrawals which are dangerous to the shaky banking structure. It is estimated that OPEC's investment in the United States, as of the middle of 1981, was approximately $70 billion, according to conservative estimates made by the U.S. Treasury. (OPEC was said to have held $35 billion of U.S. government securities plus corporate stocks and bonds and bank deposits.) Undoubtedly, the institutions that have the biggest stake in maintaining high oil prices are the multinational banks. If oil should fall to its technically projected level of $20-$24 a barrel, a banking panic could occur. OPEC's deposits are concentrated in Chase Manhattan, Citibank, Morgan Guaranty, Chemical Bank and Manufacturers Hanover.

(Bankers abhor risk. As a result, they usually take the most risk with your money and mine because they loan huge amounts for the wrong ventures at the wrong time, effectively at the top of the market, when the risk appears to be the least but is in fact the greatest. The latest example of this is evidenced by the billions of dollars that the multinational banks have loaned the oil and oil services industries right at the top of the market.)

The international oil companies, the federal government and the multinational banks all have a considerable stake in maintaining high oil prices long-term. And it's not that these vested interests don't talk to each other. The interlocking directorates among major oil companies and commercial banks are numerous.

**Indirect Interlocking Directorates Among Major Oil Companies
Through Commercial Banks, 1972**

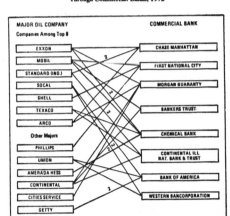

Source: Compiled from Stanley H. Ruttenberg and Associates, *The American Oil Industry—A Failure of Antitrust Policy*, Washington, D.C., 1974, pp. 83, 147–60.

Source: THE CONTROL OF OIL, John M. Blair, Random House, NY, 1976.

The financial problems caused by lower oil prices are not only domestic but also international. Great Britain loses $400 million in income for every dollar the price of oil drops. And there is definitely a domino effect because many multinational banks own each other's shares. This incestuous game of bank *"musical chairs"* ownership is practiced by J. P. Morgan, Citibank, Chase Manhattan, Morgan Guaranty Trust, Chemical Bank, Mellon Bank, Wells Fargo, Bank of America and Manufacturers Hanover. What happened to the banks as a result of the stock market crash in 1929 could very well happen to them again, this time as a result of a crash in the oil market. While the American public sleeps in its economic ignorance, the multinational bankers are breaking out in an oily sweat.

How can the price of oil be forced higher? If demand is contracting and cannot be increased, there is only one other way—reduce the supply. Destroy the primary oil producers' wells, pipelines, refineries and the like. How can this happen? Through terrorism and war, of course. There is precedent for such action.

When this writer was undergoing T-38 instructor pilot training at Tyndall Air Force Base, Florida, in our class were many Air Force jet fighter pilots who had just returned from the Vietnam War. They openly discussed how they were not allowed to bomb the oil supplies which came down the Ho Chi Minh Trail. They further commented on how the oil refinery located in North Vietnam was off limits as a strategic target. I found this quite strange at the time. This contemptible situation was further discussed in the book, ROLLING THUNDER, which had an excellent discussion on how the oil refinery in Hanoi supplied oil to both the North and South Vietnamese during the Vietnam War. The refinery was/is, perhaps not surprisingly, owned by New York banking interests.

Later on, the Middle East War and the 1973 Arab oil embargo jacked up the real gasoline prices in the U.S. considerably. BUSINESS WEEK reported that the 1973 oil embargo quadrupled oil prices. However, by 1978, gasoline prices had again dropped below earlier levels. The Iranian crisis followed in 1978, leading to increases of 165 percent in the world's crude oil price. Isn't it ironic that the Iranian Revolution occurred just after record OPEC production?

In 1978, this writer was in direct contact with the Iranian Embassy because of their expressed interest in my book, CYCLES OF WAR. It was at this time that all my crumbling illusions about the honesty of the U.S. federal government (Carter) were shattered, as I tracked Iranian source information and contrasted it with *"official"* news releases by the Carter regime. The Shah always believed that he had been sold out, sacrificed for higher oil prices. And remember, too, that Evergreen Airlines was involved in transporting the Shah around the world during his last days. (Evergreen is reputed to be a CIA operation.)

Next to Saudi Arabia, Iran was the world's largest producer from 1950-1973. Logically, if Iran's oil producing capability was knocked out, the price of oil would soar. And that's exactly what happened. What did the Shah of Iran say about it all? In an interview televised by ABC's *"20/20,"* on January 17, 1980, with David Frost, the Shah of Iran declared,

> *"Two years before the changes in my country, we heard from two different sources connected with the oil companies that the regime in Iran would change.*
>
> *"And for the last year the (multinational oil) consortium never seriously discussed their plans to purchase our oil. We believe that there was a plan that there must be less oil offered to the world market. In order to make the price of oil go up, our country should have been the one chosen for the sacrifice. Iran was producing 5,600,000 barrels a day. So, in order to have a shortage of oil, in order to make the prices go up, with what I have heard about these two people, connected to two oil companies and the oil consortium never really starting serious talk about placing an order to buy our oil—so it seems that the chosen country to drop its production of oil would have been mine. They happened to be American companies."*

Production of Crude Oil: Nine Leading Producing Countries, 1950–73

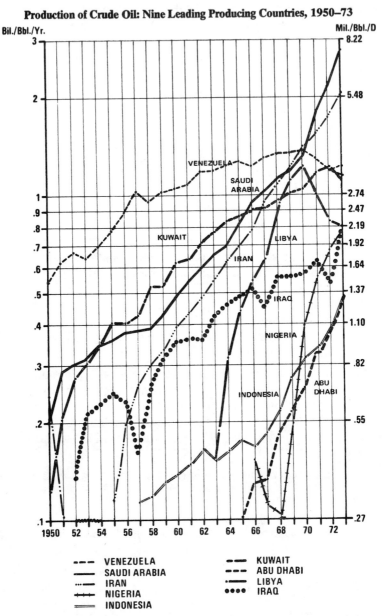

Source: Derived from Organization of Petroleum Exporting
Countries, Statistical Bulletins.

© 1975 by Middle East Research and Information Project, Inc.
Reprinted by permission of Monthly Review Press.

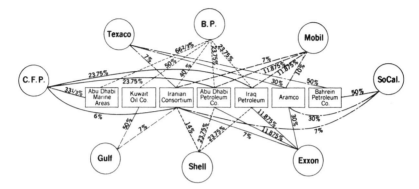

Ownership Links Between the Major International Oil Companies
(Including Compagnie Française des Pétroles)
and the Major Crude-Oil Producing Companies in the Middle East

Source: U.S. Senate, Hearings Before the Subcommittee on Multinational Corporations of the Committee on Foreign Relations. On Multinational Petroleum Companies and Foreign Policy, Part V, p. 290.
© *1975 by Middle East Research and Information Project, Inc. Reprinted by permission of Monthly Review Press.*

From the graph, it is evident how thoroughly the multinational oil companies are intertwined with the Middle East oil producers. Just withholding technology from these Middle East oil producers would do the trick of reducing world oil supply it would seem. But this is a bit too obvious. Blocking the Straits of Hormuz in the Persian Gulf would knock out (conservatively) 40 percent of the non-communist world's oil supply and eliminate 75 percent of Asia's petroleum supplies. In 1980, the United States received 14 percent of its oil, Japan—75 percent, France—87 percent, Great Britain—57 percent, and West Germany—34 percent through the Straits of Hormuz. Some two-thirds of the oil that moves by the world's oceans and international oil trade comes from five countries bordering the Persian Gulf—Kuwait, Iran, Iraq, Saudi Arabia and Abu Dhabi. OPEC is said to control 52 percent of the world's oil supply and account for 40 percent of world oil production. (OPEC was hurt badly by the 23 percent drop in U.S. oil demand alone in the first eight months of 1981.)

OPEC accounts for 80 percent of the oil traded internationally.

OPEC's record oil exports occurred in 1977—31.2 million barrels a day. They slipped to below 20 million barrels a day. In the second half of 1981, OPEC's oil production fell to an 11-year low. With current world demand at 22 to 25 million barrels a day for OPEC oil and the OPEC member states having structured their budgets based upon sales of 26 to 28 million barrels a day, the 13 OPEC countries have no choice but to continue high levels of production. Stated differently, there is little room for OPEC to drop production, given its present financial bind. By no coincidence, this financial difficulty should continue to plague OPEC for the next three years at least. Except for Saudi Arabia, the other OPEC members have mortgaged their anticipated oil revenues to the hilt. The sharp oil price drop caught them off guard. They literally cannot cut production more now. Such action would ensure financial ruin. In fact, if prices drop too sharply, OPEC may have to increase production in order to increase revenues. Nigeria, Algeria and Libya are the countries hurting the most with their high-priced oil.

High interest rates further discouraged any international incentive to stockpile oil. It is estimated that some 3.3 billion barrels of crude oil is now stockpiled internationally. Some super tankers have been circling offshore, full of oil, for over a year. There is no place to offload.

As of September, 1981, Libya's production had been cut to 650,000 barrels a day from 1.7 million barrels at the end of 1980. Nigeria's production was cut to below 800,000 barrels a day from 2 million barrels a day in December, 1980. Nigeria's foreign reserves fell to $5 billion from $9 billion in early 1981. Kuwait cut its oil output by 50 percent. Kuwait cut its oil price to $32.30 a barrel on January 1, 1982. In late 1981, Iran cut its oil price to $32 a barrel. More cuts are expected. A Standard Oil of California refinery in the Bahamas, with a 500,000-barrel-a-day capacity, is running at only 33 percent of capacity. Saudi Arabian Oil Minister, Sheik Yamani, declared that there will be no shortage of oil in the 1980s, given the world's *"economic conditions."* Algeria, Kuwait, Libya and Nigeria together cut production back 2.2 million barrels a day in the last year due to a lack of buyers. Adding insult to injury is the possibility that the United Arab Emirates plan to double oil production capacity to 3 million barrels a day by 1985. And once the war between Iran and Iraq is over, oil exports could increase from 2 million barrels a day to up to 6 million barrels a day by these two countries. Egypt could produce approximately 660,000 barrels of oil a day this year, plus gas. Egypt is also on the verge of a major oil boom, as is the Far East, including Indonesia and particularly Australia. Oil is everywhere and it's getting cheaper and more abundant as demand falls.

Saudi Arabia is the unique member of OPEC, without financial difficulties, and is being pressured to reduce production further. The ARAMCO partners, Exxon, Mobil, Texaco and Standard Oil of California were having difficulty marketing the 6 million barrels of oil daily they take of the 8.5 million barrels a day that Saudi Arabia produces. Saudi Arabia just cut production more.

Which countries are the logical targets in the Middle East to reduce, probably forcibly through terrorism and war, world oil production? Kuwait, Qatar, Bahrain, the United Arab Emirates, Oman and the jewel of OPEC, Saudi Arabia. Together, these six countries produce 11.5 million barrels of oil a day, which is approximately 50 percent of OPEC's total oil production.

Saudi Arabia seems like the most logical candidate for destruction. Like Iran, it heads the heap of oil producers and is ripe socially, politically and in terms of *"conditioned"* world opinion to be knocked off. Phillip K. Verleger, an oil scholar at Yale, declared, *"OPEC really doesn't matter, but Saudi Arabia matters a lot."* Saudi Arabia all by itself can, and has, accounted for nearly half of OPEC's total oil production. Saudi Arabia sets the world's floor oil price. OPEC set a record production of 31.2 million barrels per day in 1977, the year before the Iranian Revolution that touched off a 165 percent increase in the world price of crude oil. The 1973 Arab oil embargo increased oil prices four times. What would happen to world oil prices if Saudi Arabia conveniently, accidentally, was *"temporarily"* eliminated from the world's oil picture? Is there any question that oil prices would skyrocket?

Saudi Arabia does not have the ability to adequately defend its oil fields from invasion or terrorism. The Saudi Arabian government itself is insecure and uncertain about its ability to maintain power. There has already been one major assassination attempt on the Royal Family. In fact, some intelligence sources are projecting the present Saudi Arabian government to fall within the next five years. The timing is too convenient.

Will the U.S. government defend the Saudi Arabian oil fields when destruction or production cutbacks in those fields benefit the U.S. Treasury, the U.S. multinational banks and the U.S. multinational oil companies? Unlikely, given political reality. Saudi Arabia already plans on building bombproof oil storage facilities on the Red Sea coast which will have the capacity to hold 1.5 billion barrels of crude oil. This will be the world's largest oil stockpile facility, itself indicative of Saudi Arabian concerns.

How else could the necessary high price of world oil be maintained?

If the Soviet Union controlled Iran, the Persian Gulf, the Straits of Hormuz and the entire oil Middle East, then the U.S.S.R. could *"ration"* oil to the world, *"conveniently"* keeping the world's oil price high. Then the multinational banks and oil companies, along with the U.S. Treasury, would be off the financial hook. If the U.S. resists the Soviet Union militarily in the Middle East, Russia will attack Western Europe and World War III will be on. Watch Israel. Islam is uniting against Israel. Israel will use its nuclear and other sophisticated weapons if the Islamic and Soviet threat becomes severe enough.

The March 16, 1982 ROCKY MOUNTAIN NEWS, in a featured story by R. H. Boyce, reported that the Soviet Union is building a military base and warm water port on Iran's southern coast at Cha-Bahr Harbor. The base overlooks the oil tankers' route out of the Persian Gulf, and fulfills Russia's centuries old dream of a warm water port on the Arabian Sea. Soviet planes and warships will be stationed there.

The U.S.S.R. is also financing a number of Iran's construction projects. The Tudah Communist Party in Iran is growing rapidly in importance. It will be only a short time until Iran is a Soviet puppet. Then the stage will be set for the U.S.S.R. to attempt to control the Middle East and its oil. Look for Soviet inspired tensions to increase between the Arabs and Israelis and between Shiite and Sunni Moslems. War will become increasingly the topic of conversation when the Middle East comes up.

*   *   *

"Some startling aspects of the Israeli invasion of Lebanon have been turning up . . . What the Soviets and PLO have accomplished . . . is astounding . . . Steel-reinforced caverns and miles of underground galleries were cut through earth and rock to link up huge command and storage halls, some of them large enough to shelter fleets of helicopters. The steel doors shutting off ultra-secret chambers were designed to be opened only by radio signals from Soviet subs off the coast . . .

"Equally alarming, enough missiles, cannons, tanks, and other armored vehicles to equip a modern army were turned up in the underground depot."

DAILY NEWS DIGEST
August 4, 1982

BANKS AND BUCKS

8/1/80

Congressman Ron Paul of Texas recently wrote me expressing his alarm over the Housing Banking Committee's decision to increase U.S. taxpayer's contribution to the IMF by $5.5 billion. The vote was 34-4. This redistribution of our tax money to bail out Third World deadbeats is so the Third Worlders can pay off the big banks. Put simply, we are bailing out the multinational banks again.

Dissenting Views on H.R. 7244
Hon. Ron Paul of Texas

In The House of Representatives
Thursday, May 15, 1980

"Mr. PAUL. Mr. Speaker, once again your committee has recommended pouring billions of tax dollars down an international rathole, bringing to approximately $16.5 billion the total amount of wealth we have taken from the American people and given to the International Monetary Fund. The approximately $5.5 billion increase in our quota is the largest single increase in history, and it occurs at a most dangerous point in the history of the international monetary system.

Bailing Out the Banks

"In his appearances before the Senate and House Banking Committees on this bill, Federal Reserve Governor Henry C. Wallich had some disturbing things to say about the purposes of this massive increase in our quota. Many of these statements are allusions to the desperate condition that seems to exist and be worsening in repayments of loans by developing countries to large American, Japanese, and European banks.

" '1. In an environment of increased international financial strains and of increased sensitivity of the U.S. economy to developments abroad, the United States also benefits indirectly from the IMF's efforts to alleviate such strains. In many instances, without temporary financial assistance from the IMF, countries would be forced to take severe

63

adjustment actions that could have a disruptive effect on the international economy.

" '2. The strengthening of the financial position of the Fund resulting from the increase in Fund quotas is an essential element in preparing for the strains that may well develop on the international financial system in the next year or two.

" '3. Given the expected increases in demands for balance of payments financing, as well as the large external indebtedness that many countries already have with commercial banks, the IMF should be in a position to meet a larger proportion of the immediate financing needs of its members in the coming years than it has assumed recently. A strengthening of the Fund's financial position by an increase in members' quotas would increase the likelihood that more countries would come under the Fund's conditional lending umbrella.

" '4. The letter from the chairman of the subcommittee inviting the Board to testify has accurately pointed to the dilemma facing the international financial system: a high level of lending by banks to developing countries could lead to excessive risk concentration at banks . . .

" '5. Between the end of 1974 and the end of 1979, outstanding claims of banks from all countries on non-oil developing countries increased on average about $20 billion per year.

" '6. The rapid expansion in lending by foreign banks has caused some concern among foreign regulatory authorities. The German and British authorities have begun to require banks in those countries to maintain detailed records on a consolidated basis including, as a minimum, lending by their head offices and foreign branches. Since last fall, Japanese banks have been constrained by a request from the Ministry of Finance to limit their international lending.

" '7. Weighing all these factors is indeed complex, but, on balance, I would conclude that the general risks are somewhat greater in 1980 and 1981 than in 1974 and 1975. The situation clearly varies greatly from country to country. Recent history has taught us that the positions of some countries can improve dramatically in a short period of time. Unfortunately, in other cases, the external situation has deteriorated rapidly over time, either as a consequence of financial mismanagement or because of external (and sometimes internal) events over which the country has little control.'

"These warnings and allusions to impending crises cast some light on the perceived necessity for this massive infusion of American tax dollars into the IMF. The money will apparently be needed to bail out some banks that have made risky loans to the socialist governments of developing countries.

Worldwide Inflation

"Even since World War II, the IMF has permitted and encouraged worldwide inflation. This has been done through providing reserves to facilitate international payments problems. One of the reasons given for passage of this bill is that it will enable the IMF to handle the large imbalances of payments that now exist and are expected to persist into the forseeable future. The developing nations, like the developed nations, have to face reality. There is no free lunch. An increase of international liquidity merely serves as another source of price inflation. It is true that recipient nations can buy goods and services in the international markets at yesterday's prices, thereby gaining in relationship to those who have not yet gained access to the fiat money, but this only can be paid for by those who must restrict their purchases in the face of higher prices.

"By creating added liquidity, the IMF can indeed redistribute wealth, but it cannot create new wealth. The net trade imbalances of the nations that import more than they export can be met by gifts of new liquidity of IMF reserves, at least for as long as such reserves are honored by the producing nations. But this is simply a giveaway program.

"In effect, it steals resources from one group of citizens and gives them to another group.

"The transfer of resources from one nation to another makes the IMF just one more foreign aid bureaucracy. The wealth of middle-class citizens of the nations of the West will wind up subsidizing the grossly inefficient programs of the elitist, socialist, envious, and bureaucratized Third World nations. The middle classes of the West will have to support the educational elite of the less-developed nations. We will rob from the middle class to finance the powerful, only we will do it across borders.

"What we have seen again and again during the past 30 years is that the guilt-ridden voters of the West—unnecessarily guilt-ridden—have allowed their governments to transfer their hard-earned resources to the state planning bureaucracies of the Third World. Government-to-government aid strengthens the economics of socialism. This kind of aid is nothing less than a weapon—a weapon used by Western-educated socialist bureaucrats in the Third World to suppress economic freedom in their own countries.

"Because of the testimony taken by the subcommittee two amendments were incorporated into this bill regarding the social programs of nations which borrow from the IMF. The first would encourage the IMF not to impose conditions on its loans that would adversely affect the socialist programs of the borrowing governments. It seems that the conditions that the IMF has imposed in the past have curtailed the attempts of those governments to provide material security for their subjects, and the committee feels that these welfare programs should not suffer because of the irresponsible policies of the government.

"Important as this amendment is, the second amendment would encourage the World Bank to coordinate its lending activities with those of the IMF so that borrowing governments may receive funds sufficient to repay their loans to the banks and also maintain the welfare programs at home. Working in tandem, the IMF and the World Bank would become the main vehicle for the international redistribution of wealth. Much of that wealth, of course, will be redistributed from the American people to large bankers via Third World governments. It will not be the first time that poor Peter will have been robbed to pay wealthy Paul. If the IMF is successful in its proposed policies, we will see even greater disruption of international economic cooperation. The IMF may have failed in its attempt to create a world of price-controlled stability; it will not fail in its attempt to subsidize uncertainty-producing socialist regimes in the Third World and large banks in the First World.

"Should anyone believe that the United States needs the IMF to achieve its supposed goals of monetary reliability, price stability, and economic growth, let him consider this fact: Switzerland has never belonged to the IMF, does not suffer from price inflation, and did not contribute its gold reserves only to see its gold sold off to finance the financial follies of the Third World socialists.

"We could learn a lesson from the Swiss experience, and I hope we do. I urge my colleagues to reject this bill."

*   *   *

In the Woodstack

Did you know that the Federal Financing Bank has $65 billion in loans outstanding? Did you know that the FFB is an off-the-budget bank, since it is a part of the U.S. Treasury? Did you know it is made up of ten full-time employees, all of which are unelected bureaucrats? Did you know that its $65 billion loan portfolio is larger than the Bank of America's? Did you know that the FFB has never denied a loan request? Is the FFB representative of the will of the people? Is this the way you want your tax money handled?

*   *   *

28833

Federal Register
Vol. 46, No 103
Friday, May 29, 1981

Presidential Documents

Title 3—

The President

Presidential Determination No. 81-7 of May 20, 1981

Determination under Section 2(b)(2) of the Export-Import Bank Act of 1945, as amended—Socialist Republic of Romania

Memorandum for the Secretary of State

Pursuant to Section 2(b)(2) of the Export-Import Bank Act of 1945, as amended, I determine that it is in the national interest for the Export-Import Bank of the United States to extend a credit in the amount of $120,742,500 to the Socialist Republic of Romania in connection with its purchase of two nuclear steam turbine generators and related services and spare parts.

On my behalf, please transmit this determination to the Speaker of the House and the President of the Senate.

This determination shall be published in the Federal Register.

Ronald Reagan

THE WHITE HOUSE,
Washington, May 20, 1981.

[FR Doc 81-16217
Filed 5-27-81, 2:29 pm]
Billing code 3195-01-M

TERMS OF THE LOAN

```
Amount of sale: $142,050,000
Amount financed: $120,742,500
Percentage financed: 85%
Repayment schedule: 20 semi-annual payments beginning in July 1989
Interest rate: 7 3/4% charged to  Romania
               1/4% charged to General Electric
               1/2% commitment fee
Seller: General Electric
Item: 2 700 megawatt  nuclear steam turbine generators, spare parts and services
```

39655

Federal Register
Vol. 47, No. 175
Thursday, September 9, 1982

Presidential Documents

Title 3—

The President

Presidential Determination No. 82-19 of August 30, 1982

Determination under Section 2(b)(2) of the Export-Import Bank Act of 1945, as amended
People's Republic of China

Memorandum for the Honorable George P. Shultz, The Secretary of State

Pursuant to Section 2(b)(2) of the Export-Import Bank Act of 1945, as amended, I determine that it is in the national interest for the Export-Import Bank of the United States to extend a credit and guarantee in the aggregate amount of $68,425,000 to the People's Republic of China in connection with its purchase of steel making equipment and related services.

On my behalf, please transmit this determination to the Speaker of the House and the President of the Senate.

This determination shall be published in the Federal Register.

Ronald Reagan

THE WHITE HOUSE,
Washington, August 30, 1982.

[FR Doc. 82-24901
Filed 9-7-82, 4:35 pm]
Billing code 3195-01-M

THE FOUR HORSES OF THE APOCALYPSE
FOR THE THIRD WORLD COUNTRIES

7/17/81

Beyond a shadow of a doubt, it has been the Developing World, the Third World countries, who have suffered the most from the inflationary whipsaws, the burden of debt, high interest rates and oil price increases. Because they have no financial clout and little education, they are easily exploited. They suffer the additional humiliation of having to buy (import) at retail prices and sell (export) at wholesale prices. This ensures permanent deficits (a lesson they learned well from the American farmer). While consumer prices have risen 56 percent in the U.S. since 1975, and have increased in the world-at-large 79 percent since 1975, the Third World countries have experienced a whopping 243 percent increase in consumer prices since 1975. Talk about financial indigestion.[5]

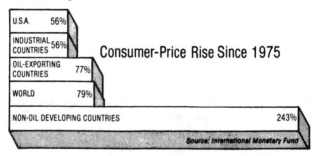

Source: THE WALL STREET JOURNAL

Third World debt now stands at a breathtaking $500 billion +. And over 20 of these 100 Third World Countries are renegotiating this debt service. The 15 largest U.S. banks, which have about half of all U.S. bank deposits, account for 80 percent of all the loans to these developing countries. The Bundesbank has concluded that the Third World's financing requirements are now unmanageable. This was also concluded during the Great Depression when a moratorium was declared on Third World debt. The more things change, the more they remain the same.

The dominoes have started to fall . . . Iran, Poland, . . . ? The international bankers, having finally recognized the error of their ways, have been scrambling like crazy, using their political clout to shift their deadbeat loans to the international financial organizations—The World Bank, The IMF, The Export-Import Bank, etc. With international loans presently accounting for 50 percent of the total lending by the ten largest U.S. banks, it is no wonder these bankers are unsettled.

The mischief conceived as of late by these international bankers include:

1. The Monetary Control Act of 1980. Under this little legislative jewel, Third World loans could (will) be bought up by The Federal Reserve, the American taxpayer, of course, picking up the tab when you come right down to it.

2. There has been some recent shuffling and switching of high-placed financial chairs. The former head of The Bank of America now heads up The World Bank, while the former kingpin of The World Bank has shuffled on over to The Bank of America. A switch in the nick of time, perhaps? David Rockefeller has become head of the International Affairs Department of Chase Manhattan, bringing along his trusty sidekick, Henry Kissinger. Paul Volcker, an old understudy of David Rockefeller, now serving as Chairman of the Board of The Federal Reserve, doesn't hurt the international schemes any.

3. On May 12, 1981, the House of Representatives voted to remove $876 million from the 1981 budget of the Export-Import Bank. The big banks' and corporations' executives went to work that very night. The next day, May 13th, 71 votes were switched and the $876 million was reinstated. That's real power in action! The U.S. taxpayers have subsidized the Export-Import Bank to the tune of $13 billion already, historically.

4. The House Banking Committee voted $13 billion total in funding for the World Bank, the International Bank, the International Development Association, the Inter-American Development Bank, the Asian Development Bank and the African Development Bank. The U.S. had only provided $8.5 billion for the World Bank in its first 35 years of existence. Adding insult to injury, this time the *"callable capital"* of the World Bank was increased by $8 billion, which will allow the World Bank to float $40 billion more in loans.

Keep an eye out for news items on the World Bank, the Export-Import Bank, the International Development Association, the Inter-American Development Bank, the Asian Development Bank and the African Development Bank. Money will be cycled from the American taxpayer to these banks, from there to the Third World countries who will then pay back their loans to the U.S. multinational banks.

Here are some interesting statistics on the status of the Third World's population:

1. The lowest 48 percent of the world's population has less than 5 percent of the world's income.

2. 36 of these Third World countries, with nearly 50 percent of the world's population, had per capita incomes of $3000.00 or less.

3. In 1980, the total fuel bill of the Third World Developing countries was $40 billion. They have stayed afloat since 1974 by petrodollar recycling, another catch phrase for throwing money down a rat hole.

4. These Third World Developing countries contain 72 percent of the world's population.

5. The debt the Developing countries owe is many times the total capital in the international banks.

CONFETTI A LA CARTE

4/30/82

This writer has consistently held that our boom/bust economy (created by the Federal Reserve's monetizing of the deficit and the creation of credit through the fractional reserve banking system, whereby each dollar is leveraged up to 6-7 times) would finally result in a topping out of the U.S. economy long-term, followed by a disinflationary interlude of approximately three years, and then an ultimate hyperinflation and destruction of the U.S. dollar. The real estate market, automobile sales and agriculture, three pillars of our economy, topped out in 1979-80, exactly as projected. The accelerating decline of the long-term debt market, the bond market crash of 1979, assured the economic downturn. Other segments of the economy experienced a rippling deterioration since then.

We have not yet felt the full brunt of the destruction of the base upon which our economy is built, the demise of the long-term bond market. We have only scratched the surface of the upcoming political and social readjustments which must and will be made as a result of the financial debacle. It is the height of folly for a society to believe that it can maintain a solid economic foundation built upon long-term debt, when its humanistic evolutionary overview is consistently and overwhelmingly short-term. It's like trying to walk on clouds. Even the first step meets with failure and an abrupt surprise.

The upcoming hyperinflation is almost assured for the following reasons: 1) The American public is economically and politically illiterate. The masses do not have the knowledge of the steps that must be taken to preserve our social order. Neither do the politicians they elect. 2) The humanistic American general public lacks the self-discipline and character necessary to undergo the pain to make the required readjustments, even if it did have the economic and political knowledge of what needs to be done.

With better than 50% of the American public dependent upon the government for a living, given the pervasive envy and selfishness which permeates our society, the American general public will not again vote against its own self-interest economically, as it did during

71

the 1980 election of President Reagan. Already, we have seen the accelerated political disintegration of this Republican administration, marked by such things as bumper stickers in California which read, *"I never thought I would miss Jimmy Carter."* Golf balls and tomatoes have been thrown at Secretary of Defense Weinberger. President and Mrs. Reagan were booed at a cultural affair at the Kennedy Center. The President's popularity in the polls has dropped sharply. Senators and congressmen are increasingly jumping the Reagan ship of state, scrambling like the political rats they are. The United Steel Workers of America took out a quarter-page ad in THE WALL STREET JOURNAL which read, *"Mr. President: You Broke Your Promise to the American People."* Tension, distrust, dismay, disillusionment and bewilderment run high at the White House as Reagan's ship of state is swamped by problems it cannot solve because it cannot even clearly see and define the issues. Reagan and his boys missed the philosophical, religious and psychological bases of the problems. The Reagan administration, with its lack of depth, is caught. It won a few battles in 1981, but started losing the war in 1982, just as this analyst projected would be the case.

Now comes *"Confetti a la carte."* A knowledgeable old banker, who understands the nuances of our financial system, recently spilled the beans on how the hyperinflation will most probably occur. Vince Rossiter is a shrewd cookie. He understands the importance of real new wealth and commodities being monetized on a local level in line with the principles of *"Wealth for All."* Rossiter understands the banking maze and how it operates detrimentally to the welfare of the average American. This writer has long pointed to the fact that, in a general sense, there are three financial factors which hold the seeds of hyperinflation, as our present banking system is constituted (political considerations somewhat aside). They are: 1. The Monetary Control Act of 1980, 2. The practice of the money center, international banks of dominating and drawing funds through the federal funds market from small, rural, liquid, country, correspondent banks and leveraging same, 3. The massive, unregulated Eurodollar market.

In the April 1982 issue of ACRES, U.S.A., Vince Rossiter skillfully explained how these factors combine to create an upcoming hyperinflation that will self-destruct not only the U.S. dollar, but all the other currencies internationally. Vince's words are worth reading and rereading. After they have been digested, it will be painfully obvious why, at the depths of this disinflation (which appears to be a deflation), we may need to move rapidly into tangibles to maintain our wealth. The *"breath"* between severe disinflation and hyperinflation could be a short one. We expect to walk through this canyon within the next three years.

For now, the American general public is tired, unable to sustain the inflationary pace of the 1970s. A disinflationary contraction has resulted, marked by a decline in the velocity of money and weakness in producer prices. The private sector has moved toward retrenchment. But, the public sector (federal government) and the multinational banking establishment (which is on the ropes with billions of dollars of bad loans) will not easily give up its rulership and long successful practice of fleecing the American general public. It is the *"death throes"* confrontation between the decadent, established, centralized order and the emerging trend toward decentralization, which could lead to a hyperinflation once this disinflation (which has all the characteristics of a deflation) has run its course.

Rossiter comments:

> *"In 1980 Congress passed a very comprehensive banking bill. It was designed primarily by the large money banks of the United States, with the blessing of the Federal Reserve. This act makes it possible for the banks of the United States to double the amount of indebtedness that we have in the United States from this point for the next five or ten years as rapidly as people are willing to borrow without increasing the deposit base one penny from profits. We can now double the volume of loans in the commercial banking system without increasing the deposit base by one dollar. If we do so it will also double the price of everything in the United States. It will happen as quickly as people are forced to borrow the money at whatever interest rates are available. Of the 100 largest banks in the United States, Citicorp of New York has 75% of its deposits from foreign sources. The large money banks of the United States control half of all the loans and half of all the deposits of all the banks in the system. There are 14,800 banks in the system, so 100 of these control half of all the assets. The other 14,700 do have liquidity and it ranges from $150 to $160 to $170 billion on a daily basis. But the large money banks have learned to leverage their banks four days of the week. They have to balance up with the Federal Reserve System on Wednesdays, but during the other four days that they don't have to balance up, they run it over from 20 to 50% of all deposits they need to meet their commitment for loans, investments and reserve for the Federal Reserve System—and by doing this they are leveraging their banks, obviously, and then at the end of the period on Wednesday, when they have to balance, they borrow the money on what we call federal funds. It has nothing to do with the federal government. They borrow from the little banks to cover their demand for these excesses they have engaged in over the years and then pay it back the next morning. The interest rates went as high as 21% last summer for this overnight money. But that isn't enough anymore.*
>
> *"As of October 1, the Federal Reserve System authorized the foreign branches of American banks to return the money from*

their foreign holdings to the United States on Wednesday to help them with their settlement problem. The computer money goes back overseas the next morning.

"But that isn't enough. On December 3, 1981, Congress passed a law which made it possible for as many banks as can qualify and make application to establish a foreign banking facility on the continental United States. These banks were previously in the Caymen Islands and in the Bahamas and no one knows what went on there, but there has been a lot of suspicion. But after 10 years of arm twisting and legislative effort on the part of the large money banks, these banks can now be made domestic. Approximately 50 of the 150 banks opened in the U.S. on the first day.

*"But despite the fanfare, all it actually opened was a few sets of books and at first the sums at the bottom of the books will be fairly small. They are a sham, facade and the government is promising not to interfere in any way with what is going on in these banks. The international banking facilities were designed to make American banks more competitive with a booming Eurodollar market. They will allow banks to take time deposits of and make loans to foreign customers only. The banks will not be required to hold reserves against these deposits nor will the money be subject to interest rate ceilings. They are also considered a tax saving source by the international bank facilities. Much of the business is expected to shift from eligible business now in the United States books or business booked at banks and other offshore locations. The most likely shift will be out of the booking centers like the Bahamas and the Caymen Islands where the time zones are the same as New York. The Federal Reserve staff has estimated that the assets and liabilities of the IBF's would grow to anything from $80 billion to $120 billion, half from foreign owned assets at domestic banks. New York's international trade representative, John B. Lindsey, New York's former mayor, says that in London the New York share of Eurocurrency market could grow to $150 billion in the first 12 months. London's Eurocurrency is currently about $285 billion. The total is $1 trillion of Eurocurrency floating out there and it is largely the same kind of smoke money that I was describing to you that has come into the rural communities. It has been loaned into the economy. If the assets in Europe were sold and the debts were paid the money would disappear. There wouldn't be any money. The headlines say **Eurodollars Come Home** if the IBF's open, and they did open December 30. That means that we have $172 billion available from foreign branches. We have $1 trillion of pure inflation coming down the pike. This is such a destructive inflationary force coming into the Continental United States without any production that it could decimate the economy of the United States, but the proportion of money being fed into the banking system and all through the financial system is in such monumental amounts that the little things that the administration is doing to save a few hundred million here and there is going to amount to nothing. The inflationary impact of $100 billion federal deficit this next year is going to be catastrophic. If we dump in another $100 billion or $200*

billion of Eurocurrency, it is going to be terrible.

"Debt carries with it the illusion that it will be paid. But can the $5.8 trillion public and private debt ever be paid, or even paid down to a sustainable level? Let's assume that the interest rate is 15% and we had 100 years to do this. Would it be possible? Or would mathematical ambition run counter to physical possibility? At 15% interest, $5.8 trillion public and private debt on an amortized basis for 100 years would come to $81.2 trillion. This computes to $87 trillion of interest and principal, all a consequence of the multiplier effect. Moreover, there is a lot of debt that isn't performing the multiplier effect. It is dead. It is sterile and it is hanging over the economy until it is paid. In the financial community they have a saying, 'If the borrower doesn't pay, the lender does.' "[6]

*   *   *

The following excerpt from the 4/12/82 WALL STREET JOURNAL perfectly illustrates our point of how money is being drained from the country to the city. Houston, *MO* (*not* Houston, TX) is a small town, which has exported its capital resources, killing itself economically in the process.

"Houston's current troubles are partly due to the nationwide recession, but its economy is also plagued by a new ailment that is laying low a lot of relatively poor town, suburbs and small cities. Houston's capital resources—it's people savings—are no longer staying home and helping finance local farmers, merchants and consumers. Instead, the deposits are being rapidly drained off to fetch higher yields at big-city banks, major corporations and even foreign countries.

"Although the Bank of Houston's deposits increased $5.5 million from the end of 1978 to $25.3 million as of last Dec. 31, about 75% of the additional money has been funneled into federal debt issues and other investments remote from Houston. Similarly, the town's only savings and loan association, Progressive Federal, has attracted $11 million of new deposits since 1978—lifting its total to $25.7 million at Dec. 31—but almost all the extra money has been shipped off to so-called money-center banks, which lend it to other large banks, giant corporations and foreign countries. All told, about 58% of the bank's deposits and about 67% of the S&L's are invested outside Houston."[7]

*   *   *

Economic Progress, Compound Interest and Banks

Economic progress only occurs when productive men and women produce goods and services. This real wealth (goods and services), when purchased with real money (a commodity or commodity-backed substitute), is the mark of a healthy economy. A contrasting, extreme economic distortion is *"funny money"* wealth, which purchases real goods and services. This wealth is obtained in part through the earning of *"compound interest."* Through *"compound interest"* wealth, no goods and services are produced, and thus no real economic benefit is *"earned"* into society.

In 1982, investors, rather than investing in businesses which could bring real economic benefit to society, instead opted to place their investment dollars in money market mutual funds, to the tune of over $200 billion. The *"compound interest"* earned on this $200 + billion, just like the $100 billion plus in *"compound interest"* paid on the federal debt, is a terminal cancer, eating away at the economic substance of this country. Error prone, limited, reality-based man was never intended to do battle with absolute, infinite, abstract *"compound interest."*

Businesses have been/are borrowing to prevent bankruptcy, not to produce new goods and services. The federal government is borrowing to finance its deficit. (Governments, economic parasites, are never primary producers of goods and services.)

Financial institutions are the creators and promoters of *"compound interest."* Unfortunately, most *"bankers"* know about as much about economics and investments as car salesmen do about automobiles. *"Bankers"* are neither engineers or mechanics. They are money salesmen. So, today's 20th century financial institutions not only separate and alienate men from the symbol of their productivity (money), they also, through loans, create inflation, promote class warfare and social instability, promulgate the burden of *"compound interest,"* and also squander their clients' funds on poor investments. *"Wealth for All"* can only be established when we again have free market, honest and moral, commodity money and men take personal responsibility for the direct, non interest bearing investment of their funds.

*   *   *

"So, why do we give our money to bankers in the first place to have them engage in periodic potlatches? The notion of 'safekeeping' is the rationalization, similar to the reasons why primitive groups give their valuables to their headsmen to smash. But if we look at banks as temples and bankers as priests who handle this 'dangerous' poison-magic-money for us because only they are potent, holy enough to touch such great sums without guilt infecting them, then it becomes more understandable that they send it off to risky ventures, at home or abroad, which periodically cause disastrous crashes in the 'circula-

tion system.' (Of course, by now millions of us are miniature priests, extending and contracting our risky ventures along with the banker-priests and contributing to the manic and depression wishes of the group—but it is still useful to see the banking and in general capitalistic system as delegates of the group which handles our accumulated poison-money.)"

Lloyd DeMause, Editor of
THE JOURNAL OF PSYCHO-HISTORY

*   *   *

Compound Interest
11/6/81

". . . To illustrate the power of compound interest we asked a mathematician to figure out what one cent would be worth today if it had been loaned out at 6% interest compounded annually by one of the three wise men who attended the birth of Christ, 1977 years ago. With the aid of his 9-digit calculator he soon came up with the answer: 1.07 × 10 to the 48th power or $1,070,000,000,000,000,000,000,000,000,-000,000,000,000,000,000,000,000.00, or one quindectillion, seventy quatrodectillion dollars.

"The above amount would pay for a sizeable gold nest egg. Let us attempt to comprehend that inconceivable sum. At $150 per Troy ounce, it would pay for 2.22 × 10 to the 41 tons of gold. Since the earth weighs in at a mere 5.98 × 10 to the 21 tons, it weighs roughly 0.37 times one trillion times one millionth of one percent of the weight of the gold, or 1 divided by 2.7 × 10 to the 18°.

"As for the size of the gold ball, its radius would be 2.2 million times that of the earth. If its center were placed at the center of the sun, all nine planets would be pushed out of the way. In fact, the orbit of the outermost planet, Pluto, would only be 2/5 as large as the diameter of the gold sphere, which would have a radius of 8.76 billion miles, 100 times larger than the radius of the earth's orbit, which is a mere 93 million miles. Looking at it still another way, if the earth were placed on the surface of this vast mass it would be proportionally the size of a modest house on the surface of the earth.

"Incidentally, all of the gold ever mined in 6,000 years of history weighs only about 100,000 tons, and if melted together, would make only an 18-yard cube."

Source: Hard Money & Soft Leaders (P. O. Box 2756, Durango, Colorado 81301), from Government Educational Foundation, Inc. (P. O. Box 1622, Washington, D.C. 20013)

DEBT CAPITALISM: THE NEMESIS OF FREE ENTERPRISE

11/13/81

When we get down to the way the world really works, we find that the abstract precedes the concrete; the eternal, the timeless, rules over time; thoughts, ideas, precede action; the pen is mightier than the sword; theory, plan and principle precede practice. An example (truism) of this can be readily seen by examining the economic subject of *"property rights." "Property rights"* are sacrosanct because property rights are finally *"human rights."* A man uses his brain for either intellectual effort or to direct his motor skills in physical labor. Both are *"work."* To accomplish his *"work,"* a man requires *"property."* This *"property"* may be simply pencil and paper; it may be monetary capital—savings; it may be a fleet of trucks or garden tools, etc. These *"tools"* are sacred *"property rights"* which enable a man to be productive by working out his thoughts in time. His ultimate production, the net product of his ideas and action, is thus a *"property right"* and also a *"human right."*

The starting point in the whole chain of production is an abstract, eternal, timeless *"idea,"* a *"human right."* The *"property right"* is the end product. It follows that to protect *"property rights,"* the abstract, timeless principle of *"theft is wrong,"* applies. From our religious heritage, *"Thou shalt not steal."*

Since consistently in the abstract and concrete realms, *"property rights"* are sacred as an extension of *"human rights,"* it thus follows that free enterprise is the correct economic modus operandi for society. Free enterprise is contractual in nature. Men exchange goods and services for their mutual benefit, by contract, freely determined. Thus, *"property rights"* are freely transferred. *"Human rights"* are protected. Self-interest is thus best served by service (exchange) with one's fellow man in a free market. The balance between the individual and the group is maintained. The *"greatest good for the greatest number"* is realized because an individual only maximizes his self-interest in a free market long-term by service (exchange) with his fellow man. Unethical business practices, by contrast, soon lead to a loss of customers as word of the bad reputation spreads in the general community, particularly where there is geographic proximity and

78

decentralized accountability.

It should become evident, upon examination, that debt capitalism is a far cry from free enterprise. The mammoths of debt capitalism in our mature culture, the *"Fortune 500s"* and other multinational corporations, exercise their financial and political power, akin to that of kings and lords in times past. Workers, subjects and serfs are on the opposite end of the spectrum. The world of big business and multinational corporations, New York Dow Jones Industrial style, is one of centralization of economic power, not decentralization. It is one of limited accountability and geographic distance. It is one of debt—debt capitalism. (And poor organized labor doesn't understand that its leadership sold out long ago.)

Because it is often impersonal and oppressive in nature, debt capitalism works very well in such tyrannical regimes as the Soviet Union, where some 200 U.S. multinational corporations carry on business. It stands to reason that the Soviet Union is then not the enemy of these multinational corporations, particularly since they do business with the Soviets. Yet, the Russians are **our** enemy. Strange, isn't it? The number one beneficiary of U.S. aid in this century has been the U.S.S.R.

NETWORK, perhaps, said it best:

> *". . . There is no America. There is no democracy. There is only IBM and ITT and AT&T and DuPont, Dow, Union Carbide and Exxon. Those are the nations of the world now. What do you think the Russians talk about in their councils of state—Karl Marx? They pull out their linear programming charts, statistical decision theories and minimax solutions like the good little systems-analysts they are and compute the price-cost probabilities of their transactions and investments just like we do.*
>
> *"We no longer live in a world of nations and ideologies, . . . The world is a college of corporations, inexorably determined by the immutable bylaws of business. The world is a business . . . It has been that way since man crawled out of the slime, and our children . . . will live to see that perfect world without war and famine, oppression and brutality—one vast and ecumenical holding company, for whom all men will work to serve a common profit, in which all men will hold a share of stock, all necessities provided, all anxieties tranquillized, all boredom amused. . . ."* [8]

"Companies" are playing the role of God. They are the *"survival of the fittest"* in the evolutionary spiral.

Let's get back to principle. Debt capitalism violates the principle that *"theft is wrong."* We have seen this very clearly in its evil financial effect on small businessmen. The recent scramble by these financial dinosaurs to borrow billions of dollars for mergers and acquisitions squashed the small businessman in the capital markets. While the issuance of stock, partnerships, and joint ventures establish contractual, decentralized, free enterprise responsibility, debt capitalism, built upon loans, does just the opposite. Under debt capitalism, when (particularly) a large multinational corporation borrows huge sums of money from a bank in the fractional reserve banking system, each dollar can be multiplied six to seven times through the system. This is effectively counterfeiting the original dollar. Counterfeiting is a form of theft. *"Theft is wrong."*

Debt capitalism also violates the laws of economic thermodynamics concerning the exchange between energy and matter. The fractional reserve banking system is, by its very nature, inflationary. Inflation is also a form of theft. *"Theft is wrong."*

The velocity (turnover) of money in the fractional reserve banking system further helps wealthy borrowers pirate funds so they can get first access to new goods and services before prices increase in the inflationary cycle. Workers or laborers are the last in the economic chain to be compensated for inflation. So, the rich get richer and the poor get poorer.

Banks only loan to those who already have assets and collateral. When the rich get too rich and the poor get too poor, a revolution occurs. Communism has a natural appeal for the ignorant masses in the anarchy and confusion of a revolution.

Loans to debt capitalists alienate labor from the means of production. It promotes Marx' class friction between the bourgeois and the proletariat. Under debt capitalism, labor no longer shares in wealth creation because it does not have a stake in stock, joint ventures or partnerships. Decentralized accountability is, thus, also missing. Money borrowed is not necessarily tied to a particular project. Even the buyers of bonds, particularly today, are primarily institutions who operate through third parties—brokers—who, like bankers, accentuate the alienation of the natural affinity which should exist between owners, management and labor. Men need to control the fruits of their productivity (money).

As mentioned, bankers loan to the rich who have assets to collateralize so they can become increasingly rich in an inflationary cycle. Loans are, by their very nature, inflationary in our fractional reserve banking system, as each dollar multiplies itself up to seven times, its inflation accelerated by the velocity of money. The poor, however, in a mature civilization such as our democracy, use their political clout to see that this unearned wealth is redistributed among the masses. They also look to government subsidies and doles to bail them out, such as from the Small Business Administration, the FHA, CETA and the many other government alphabet agencies. Government redistribution of wealth is legalized theft and produces social conflict between the *"haves"* and *"have nots."* The abstract principle that *"theft is wrong"* is, thus, violated by government. Government's seemingly benevolent efforts therefore become a curse to the social structure. A truism of government action is that government's best income redistribution intentions, when legislated, become a curse. They achieve the opposite result of what was originally intended. Both debt capitalism and government transfer of wealth are theft. Both concentrate political and economic power in the hands of a few elitists. Immorality has been legislated. *"Theft is wrong."* The bankers, corporate managers, and government bureaucrats become the ruling elite. Such elitism is particularly dangerous in our day and age with our advance state of technology. For the first time in human history, such *"do good planners"* have the means to control the general population. Satellites and computers have made it possible.

Are we on the verge of a BRAVE NEW WORLD? Will FAHRENHEIT 451 become reality? I hope not. Are we living at the end of the age of debt capitalism? The *"kings of the hill"* have maximized their power for all it's worth. We have the *"Big Three"* in the automobile industry, soon to become the *"Big Two"* with the demise of Chrysler. We have the *"Seven Sisters"* in the oil industry. We have the few, big (approximately 10) multinational banks, led by Chase Manhattan, who have interlocking corporate directorates with the other *"biggies."* We have industrialists, like Armand Hammer, who is Soviet Russia's greatest capitalist friend. We have real estate developers and companies like Trammell Crow and Vantage Co. The likes of Crow are the few who can still obtain loans these days from the big insurance companies like Connecticut General. Sears buys Dean Witter. It's a brotherhood of mammoths, created by debt capitalism. And its evolutionary, satanically so.

How many individual Americans now really own the means of production? How many Americans today can truly be called *"capitalists?"* We're told that we live in the richest nation on earth. Oh, really? How many Americans would have a positive net worth if they had to liquidate their *"assets"* now? How many Americans, due to debt, are net in the red? How many more if real estate prices crater? How many more will be in the red as a result of this recession/ depression? At retirement, only 3 percent of Americans are financially self-sufficient now in a bare bones sense. **Only 3 out of 100 retirees have enough investment income to provide themselves with $3,000 a year at age 65.**

How many small businessmen have been squeezed out of the loan market as a result of lofty interest rates and due to federal government and multinational borrowing crowding them out? Who will have the financial assets loaned to them in order to purchase, at bargain dollar prices, the assets of these victims of Volcker? The multinationals, of course. The loans will be there from their fraternity brothers, the multinational banks.

We are all conditioned in our culture to be *"company"* men. The public schools are the *"company"* schools that teach us to *"fit"* into the *"company."* Trade schools are more blatant about it. Colleges are more subtle. But today's MBA is not trained to be an entrepreneur. He is trained to be a manager in a *"company."* We are educated to be square pegs that fit into square holes. Our unique individual talents are not developed. Such individualistic education is contrary to the end goals of debt capitalism although obviously in the best interest of free enterprise. CBS, ABC, NBC and PBS, monopolies in and of themselves, don't tell us the truth. How can they? Their multinational sponsors, who provide them with tremendous advertising income and profits, wouldn't support the truth. (Mrs. Sharon P. Rockefeller is Chairman of the Board of Directors of the Corporation for Public Broadcasting.)

What's left to be conquered? Industry, transportation, banking, investment firms, retailing, the oil industry, education, and real estate have all succumbed. The small businessman is out cold. Farmers are on the mat, too. In keeping with our city versus country analysis, it is logical that the farmers would be the target of the final attack, just like the Third World countries. Both are basic producers of real new wealth.

With such awesome power and well-wired political connections, how can the debt capitalists lose? The same way a bull market yields to a bear market when it seems most unlikely. Every bull market sows the seeds of its own self-destruction through excessive bullishness. Such is the state of debt capitalism now. The multinational bankers shake over the sure upcoming loan defaults by the Third World countries and communists. They are counting on The Monetary Control Act of 1980 and their lackeys at the Federal Reserve to bail them out. The anarchy of humanism, with each man as his own god, is promoting revolution and disrupting business worldwide. The black market and the underground barter economy now make up as much as one-third of our GNP. Women, who have to work, have destroyed the basic security of the classic American family. As such, the middle class, which is the stability of society under a social bell-shaped curve, is disrupted not only economically through inflation but socially as it is riddled by divorce. Now only 7 percent of American families have a working father and a mother at home with their natural children. Illegitimacy has hit 50 percent among some groups. These offspring are not interested in *"fitting"* into the *"company."* Their basic insecurity scars are the breeding ground for entrepreneurs. And so the system, instead of turning out more *"company"* men, is now producing future entrepreneurs, antagonistic to the *"company."* Remember, too, that approximately 80 percent of new jobs and new inventions are created by small businesses. By choking small businesses out of existence the mammoths have killed the goose that lays the golden egg. The upcoming severe climatic changes should be the final nail in the *"companies'"* coffin. Within the realm of apparent omnipotence comes glaring weakness.

The cities where these mammoth *"companies"* reside are crumbling in waves of crime and social service bankruptcies. Meanwhile, throughout the country, both urban and rural Americans seek their roots, which is why country music is the craze. Country music speaks to the soul of America. And, ironically, debt itself is the acid destroying debt capitalism. Compound interest is the culprit. In 1980, interest expense amounted to 45 percent of corporate net profits before taxes.

George Knupffer, in a well-written but black-balled book entitled, THE STRUGGLE FOR WORLD POWER (The Plain Speaker Publishing Company, 43 Bath Road, London, W.4.), presented a well-documented explanation of the economic travesties promulgated by debt capitalism. Knupffer is, interestingly enough, an elderly Russian aristocrat who knows the workings of debt capitalism all too well. He noted that the financing of the Russian Revolution came from multinational bankers located in New York and Berlin. From New York, for the Marxist Russian Revolution, came funds from Kuhn, Loeb & Co., whose directors included Schiff and Warburg, founder of the Federal Reserve System. Commenting on this tragedy, Knupffer wrote:

> *"Do not be misled by those who tell you that the enemy is only in Moscow. It is quite true that one of the enemies is there, and it is an enemy of a kind with whom there can never be compromise of any sort. But we must realize that if we continue to see the enemy only in Moscow, we will be stabbed in the back by the enemy in New York, who wants to lead us. But that enemy, like the one in Russia, is only using America as a base. The American nation is no more guilty than the Russians. Both are victims of a subtle and powerful subversive force which they have not recognized in time."*

In his stimulating chapter 3, *"Economic Roots of Power,"* Knupffer commented:

> *"The present-day system, still in force outside the Iron Curtain, is based on usury, ie. the lending of money at interest, the ownership of economic factors not only by individuals directly, but especially by a more or less anonymous set of ever-changing people indirectly, through shares, and by the transfer of the powers of monetary coinage, i.e. issue, from the sovereign State to private individuals and corporations, to whom both a large part of the*

public and even the State is indebted, in part because all money thus created comes into being as a loan at interest. The bankers are able to create money, credit, the means of exchange, out of nothing, by mere book entry. They thus control all aspects of economic and political life."

In chapter 5, "*The Nature of Capitalism and Banking,*" Knupffer wrote:

"*The distinguishing characteristic of capitalism is that it is concerned with the means of exchange, that it is a system in which usury—the lending of money at interest—plays a leading role; it is the essence of capitalism, in addition to the private issue of money. Capital is not land, or money as such, or a factory, if we consider it under the heading of capitalism. Under that heading, capital is not an asset, but a liability; it is not property, but a debt burdened by interest payments. The capital of a company is not what it owns, but what it owes. Capitalism is a system which has been created by the moneylenders, by the parasites. It is not the system of the constructive owners, the true creators of wealth by work and invention. It is a system of those who 'use idle money and put it to work for them,' to use a piece of typical capitalistic jargon. . . .*"

In chapter 6, "*The Nature of Socialism,*" Knupffer discussed socialism.

"*. . . Socialism has never seriously attacked Capitalism, it has never dealt with its root characteristic of usury. Attention has always been diverted by the Socialists from the basic essentials, from the private issue of money and its loaning at interest, to the question of the private ownership of the means of production, distribution and exchange. The Socialists claim that it is the so-called 'nationalization' of property which is a cure for all ills. The reason for this formula is obvious; to attack usury would be to attack the true bosses, while to preach confiscation is to assure the transfer of all that we own to the control of the materialistic messianists . . .*

"*The ultimate real aims of Capitalism and Socialism are identical: the centralized rule of a political group, which owns all the means of production, to say nothing of controlling all money, and which thus achieves the ideal of the materialistic messianism. It is a natural attribute of this conception of power that it must be international, worldwide. And, it is not so much the case that Socialism cannot survive in one, or a few, countries . . . The real trouble is that Capitalism cannot survive at all, either in one country, a group of countries, or in the whole world. If the Soviets are alleged to be sitting back now, and waiting for the collapse of Capitalism, they are right. But we must not fall into the trap of assuming that the Soviet tyranny is Capitalism's enemy and alternative; it is its product and its completion. . . .*"

R.I.P.

Gulf Oil, a U.S. multinational corporation, has valuable oil interests in communist Angola. Cuban communist troops have been protecting Gulf Oil's energy installations in Angola against terrorists. Recently, a Cuban general was killed during fighting between Cuban communist troops which were defending Gulf's interests against guerrillas. May the Cuban general Rest In Peace. (R.I.P.)

It is heartwarming that a Cuban communist general, a Russian surrogate, would give his life for a *"capitalist imperialist"* like Gulf, a United States multinational corporation. It just goes to prove that there is true peace in the world. How can it be otherwise if U.S. multinational interests and Cuban communists are cooperating? Or, could it be *"Debt Capitalism: The Nemesis of Free Enterprise"*?

*   *   *

Multinational Debt Capitalism, the Nemesis of Free Enterprise

". . . Romania and Yugoslavia are the only Eastern European Communist countries in the IMF and the World Bank.

"Poland would like to obtain IMF financial assistance in working its way out of its economic crisis. Hungary's international payment needs aren't as pressing. But it would like to qualify for World Bank loans . . ." [9]

*   *   *

"Mexico's new central bank chief . . . a Marxist!"

DELIBERATIONS
September 15, 1982

*   *   *

"Of America's 500 largest corporations, 115 have been convicted in the last decade of at least one major crime or have paid civil penalties for serious misbehavior.

"Among the 25 biggest firms—with annual sales that range from 15 billion to 108 billion dollars—the rate of documented misbehavior has been even greater."

U.S. NEWS
September 6, 1982
Reprinted from U.S. News & World Report,
Copyright 1982, U.S. News & World Report, Inc.

DEBT CAPITALISM: ITS FINAL ATTACK

11/20/81

The master psychologist, A. Maslow, in his *"Hierarchy of Needs,"* listed man's basic need as *"biological."* The last frontier left for debt capitalism to conquer is the institution which has been historically the backbone of the American free political and economic system, the institution of American agriculture, a *"biological"* institution. Recognizing the successful reality of debt capitalism's attack against agriculture, the October, 1981 issue of COMMODITIES Magazine declared editorially,

> *"COMMODITIES Magazine is moving from the heart of the nation's farm belt, Iowa, to the centers of futures trading, Chicago and New York City."*

That quote says it all. Paper corn is more important than the real thing. It's city vs. country.

The cold, harsh reality of the elitist control of food, the ultimate resource, *"protein gold,"* is almost at hand. A few mammoth multinationals eventually controlling U.S. food production would be the cartel of cartels, making OPEC look like child's play. The whole world is looking to North America for food in the 1980s and 1990s.

Farmers are vulnerable. They are already on the multinational energy hook via intensive use of big agribusiness' herbicides, pesticides, chemical fertilizers, seeds and motorized irrigation systems. Farmers have also sold their souls to country bankers for operating loans, mortgaging their real wealth, their farmland. They have become locked into reporting requirements for the U.S. Department of Agriculture. They have taken out prostituting loans from the Farmers Home Administration. Farmers have been indoctrinated (brainwashed by the federal government and multinational corporations' sponsored university agriculture schools which have done any and everything they could to discourage the farmer from using organic farming techniques). Forget crop rotation, land terracing and minimum tillage. So what if the land is worthless in 20 years. Rape and reap is now the theme of evolutionary, get rich quick agriculture.

Farmers are receiving prices at Great Depression equivalents. With

86

agricultural land prices now dropping, their basis for ever expanding loans has dried up. And with it will come the foreclosures and the subsequent multinational takeover of country banks. Who will bail out the country banks and the assets (farms) foreclosed on by the country bankers? Multinational bankers and multinational agribusiness corporations. Who else? The Fed is behind them.

The U.S.D.A. announces grain sales made by multinational corporations. Multinational agribusiness already dominates world grain trade. Dan Morgan's book, MERCHANTS OF GRAIN, discussed the five multinational corporations that control world grain trade—Continental Grain, Dreyfus, Andre, Bunge and Cargill. Cargill and Continental handle better than 50 percent of U.S. exported grain. Monopoly is no game.

The infiltration and continuing domination of agriculture by big agribusiness has progressed in ways you and I could never have imagined. Gary North, in his REMNANT REVIEW, exposed how the multinationals are buying up the seed businesses. Talk about controlling the seed corn. Gary, in a brilliant piece of investigative journalism, discovered that not only have the multinational agricultural corporations been buying up the old, small, family-operated seed companies; they have more insidiously *"canned"* the continually reproductive seeds and replaced them with sterile hybrid seeds. These hybrid seeds, promoted by the multinationals, must be purchased by the farmers year after year. You see, the hybrid seeds do not reproduce like the old fashioned seeds developed by the small, family-operated seed companies. Those seeds, the old reliable kind, produced crop after crop with their *"offspring"* producing yet more seeds. These newfangled hybrid seeds, in addition to being sterile, and ensuring the farmers' dependency upon the multinational corporations, have not developed the immunities to local pests and blights in many cases either.

The good old U.S.D.A., consistent with big business' self-interest and the principle that the government always does the wrong thing, is tightening the genetic noose on these old-time, reliable, family seed companies. They are being driven out of business or gobbled up by the multinationals. Gary reported that the small seed companies could not meet all the registration and bureaucratic labeling requirements fostered by the federal government. All too willing to step in and buy up these seed companies have been the likes of Cargill, ITT, Purex and Altantic Richfield, which recently bought out Dessert Seed Company. What's worse, these multinational corporations, with no love for the land, with only their own short-term financial self-interest at heart, have developed seeds of only a handful of varieties. Less than half a dozen varieties of seeds account for 100 percent of the millet, 96 percent of the peas, 76 percent of the snap beans, 72 percent of the potatoes, 71 percent of the corn, 69 percent of the sweet potatoes, 60 percent of the dry beans, 53 percent of the cotton, 65 percent of the rice, 56 percent of the soybeans, 42 percent of the sugar beets, 95 percent of the peanuts, and 50 percent of the wheat produced. What this means is that if these limited special seeds are hit by disease, crops worldwide will be wiped out. Millions will starve. With agricultural centralization comes an all or nothing situation. Are multinational profits worth gambling on the basic biological survival of the world? Small decentralized farms with various crops and different seeds and methodologies provide better protection against a horrible agricultural nightmare.

There is a battle underway for control of agricultural land now. The small farmers are losing in a big way. Two-thirds of this country's food supply is now produced by only 10 percent of this nation's farms. The actual number of farms has declined 54 percent since 1945. Approximately a third of today's U.S. farms are so small that their annual sales are less than $2,500. The average farm size now is 450 acres, up from 196 acres in 1945. Over 50 percent of all farms are operated by partial owners.

In an excellent documentary on the plight of the small American farmers, Carol Monpere and Sandra Nichols did a presentation on PBS in cooperation with KTEH, San Jose, entitled, *"The Battle of Westlands."* This documentary began:

> *"We Americans take farming pretty much for granted. We eat the food, wear the cotton, and don't question where it comes from, so what goes on out here, well it just doesn't concern us much. But to the rest of the world, agriculture is America's bright success story . . . Our place as a power in the world depends in good part on this. Today, though, something seems to have gone wrong with the great success story. Part of the problem could be that the farmer himself is disappearing. 100,000 leave our country's farmland every year. But, whatever the cause, there's trouble on the farm . . ."*

Monpere and Nichols took a line from *"Wealth for All"* and reworked it: City vs. country revisited.

What's at stake in the Westlands (California), one of the richest farmland areas in the world? The federal government financed the water development project which allowed the Westlands, formerly a desert, to bloom. The landowners in the Westlands, when they signed a contract to accept water from the Westlands Water District, agreed to sell their land holdings over 160 acres per person within ten years of the time they received the water, at a price for the land that did not include the value of the water. Now, the big land owners want to repudiate their contracts. In 1960, when Congress authorized the Westlands project, the stated purpose was to *"make our great land resource available to more people."* It was estimated that there would be 27,000 farm residents on 6,000 farms. Of course, we know that when government initiates *"do-gooder"* wealthy transfer programs, the end result is the opposite of what was intended. Government action is cursed. It violates the principle that *"theft is wrong,"* for that is exactly what wealth redistribution is—theft! Now, 20 years later, one-third of the rich Westlands farmland belongs to just ten companies. 94 percent of the farmers' annual profit in the Westlands is subsidized according to a U.S.D.A. estimate. Tenneco and Southern Pacific are some of the *"needy"* multinationals that receive the benefit of subsidized water rates, canal systems and dams. Southern Pacific receives a $3 million annual subsidy. Southern Pacific farms 106,000 acres. Standard Oil is also an unlikely megabusiness involved in farming in the Westlands. There are only 200 farms in the Westlands, a far cry from the government's 1960 estimate of 6,000. Will these multinationals take care of the land, long-term, like small farmers? Unlikely.

Those farmers who have sold their large operations in keeping with the letter of the law of 160-acre maximum farms have violated the spirit of the law. There have been sales, but immediate lease backs to trusted friends and family members which have left, when the dust settled, one large farm operator again in control. Effectively, nothing has changed.

How have these *"biggies"* been able to so dominate agriculture in the Westlands? By borrowing money to buy land! Debt capitalism is proving to be just as effective in agriculture as it has been in gobbling up industry, oil, real estate, small businesses and everything else. Bank of America, a banking giant by any standard, has lent millions of dollars in the Westlands.

Now, Monpere and Nichols, in their documentary *"The Battle of Westlands,"* of course didn't observe that the battle over farmland in the Westlands between the *"haves"* and the *"have nots"* was basically the result of government intervention in the marketplace **and** debt capitalism, both a violation of the moral principle that *"theft is wrong."* But giving these two gals credit, they did rightly observe the end result of the violation of this moral principle. The end product via the insidious theft of government wealthy redistribution **and** debt capitalism has not come anywhere close to providing *"the greatest good for the greatest number,"* **or** promoting free enterprise. In fact, it has done just the opposite. It has achieved *"the greatest misery for* *the greatest number,"* and promoted monopoly.

Monpere and Nichols discussed and confirmed a well-substantiated anthropological study that reveals that in small farming communities, business thrives and social services are readily available. However, in farming communities surrounded by the big multinational farms, the opposite is true. The multinationals that own the land don't spend their profits that they earn from that land in the local region. They ship them back to Los Angeles and New York. City vs. country again. There are a few very rich and many very poor in agricultural communities dominated by large corporate farms. The very poor end up moving to the cities and/or going on welfare.

And so, the small American farmer, the original and last bastion of America's freedom and roots, too, falls victim to the multinationals' *"survival of the fittest"* program. Pretty soon the masses will have only one alternative left—revolution. And with that will come the attempted tyranny of a communistic state and/or the concomitant technological dictatorship. America will have become one big all encompassing multinational *"company,"* if the powers that be have their way. The *"Fractured Financial Fairy Tale"* will have become a harsh reality, a nightmare come true.

Is there any hope for the farmers? Sure. Farmers are a fiercely independent, God-fearing, nationalistic family-oriented bunch. They will revolt against the multinationals. Actually, since farmers make up only a little better than 1 percent of our country's population, if they weren't so stubborn, they could form one heck of a cartel. North America is the 1980s breadbasket. They could even turn the tables on the multinationals by beating them at their own game. Imagine, just imagine if the farmers collectively made turnabout fair play. What if the hog and cattle producers refused to raise livestock and instead went long in the futures market. Just imagine the implications of the wheat, corn, cotton and soybean growers refusing to plant their crops and instead planting paper crops by buying long positions on the futures markets in Rotterdam, Chicago, Winnipeg, and/or Kansas City. They could bring the cities, the cities' politicians, bankers, multinationalists, the welfare state, the military/industrial complex, the communists, the oil cartel, and all the other *"companies"* to their knees—all in less than a year. The world had only a 7-week supply of grain. Farmers could turn the whole country around. By controlling the world's hungry tummy, they could establish sound money, free enterprise and restore the U.S. Constitution. This farming cartel is forming in an elementary way now.

U.S. farmers provide the Japanese with over half of their wheat, corn and soybeans. The Soviet Union's oppressive multinational dictatorship depends ultimately on the food imported from American farms. The Russians haven't been self-sufficient in agriculture for over 60 years. Agricultural producers in Australia, Canada, Brazil and Argentina might join the American farming effort. Climate is changing for the worse, which would be supportive of such an agricultural movement. Farmers are decentralized, geographically separated, and have many friends and family in local communities. They would be difficult to round up and force to produce.

World food production is still within only a few percentage points of world food demand. Farmer revolts are a part of this country's history. There was Shay's Rebellion in 1788 in New England and the Whiskey Rebellion in western Pennsylvania in 1793. Land erosion and lack of water will reduce significant percentages of the agriculturally productive land in the next 20 years. Petroleum fertilizers will become more scarce. Only 24 countries export grain now. The United States produces 60 percent of the world's soybeans and exports 79 percent of the world's soybean exports. The United States' farmers produce 27 percent of the world's corn and export 80 percent of the world's corn available for export. U.S. agriculture is responsible for approximately 15 percent of world wheat production and 45 percent of world wheat export, as well as over 1.5 percent of world rice production and 24 percent of world rice exports. Overall, 58 percent of all the world's grain exports come from this country.

In summary, the stage is set as never before in history for the world's great *"protein gold"* cartel. The big question is, *"Who will run this ultimate cartel?"* Multinational agribusiness is rapidly gaining the upper hand. But the small farmers and operators (for big agribusiness) are sleeping giants. They could be the last and best hope America has at regaining her constitutional freedoms and reestablishing *"Wealth For All."*

*　　*　　*

More Beef for Russian Bureaucrats

The June 26, 1981 REAPER stated,

"Soviet per-capita meat consumption is approximately 128 pounds per year. Soviet bureaucrats would like to raise the per-capita meat consumption to 180 pounds per year. Because the Russians have been unable to raise the desired quantity of meat at home, they have ventured out into the international market . . .

"Being cynical, we would expect U.S. multinationals to horn in on this export opportunity. And, lo and behold, what do we find but that the old trading partner of the Soviets, Occidental Petroleum's Armand Hammer, has spent $800 million to purchase

Iowa Beef Processors, which operates 11 packing plants in 7 states. Keep an eye out for the Russian brand on the hind quarter of some American beef."

Some 4½ months later, we read,

"Occidental Petroleum Corp. Chairman Armand Hammer will go to the Soviet Union in December where he will meet with Soviet President Leonid Brezhnev and other Soviet trade officials. Accompanying him will be Robert Peterson, President of Iowa Beef Processors, Inc., the nation's largest beef processor, which was purchased by Occidental in August."

*   *   *

In "Protein Gold" Multinationals Must We Trust?

From the November 13, 1981 WALL STREET JOURNAL:

"Federal prosecutors charged Cargill, Inc. with filing false tax returns in 1975 and 1976 understating its income by a total of $7.1 million . . .

". . . failing to report dividends from foreign subsidiaries totaling $5.1 million in 1975 and $2 million in 1976 . . .

"Criminal informations are filed only when the accused waives its right to have the charges weighed by a grand jury, and usually result in a guilty plea. Mr. Rosenbaum said he expected Cargill to plead guilty in a hearing today . . .

"In Minneapolis, a Cargill spokesman declines to confirm or deny Mr. Rosenbaum's statement that the company plans to plead guilty . . ." [10]

*   *   *

Multinational Debt Capitalism: Closing in on the Third World
11/20/81

While *"Debt Capitalism: Its Final Attack"* focused primarily upon debt capitalism's attack on American farming, it was parenthetically stated that this same attack should be expected by the natural resource rich Third World countries. The November 23, 1981 U.S. NEWS AND WORLD REPORT noted:

"American banks are clustering in Kenya, following corporate investors in their advance on that African center. . . .

"Several major U.S. banks have recently established regional bases or representative offices in Nairobi. Big names with footholds in Kenya now include New York's Citibank, Chase Manhattan, Chemical Bank and Manufacturers Hanover, and the First National Bank of Chicago.

"Add California's Bank of America, which has acquired a majority stake in the Commercial Bank of Africa (CBA). . . ." [11]

The multinational debt capitalists' march goes on.

MERCHANTS OF GRAIN

12/7/79

Whether you are a consumer, commodity trader, elevator operator or primary producer of agricultural products, Dan Morgan's book, MERCHANTS OF GRAIN, is important reading. As Lenin astutely observed, *"Grain is the currency of currencies."* And, there are five multinational corporations that control the grain trade in this world: They are: Continental Grain Company (New York City), Louis Dreyfus Company (Paris), Andre (Lausanne, Switzerland), Bunge Corporation and Cargill, Inc. (Minneapolis). Continental and Cargill are the two largest privately held companies in this country. Bunge is probably the largest privately held company in the world. These multinationals have interests in steel, shipping, real estate, hotels, paint manufacturing, cattle ranches, glass manufacturing, banking, animal feeding, commodity brokerage, flour milling, and mining. (All five of these multinationals have their origins in Europe.)

Because grain is more important than oil, the influence of these multinationals can in no way be underestimated. Today, we take bread for granted. However, in 1800, laborers in Manchester, London and Paris paid 50% of their wages for bread to eat. In fact, having bread to eat was a sign of social status and achievement.

Dan Morgan, in a summary of his book in the October, 1979 EAST WEST JOURNAL, *"Who Manipulates Your Food Dollar?"*, observed that these five food-controlling multinationals tend to stay in the shadows of international trade. Their influence, however, extends over three continents and has survived *"wars, famines, economic crashes, and revolutions."* They have done whatever is necessary to survive, *"forming alliances with kings, queens, and communist rulers."*

These five powerful multinationals are a necessary part of world trade because they control the distribution system, technology, processing plants, capital, and have the contacts with the international buyers and sellers.

Cargill and Continental handle better than 50% of the grain exported from this country. It must be remembered that the United

States exports better than 50% of all the grain involved in world trade. Morgan stated, *"The Big Five dominate the grain trade of the Common Market; the Canadian barley trade, the South American maize trade; and the Argentine wheat trade."* These multinationals control shipping, communications, processing plants, grain elevators, all the vital connections necessary in international grain trade.

The Big Five are family dynasties. Continental is controlled by the Fribourgs. Bunge is run by the Bornes and Hirsches. Cargill is handled by the Cargills and MacMillans. The Andres runs Andre. The Louis-Dreyfus' command Louis-Dreyfus.

Morgan observed that by 1970, animals ate as much grain as humans. In the United States and Soviet Union, livestock and poultry consume 20% of the annual grain harvest. Iowa raises 10% of all the corn in the world. Kansas and South Dakota raise more wheat than Australia. Of the grain raised in this country, large percentages of the wheat, the soybeans, the corn, and the rice are sold abroad.

Regarding the Soviets, Morgan wrote: *"The Russians understand the realities of food politics better than any other people in the world. They have been educated to this lesson by harsh, direct experience. Virtually none of the elders in power in Moscow is a stranger to the experience of actual starvation. It is not surprising that harvests are front-page news in Soviet newspapers."* Only if this country was so aware of the importance and power of food.

From reading MERCHANTS OF GRAIN, we can also obtain a better understanding of the psychology of markets. When crops are believed to be in abundance, international buyers hold off purchases, waiting for lower prices. However, when there is a perceived scarcity, they buy with both hands, whether the scarcity is real or imagined. In other words, expectations of supply influence buying by international buyers. This is just like the expectations of commodity traders for higher or lower prices. People are still people. It doesn't matter if one is running a multinational grain corporation or speculating in a $5,000 commodity account. Very few businessmen or commodity traders understand the psychology of markets, but all react similarly.

The Soviet grain purchases of 1972 resulted in $2 billion increased food costs for Americans. This $2 billion food cost increase to American consumers was a direct result of quiet actions taken by President Nixon in June, 1971. Nixon also removed the requirements that exporters obtain licenses for grain purchases. Nixon also eliminated the policy that 50% of the U.S. grain had to be transported on U.S. ships. President Nixon kicked our food budget around pretty well, didn't he?

Another fascinating section of Morgan's book discussed the day-by-day developments and news releases during the time of a Soviet grain purchase. President Ford had no knowledge of the purchases. Trade publications announced that the Soviets were buying grain. Continental denied that it was making any sales to Russia. The U.S.D.A. confirmed the sales after the fact! The bottom line for us as primary producers, elevator operators, consumers, and commodity speculators is: Don't believe the news! Technical price action will be the first indication of accumulation, of multinational corporations buying for sales to foreign powers. Once we know the news, it's usually too late. The markets have already moved in anticipation of the news announcement. In this sense, the markets are rigged.

Morgan gets off on the fact that the *"Big Five"* grain multinationals are not interested in the world's starving people, just profit. His discussion makes interesting reading. Also fascinating were his disclosures of how, throughout the 1960s, the U.S.D.A. and Cargill (collusion between government and multinational corporations) developed *"Asian poultry industries, baking industries, cattle-fattening yards, and fast-food chains"* to promote markets for U.S. grain.

Morgan's discussion on the machinations and collusion between the U.S.D.A. and these multinational corporations in influencing the internal and external affairs and policies of Iran are indeed sobering. Iran has some sound reasons to despise the United States. Until 1970, Iran imported little grain. Its people (30 million) lived off home-grown crops and meat. Now approximately 25% of the grain used in Iran comes from the United States. Chemical oriented agriculture, U.S. machinery, vast dairy and poultry industries that rely upon U.S. grown soybeans and corn, as well as wheat bread, have become more popular in Iran—all as a result of U.S. meddling in that market. *"Iran, which spent only $15 million on American wheat ten years earlier, had become a $325 million customer by 1975. . . . Iran, in effect, had surrendered to the United States a good deal of its agricultural sovereignty. . . . The U.S.D.A. even won a contractual right to meddle in Iran's internal agricultural affairs."*

Source: Dan Morgan's MERCHANTS OF GRAIN, Viking Press, 625 Madison Avenue, New York, NY 10022, 1979, 387 pp.

CROPEC: A CIA/NY CONNECTION?

1/21/82

As this CROPEC table clearly shows, the United States, Canada, Australia, and Argentina control 80-90% of all the world's grain trade. If that doesn't hold the potential for a *"protein gold"* cartel, what does?

CROPEC vs. OPEC
Control of Key Agricultural Crops in World Trade

	U.S.	Canada, Australia, and Argentina	Total
Wheat	45%	33%	78%
Corn	80%	7%	87%
Soybeans	79%	11%	90%

While only 4 countries control 78-90% of world grain, it takes 13 OPEC countries to control 71% of world oil.

Source: W. R. Grace & Co., Grace Plaza,
1114 Avenue of Americas, New York, NY

With the city vs. country conflict coming to a head, particularly in Western civilization, the issue of *"protein gold"* becomes one of *who controls food!* It's power that's at stake here, just like power and resulting wealth is/was at issue over the control of oil. Control of food is ultimate control. The importance of food in Romania, where hoarding results in five-year jail terms; Poland's slide down to the use of tobacco and alcohol as money; food rotting in rural Ghana while people are starving in Ghana's capital city of Accra; the multinationals' growing control of Third World resources, world grain trade, and U.S. agricultural land; U.S. technological and agricultural trade (subsidies) to the Russians and Chinese, our so-called enemies; the pesticide, the hybrid seed, fertilizer, and herbicide controversies—all speak to this *"protein gold"* question.

Now we find that Poland may be granted credit to buy as much as $200 million worth of U.S. feed grains. And, Beatrice Foods has entered into a joint venture with the city of Canton, China and the China International Trust and Investment Co. This Beatrice Foods/ Chinese company will be known as Guangmei Foods Corp. This corporation will develop the export and domestic Chinese markets for canned fruits and vegetables, citrus juices and soft drinks. It is the first joint venture a U.S. company has ever signed with China. (Does Beatrice Foods know that China is expected to be the next great civilization according to the 510-year civilization cycle?) Of course, we know that Armand Hammer of Occidental Petroleum bought Iowa Beef so he can sell beef to the Soviets.

The U.S. multinationals' growing control of agriculture is similar to the large multinationals' dominance in the oil industry. Controlling the refineries and distribution systems, the multinational oil companies lay off most of the risk on the independent and wildcat drillers, who drill better than 70% of the wildcat wells in this country. So it is becoming with agriculture. And, can you imagine, if you were a multinational agricultural conglomerate, what kind of a stacked deck you would have in your favor in the commodity futures markets when you control the adjuncts, production and distribution of food, and know who is about to make large purchases that will drive up commodity prices? What a racket! Recall that last year the commodity king, Philbro, merged with a finance king, Salomon Brothers. And Goldman Sachs & Co. joined with J. Aron and Co.

Let's turn to the other members of CROPEC. In Australia, wheat is a primary export. The Australian Wheat Board rules supreme down there, much like the U.S.D.A. here. The noises that Chase Manhattan has been making recently about investment in Australia speak loud and clear about the critical protein domino falling into place. Willard Butcher, president of Chase Manhattan, thinks Australia is a wonderful place to invest. In fact, Chase has been financing projects in Australia for decades. When David Rockefeller recently took his Chase Manhattan Advisory Committee to Australia, we should have known something foul was in the wind. Henry Kissinger went along in the entourage. America's old Soviet ally, Armand Hammer, has also been visiting and aggressively promoting Australia recently.

(It's interesting/important to note that one of the largest CIA bases in the world is located in the middle of Australia. Pine Gap, Australia, officially named Joint Defense Space Research, located at the southern foot of the MacDonnell Ranges, 12 miles from the center of Australia, is one of three top-secret U.S. government operations in Australia, about which the American public knows absolutely nothing. We have 700 military-types in Australia. How convenient for CROPEC.)

(Beyond a doubt, one of the government's foremost sacred cows is science. Almost totally financed with government money and institutionally the high priests of evolutionary humanism, we must wonder just how much technology has been developed that has not been made available to mankind. Joseph H. Carter, in his book, AWESOME FORCE, presented some mind expanding and shocking evidence in this regard [if Carter can be believed]. [Carter, Joseph, AWESOME FORCE, P. O. Box 9478, Winter Haven, FL 33880, $14.95, 400 pp.])

What about the third link in the CROPEC chain? Guess who, in April, 1981, took the directors of Chase Manhattan to Argentina for a meeting. None other than David Rockefeller. Argentina has been the recipient recently of millions of dollars of loans from the World Bank. Due to the social, political and economic turmoil in recent years, multinational banking and corporate interests (multinational debt capitalism) is rapidly gaining control of Argentina. No one else has the bucks or the clout to finance that critical agricultural country. And, in today's world, control of finance is political and economic control. Argentina is self-sufficient in energy. Agriculture there accounts for 90% of foreign exchange. Central bank (Banco del a Nacion) creation of money has recently accelerated inflation to over 100%. How convenient for cornering a country's natural resources.

The devaluation of the Argentine peso, the result of a loan condition imposed by the IMF and Inter-American Development Bank, has created *"national poverty."* Guess who is buying up Argentina's assets?

Meanwhile Brazil, which is no agricultural slouch, has allowed only a dozen or so foreign banks to operate there. These foreign banks' profits averaged an incredible 85% return on equity in 1981. Two of the elite U.S. banks which recorded this bonanza were Citibank and, of course, Chase Manhattan.

The fourth and final domino in the CROPEC chain is our socialistic neighbor to the north, Canada. It is very possible, if climatic conditions deteriorate in the next two decades, as some climatologists are projecting, that Canada could lose its protein producing capability. But, for now, Canada is a solid number four in the emerging *"protein gold"* cartel. The incredible fight that has taken place between Trudeau and the Canadian provinces over the new Canadian constitution speaks of the classic struggle between centralization and decentralization, which is occurring worldwide. Trudeau has long been acknowledged as a wild-eyed socialist. Yes, truly, CROPEC is coming together.

Back to the U.S. It won't be long before the 500,000 largest farms in this country that produce 80% of all farm products are owned lock, stock and barrel by the multinational debt capitalists. Worldwide, the organization that is pulling control of all commodities/raw materials under this international umbrella is the New International Economic Order (NIEO). GLOBESCAN reported that the NIEO general fund for buying commodities was initially funded with $750 million. Tyranny is closing in around us quickly as the sun of freedom sets.

Stateside, it will be important once again to carefully monitor the activities of the CIA regarding this CROPEC matter. The CIA has long operated in South America. The expanded powers given the CIA for internal surveillance in this country recently by President Reagan will open up the floodgates of potential KGB-type activity on the part of the CIA.

Novelists, poets and writers generally are sensitive members of society who predict the future. Along this line, remember Robert Redford's movie, *"Three Days of the Condor?"* The punch line of that movie was something to the effect that while in the 1970s energy procurement was the issue for the CIA, within the next 20 years, the issue will clearly be food! And, the people of the United States won't care how they get the food, just so the CIA gets it for them. Fiction is fast becoming fact. Getting what the *"people"* want when they want it was the justification for all the secrecy surrounding ruthless CIA activity in the movie, *"Three Days of the Condor."* Written projection is becoming reality.

It's important that we also note that there is emerging evidence suggesting that Jonestown had CIA involvement by way of brainwashing experimentation. Is this possible? Furthermore, forces who possibly are credible in Arizona and California, have been investigating Evergreen. Is Evergreen a CIA airline? You remember Evergreen. That's the airline that carried the Shah of Iran all around the globe during his last days. Well, it has been purported that good old Evergreen (our CIA?) has been heavily involved with the Medfly spraying in California, and possibly during this Medfly fiasco, has done some *"test"* spraying of other chemicals in order to evaluate their effect on large population numbers. American guinea pigs? (Popular attention has been brought to bear on these CIA matters by the controversial Mae Brussell.)

One final thought on this matter. You remember the man who was elected vice-president of the United States. Wasn't George Bush his name? We haven't heard much about him recently. But George Bush is still only a heartbeat away from the presidency. And George Bush is a former director of the CIA. Now, wasn't it at a dinner this past year that George Bush stood up and put his arm around David Rockefeller and said something to the effect that, *"All that I am I owe to this man."* Wonder if good old George could help make CROPEC a real-

ity? Intrigue of the highest order? Ian Fleming, creator of James
Bond, couldn't have written a better script.

*   *   *

*"The high office of President has been used to foment a plot to
destroy the Americans' freedom, and before I leave office I must inform the citizen of his plight."*

> *John F. Kennedy at Columbia University,*
> *10 days before his assassination.*

*   *   *

*" . . . Inside the car, slumped across the front seat in a puddle of
blood, was the body of a 37-year-old man with a new rifle in his hands.*

*"They searched his pockets and found the business card of William
Colby, the former U.S. director of central intelligence. . . .*

*"More perplexing yet, evidence has turned up that Nugan Hand
bank was deeply involved in moving funds around the world for big
international heroin dealers and also might have been involved in the
shady world of international arms traffic. To cap it off, the offices of
Nugan Hand and its affiliates were loaded with former high-ranking
U.S. military and intelligence officials.*

*"This has convinced many Australians that the company was in-
volved in secret work for the U.S. government. . . . "*

"Australian Mystery" by Jonathan Kwitny, in THE WALL STREET JOURNAL,
August 24, 1982. (Reprinted by permission of THE WALL STREET JOURNAL,
Copyright Dow Jones & Company, Inc., 1982, All rights reserved)

*   *   *

*". . . the CIA is engaged in independent operations against various
officials in Canada . . .*

*"Canada attracts American special services as turf for conducting
'delicate experiments.' After the scandalous revelations about the experiments on humans in the U.S. ('will suppression,' 'thought
control,' 'new thought pattern programming,' creation of 'robots,'
'removal of moral principles'), the CIA took a decision to conduct
further experiments in Canada."*

"Dossier on 800 Thousand Canadians" by N. N. Agashin, in U.S.A. ECONOMICS,
POLITICS, IDEOLOGY, from HUMINT Network Report, September 4, 1982

CONCLUSION: There is a finite amount of real new wealth produced by agriculture; that wealth has been confiscated by the banks in exchange for . . . debt slavery.

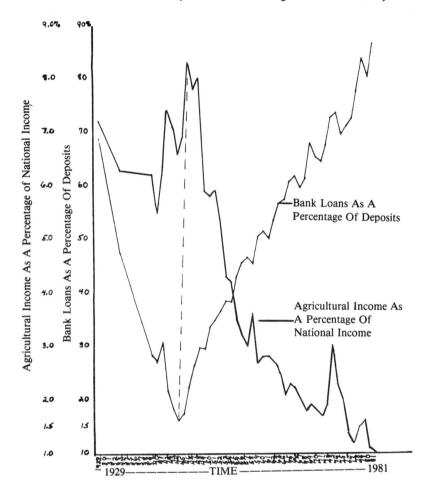

Source: THE REAPER

*   *   *

Source of much information on the CIA, courtesy
of Vernon Walters and George Keegan

WORLD TRADE - ON THE FADE

6/26/81

World commerce today is interdependent as never before. The United States' industrial machine is dependent upon imported oil and strategic metals. Without imported chromium, for example, our industrial plant would literally grind to a halt. Machinery imports and Japanese automobiles are now an integral part of our way of life, too. U.S. exports of high technology items, like computers, as well as grain and coal exports, keep the rest of the world humming. International airline travel and communication satellites have accelerated the specialization of labor and this economic interdependence.

Free trade by free men is a good thing. The essence of good business is that both parties benefit from the transaction. There is a great reluctance for a government to go to war with a country with which its citizens trade heavily.

At first blush, it would seem that what the world needs is an international government, an effective United Nations, a One-World Order, in order to solve the problems that individual nations present in stymieing world trade. This is the end for which the international bankers have worked in their own profitable self-interest. To their way of thinking, their efforts are also geared toward providing *"the greatest good for the greatest number."* And, on the surface, their perspective looks good. Nations do gum up the works in international trade. The import and export restrictions of the world's nations would literally fill a library. The problem comes with human nature. Men have not been able, historically, to handle too much power. While the best of governments, philosophers argue, are benign dictatorships, how many of them have we seen in world history? They have been few and far between. Why? Because power corrupts and absolute power corrupts absolutely. **We can't trust a One World Order to be benign.**

Beyond question, multinational banking and corporate activity, under the philosophy of social Darwinism (the survival of the fittest), have raped Third World countries, promoted communism, abused the economic and educationally less fortunate and promoted detestable international drug traffic. Many books testify to this harsh reality in-

102

cluding BANK CONTROL OF LARGE CORPORATIONS IN THE UNITED STATES by David M. Cotz; DOPE, INC.: BRITAIN'S OPIUM WAR AGAINST THE U.S. by a U.S. Labor Party Investigating Team; Herman H. Dinsmore's THE BLEEDING OF AMERICA; W. Cleon Skousen's THE NAKED COMMUNIST and THE NAKED CAPITALIST; Howard S. Katz's THE WARMONGERS; and Antony C. Sutton's NATIONAL SUICIDE.

While no one will argue that nations are totally efficient (far from it), they do decentralize power. Decentralization of power leads to a spreading around of responsibility and authority as well as, hopefully, economic goods and accountability. In such a decentralized environment, men are more free and are more in touch geographically, educationally, economically, and socially with the locus of power. Pressure can be brought to bear on the ambitious bureaucrats who seek, in their own unique ways, to reestablish the *"feudal age"* or reinstitute the *"divine right of kings."*

But now, world trade has started to slide in a major way. Europe is in recession. The United States' economy is slumping. The Third World developing countries' economies are on the chopping block. Even the high-flying Far East Pacific Basin is feeling the effects of the global contraction. A key business indicator, international airline travel, has slumped badly. The international airlines suffered the worst operating losses in their history in 1980, a combined loss for all international air carriers of $2.53 billion. It was the first year-to-year decline in over two decades.

Technically, what we are witnessing is a rounded top. This is the most severe downturn in 20 years and marks a major deviation from the long uptrend, which was only stalled by the '74 global recession. The *"World Trade Volume"* graph traces out the pattern of the growth-completing "S" curve. (See next page.)

In 1925, Dr. Raymond Pearl of John Hopkins University wrote a fascinating book, THE BIOLOGY OF POPULATION GROWTH. Dr. Pearl discovered that there is a law of growth which proceeds along an "S" curve. There is a slow beginning, a rapid rise, and then a levelling out. The "S" curve applies to such things as white rats, pumpkins, yeast cells, businesses and nations.

The economist, Robert L. Heilbroner, in his work, BUSINESS CIVILIZATION IN DECLINE, commented along these same lines:

". . . Industrial growth, or capitalist expansion, is an exponential process—a process that proceeds like a snowball, requiring continuously increasing quantities of resources and spewing forth continuously increasing quantities of wastes, simply to maintain a constant pace of expansion. No social processes of an exponential

character are capable of indefinite continuance. Sooner or later all such processes must overload their environment, consuming all its nutrients or poisoning it by the waste products associated with growth. That is why curves that originally shoot upward in near-vertical fashion sooner or later bend into "S" shapes, or actually reverse themselves and go into decline."

Edward R. Dewey and Edwin F. Dakin in their book, CYCLES: THE SCIENCE OF PREDICTION, observed:

"A growth trend amounts to a pattern; and the pattern is similar for almost all organisms, whether a group of cells in a pumpkin or a group of human beings in a nation."

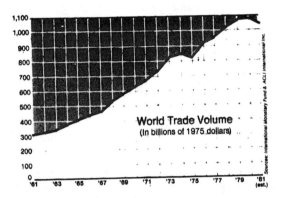

The "S" curve is truly nothing more than a natural law of growth. Businesses and nations are living organisms just like humans, plants and animals. They are born, grow, experience accelerated growth, maturity and then old age. It takes a great deal of energy to get to the top of the "S" curve. At that point, fatigue sets in. Distractions are common. Only an approach to life which is spiritual, first and foremost, can save the collective activities of man from the fate of the "S" curve.

The kingpins in any field of business are continually distracted by negative press, bureaucratic alphabet agencies' regulations, a consuming tax system, not to mention the potshots which are taken at them by the competition due to a desire for, and envy of, their *"No. 1"* status.

It's difficult to stay *"No. 1."* Theoretically, it would seem easier, because all the organization or individual needs to do is maintain its/his achieved momentum. But times change, and people aren't machines. Men and organizations get set in their ways, lazy, proud, too comfortable, lose ambition and tend to coast. When an individual or an organization is coasting, they are going downhill. Thus, the "S" curve.

Such is the status now of international world trade. It is coasting, downhill! We have turned the corner on painless, constructive, expansionary, inflationary good times. As management expert Peter F. Drucker observed in THE WALL STREET JOURNAL, *"In every inflation since the 16th century the 'smart boys' have managed short term. When the inflation stopped, they always crashed in flames."* Drucker says a lot about the death spiral awaiting strung out multinational corporations, banks, our federal government, Third World countries, Iron Curtain countries and consumers. His use of the word *"flames"* is more than symbolic. When worldwide economic hard times hit, nations will institute the destructive policy of protectionism. Protectionism is the horse pulling the chariot of war.

DEBT WOOD

3/27/81

Just as mature bull markets accelerate their price rise before they come crashing down, so also does the public trend toward self-destruction at the end of a good economic era. The analogy between markets and the economy holds because both are the result of mass human action in a specific and the general economic arena. Consistent with the concept of the coexistence of apparent opposites, that there is strength in weakness and weakness in strength, both markets and economies, when they are apparently their strongest, spill forth the seeds of crippling weakness.

Astute human thinkers have recognized this collective tendency to self-destruct down through the ages by such expressions as: *"Life on the surface is a comedy, but beneath the surface is a tragedy;" "A cynic is someone who is correct nine out of ten times;" "If you're not a liberal at 20, you have no heart. If you're not conservative at 40, you have no head;" "Humanity never solves its problems; it just luckily lives through them."* Regarding these adages, and the last adage particularly, that *"Humanity simply survives its problems,"* one only needs to point out the world energy crisis. In fact, crisis management is clearly the state of affairs globally. Man refuses to plan long-term.

The *"Peter Principle,"* the idea that men will promote themselves to their level of incompetence, can be easily seen by government, business and consumer over assumption of debt during the 50-year debt cycle. The idea that men promote themselves to their level of incompetence is simply a variation of the old economic theme that human animalistic wants are inexhaustible. Men collectively leave themselves no slack. Their pride, lust, insecurities or other weaknesses drive them until the pace becomes so white-hot that the choice becomes either permanent extinction or temporary self-destruction. To this point in history, the choice has been the latter. (We're still here.) Today, however, with the abuse of our technological achievements being potentially so great, survival is no longer so easily assured.

We do not limit the demands on our time. Time dictates to us, rather than vice versa. We do not limit our human wants. Rather, they run us under. We are undisciplined when we chase madly after goods. In economic terms, because our institutions have refused to discipline the use of credit, we have run amuck on an ever-accelerating inflationary treadmill. Our consumption of goods and services far exceeds our needs or our ability to pay. Personally, on a municipal and state level, in the business world and on the federal level, our excessiveness is crystal clear. Debt has become unwieldy. We have run too far, too fast, and are now facing exhaustion at a time when the debt load is becoming heavier. The *"debt wood"* continues to stack up. Pretty soon we will have enough for a *"bond"* fire.

Debt is a form of slavery. It blocks economic freedom. It takes time to be worked off. Debt yields a short-term benefit, but is a long-term liability. Borrowing takes place for consumption in the present (boom). It leaves a vacuum in the future (bust). We are mighty close to that vacuum. Sometimes we have trouble seeing this. The boom/bust, prosperity/depression cycle must be primarily seen as a debt cycle. Due to our fractional reserve banking system, what effectively occurs is that the economy moves from liquidity through a debt expansion phase to the point where it is loaded up with debt (illiquid), which triggers the depression.

It is all so unnecessary. The *"Wealth for All"* economic system promotes a stable, growing, prosperous economy long-term. But, such an economy does not allow insiders and elitists to get rich quick by preying on their fellow man's economic misfortune and ignorance.

What about this idea of a depression? Assuming human nature is a constant over time, are there any lessons we can glean from previous economic depressions that will give us clues to our present state of affairs? Let's look:

1. One of the primary explanations given for the Great Depression was too much debt. People had borrowed all they could borrow, and they simply stopped spending. Remember that the private sector accounts for 70% of all borrowing. But, major turning points are seldom triggered by just one factor. There are usually many causes, much like a multitude of spotlights focusing together at one point on a stage.

2. The Great Depression has been blamed upon the Federal Reserve's contraction of the money supply.

3. Public confidence collapsed in 1929. This led to people pulling their money out of banks, hoarding of gold and cash, and the calling in of loans.

4. Third World debt was a problem in the 1920s. In 1931, a moratorium was declared on all Third World debt repayment.

5. Some economists blame the Great Depression on the Smoot-Hawley Tariff. This protectionist measure was a severe blow to international trade.

We notice that evidences 1-5 are with us today. We are a credit economy which is attempting to get liquid, both in the public and private sector. The Federal Reserve is contracting the money supply. Public confidence is low. Third World debt is a problem again. The demand for protectionism is on the rise and, interestingly enough, our economic hostility is again directed toward the Japanese.

6. We entered a dry period in the 1930s. We had a dry period in 1980.

7. In the 1920's there was a panicky search for oil. History repeats today.

8. There was a real estate and stock market boom in the 1920s, preceding the Great Depression. We have just experienced a real estate boom and a commodity boom, the equivalent of 1929 stock market speculation.

9. In the late 1920's, public sentiment forced politicians to shift from liberal to conservative monetary and fiscal policies. The Reagan election is a replay of that same experience. Is Reagan a Hoover?

10. The world economy, overall, deteriorated in the late 1920s. This is the case today with Europe in recession and Third World countries on the ropes with low raw material prices (exports) and high import costs (oil), not to mention Third World exploding debt and debt service ($500 billion).

11. In the late 1920s, industry was eating its own tail, so to speak, through mergers and acquisitions. The same thing is true today. Monopolies are effectively created through mergers and acquisitions. Monopolies stifle creativity and productivity.

12. Big corporations, big banks, and wealthy speculators got rich in the late 1920s. This is true today. The middle class and lower income working groups suffered the most then and now.

13. The bond market losses we have witnessed in the last four years are only matched historically by the bond market losses from 1929-1932. The bond market today is our most important financial market.

14. The price of raw materials in 1929 was out of line (parity) with the cost of other goods and services. This problem exists today.

Sad to say, it looks like history is repeating itself again. Because man has not learned from history the easy way, it appears as though he will again learn history's lessons the hard way.

REAL ESTATE . . . REALLY?

11/3/78

This writer does not *"dig"* the real estate market at this point in time. It's true that there is nothing hidden or underground in my motivations either. It's just that I do not want to serve as undertaker at your financial burial which might well be the case if you are now heavily leveraged in real estate. Real estate is vulnerable presently. And because so few members of the general public recognize this is so, the market is even more susceptible to a correction.

Let's see if I can cover some old ground and plant some new seeds which will increase your understanding.

Real estate investment has become a mania in this country. The benchmarks of a mania are: (1) Everyone believes it is a sure thing; (2) No one believes they can lose; and (3) Leverage becomes the norm (consumers are refinancing their homes and taking second mortgages in order to finance other purchases). (4) Headline stories appear on the front page of THE WALL STREET JOURNAL (wherein consumers state that home ownership is the only sure thing).

The Robbins Report, an informative real estate report, declared, *"The housing boom of 1976, 1977 and most of 1978 is all built on shaky ground. Buyers are committing up to 33% of their income to support their ego status new homes. Twenty nine percent is the maximum the average family should afford to pay in today's economy and life style. Lenders will soon feel the delinquency and foreclosures will begin. For the cash rich, the opportunities are coming!"*

It is the South Sea Bubble and the Mississippi Land Scheme all over again. (MacKay, EXTRAORDINARY POPULAR DELUSIONS AND THE MADNESS OF CROWDS). The American consumer, who is up to his eyebrows in debt, has been at the forefront participating in this mania. The mountain land buying mania in Colorado in 1972-73, the overnight lines in California to buy underdeveloped lots, the home buying syndications made up of doctors and attorneys—all are calling cards of a mania. It has permeated the entire country. Some 77 million of America's 81 million family households live in single family or multi-family housing. What happens when unemployment increases? What happens when the consumer has to cut back because inflation is causing the price of necessities to rise? What happens when interest rates continue to rise in the face of falling demand in order to maintain foreign deposits and stay even with inflation?

There is a well established 18-1/3 year real estate cycle in this country. It has been traced from 1795 through the late 1950's. There have been eight repetitions of the 18-1/3 year real estate cycle according to Gertrude Shirk, a sparkling analyst at the Foundation for the Study of Cycles. Guess what? We are at the peak of the 18-1/3 year real estate cycle presently.

The elder stateman of U.S. real estate, Roy Wenzlick of St. Louis, confirmed this cycle in six separate studies covering building activity, foreclosures, vacancies, new family accomodations and real estate transfers. Other researchers, such as Maverick, noted a 17 to 18-year cycle in deeds recorded per capita. Maverick's work took place in San Francisco. Hoyt confirmed the same 18-year cycle in his studies in Chicago. Colean, Fisher and Gaffney, using Urban Land Institute data, also found an 18-year rhythmic cycle in urban real estate in the United States. Downs found an 18-25 year real estate cycle in foreclosures, real estate activity, real estate sales, real estate security prices, rent prices and residential occupancy. Others, who have confirmed the 18-year real estate cycle in this country, are Edward R. Dewey, deceased head of the Foundation for the Studies of Cycles, King, and Bodfish, who found a 54-year rhythmic cycle in real estate which contained minor cycles averaging 18 years in length.

It is perfectly clear as well that all the *"fundamental"* data confirms this peak. If real estate prices were plotted on a vertical scale with years on a horizontal scale, during the 1970's, and particularly since 1976, the chart of real estate prices would be approaching the vertical. This is a classic warning signal that prices are about to peak and break. What is most dangerous is that markets that approach the vertical often break badly as well.

The life blood of the real estate market are the money markets. The money markets are the mother. The funds flow through the umbilical cord, as it were, to the baby (real estate). Once the interest rates get too high, buyers withdraw from the market. Who feeds the baby? Worse yet, during a credit crunch, when short-term rates rise faster than long-term rates, or when short-term rates exceed long term rates (inversion), some disintermediation takes place. Investment funds are withdrawn from the long-term capital markets for more favorable and less risky short-term instruments. In short, the baby dies.

Presently, in this country, homes that are selling for over $100,000 are becoming very difficult to move. The inventory of listings for sales has skyrocketed. It is now a buyer's market. Commercial loan demand is dropping sharply. Large builders (with whom I have talked personally) in Chicago and Dallas are pulling in their horns. The coming energy crunch and/or OPEC price increase will be an additional blow to real estate. The chart of the annual rate of change in mortgage debt is topping out. According to Dr. H. A. Merklein's study at the University of Dallas (Professor of the Graduate School of Management), during 1982-83 the cost of servicing the national debt will exceed $100 billion. This cost is greater than the net capital generating capacity of the entire U.S. markets. In other words, at that time there will be no money available for anything other than servicing the national debt. There will be no money for real estate development or mortgages.

There are tremendous similarities between real estate today and real estate in the 1920's. In a six year period, between 1920 and 1926, the price of land for housing doubled. Then, the speculation was in Florida. Today, it is in Southern California primarily, but it has spread to the rest of the nation. During both periods of time, frantic buyers spent the night on the steps of real estate offices. Fights broke out. People sold their place in line for hundreds of dollars. Reckless speculators and unsophisticated investors became rich in housing and land speculation. Then, the market died.

Seventy five percent of the platted ground in Burbank, California was vacant in the early 1930's. Similar statistics applied across the country. The October 11, 1978 WALL STREET JOURNAL reported, *"the cost of land, as a percentage of the total cost of a new house, is about where it stood in the 1920's."*

The April 3, 1978 issue of *Barrons* reproduced a report by Charles D. Kirkpatrick, II, from the *Burns-Kirkpatrick Letter,* a marketing division of Lynch, Jones and Ryan, a New York Stock Exchange member firm. It concluded, *"An enormous price rise, faster and further than any other segment of the economy has occurred over the past 33 years . . . We feel very strongly that the house price mania will break, and break soon."* The study discussed the reasons that have been given historically for the rising price of real estate, namely population growth, inflation and spendable income. But according to the Kirkpatrick study, the rise in the price of real estate has been double the population growth. And recently, from 1940 to 1970, the price rise in real estate has been way in excess of the population growth. Population growth from 1890 to 1970 increased at a compounded 1.4% rate. Real estate, during the same time, increased at a compounded rate of 2.89%.

What about inflation? From 1890 to 1970, wholesale prices rose at a compounded rate of 1.69%. Housing prices during the same time rose at a compounded rate of 2.89%. From 1940 to 1970, the compounded rate of inflation was 3.4%, while housing prices rose at a 6.98% rate.

With regard to spendable income, from 1947 to 1970, spendable income increased at the compounded rate of 2.55%, while housing prices rose at the compounded rate of 6.55%.

Some other scary statistics are: (1) 1944 mortgage debt on single family dwellings—$17.9 billion. 1977 mortgage debt on single family dwellings—$588 billion. (2) 1940—45.3% of U.S. single family dwellings were mortgaged. 1970—60% of U.S. single family dwellings were mortgaged.

What about the demographics? Approximately 70% of the new home purchases are made by individuals between 25 and 44 years of age. This age group will be increasing at a rate of 26% during the next ten years. Just because these individuals want to buy homes doesn't mean that they will be financially able to buy homes. If those who always wanted to buy homes could do so we would see a never-ending housing boom in India. Certainly, the number of households has increased, due partially to divorces and separations. But it has also been due to our robust economy during the last 3 decades. The major economic contraction which we are expecting within the next six years should result in a wholesale retrenchment. A precedent was set in 1974. In 1972-73 there were 2.2 million housing starts. In 1974 the number dropped to 1.3 million. With the decline in supply, and an increase in population, one would have expected 1974 to be a tight market. But, in fact, this was not the case. Vacancy rates were higher in 1975 than they were in 1973.

Will the coming economic crunch cause more children to remain at home with their parents? How much longer can the already illiquid consumer afford the increasing price of housing? Not long!

ELEGANT SUICIDE

9/25/81

We have watched the economy through our predicted *"rounded topping out process"* since 1979. The crash in bonds and automobile sales, the peak of the 18 1/3-year real estate cycle, the subsequent hard times which have come upon the construction industry, the desperate condition of small businessmen and farmers, the 1980 commodity market crash carrying into 1981, and the full weight of high interest rates have made themselves known even to the stock market.

The markets are having their say. No political power on earth can withstand the force and fury of the free market! And, interestingly enough, American art reflects all of this.

An American art critic and client observed that American *"art"* is *"somewhat prophetic and always supersensitive about the present."* He observed that art's theme now *"reflects the attitude of giving up in the face of a threatening future. It is the desire to perfect the present because the future will surely bring us down. . . . Modern art which also includes, unfortunately, advertising, caters to this attitude. . . . J. R. Ewing and Ronald Reagan both fall into 'art' role models. Reagan is an ambivalent symbol. He is an ex-movie star, withdrawn, a ruler who is remote from the ruled, except when he is pleading 'for the good of the country.' His riding outfit, his ranch, his perfect ease fits with what most people would like to be but for the wrong reasons.*

"Stable and enduring societies maintain a healthy balance between the present and the future. Present needs are fulfilled modestly and balanced against an instinct for future preservation of the race/family, etc." He further observed that American society is committing *"elegant suicide."*

Reflecting upon these observations, this writer made special note of an article in the September 21, 1981 issue of U.S. NEWS: *"Flaunting Wealth. It's Back in Style."* From that article, *"There is almost a sense of desperation, that if you don't do it now, you won't have the chance again."* [12] That says it all! Confirmation!

We are consuming our capital. We are present oriented, as indicated by our unwillingness to undergo any real economic pain to reduce the federal budget. Our frantic desire to consume in the present is demonstrated by consumers' general refusal to save and the addiction to borrowing. Our advertising, as a form of 20th century art, does cater to a short-term, pagan, hedonistic philosophy which is successfully captured by the ads, *"The lazy man's way to riches,"* and *"What kind of man reads Playboy?"* The lack of interest in politics on the part of the general public, the repudiation of the *"Great Faith"* that made this country great, the refusal to recognize our military and political enemies, the public opinion polls which consistently show that Americans are **not** interested in providing for the welfare of their children and future generations—all of this reveals the short-term, selfish perspective of a society concerned only with the here and now. We know, in our collective subconscious, that the roof is about to cave in. But we intend to throw one hell of a party until it does. It is *"elegant suicide."*

Reflecting upon the truth of the foregoing observations, Colin M. Turnbull's THE MOUNTAIN PEOPLE comes quickly to mind. Turnbull, a first-rate anthropologist, shattered the illusions of contemporary, light-weight American anthropologists.

> *"In THE MOUNTAIN PEOPLE Colin M. Turnbull describes the dehumanization of an African tribe that in less than three generations has deteriorated from a group of prosperous and daring hunters to scattered bands of hostile people whose only goal is individual survival. Walled in their compounds, living in fear of each neighbor, they have created a society that frighteningly mirrors the cold and lonely selfishness of our own. Not since Oscar Lewis' La Vida has there been so remorseless a description of the social collapse and decay of people."* [13]

It has been nearly a decade since this writer first read Turnbull's illusion shattering narrative on how the *"Ik,"* a relatively civilized tribe, declined into total decadence. In its decadent state, the *"Ik"* epitomized two of the most devastating characteristics of man: The *"Ik"* were totally selfish. This selfishness was manifested by a comprehensive here and now, do your own thing, live-for-the-day orientation. This is exactly the orientation of the American people today. The only reason we are not yet living in lonely, frightening, crime ridden, violent, and abject poverty is that we have not yet consumed all of our capital. But we have been on the road to there in a hurry! Our own art declares it.

Now, let's tie this anthropological observation back into the economy and the markets. Let's loop together our relentless run toward *"elegant suicide"* with our market, economic and political observations. We are at a turning point. Gold, commodities, interest rates, the stock market, and political action all clearly speak to it. What little capital we have not yet consumed, what few monetary morsels we have still set aside for consumption by future generations, the best nest egg we can *"track"* that still differentiates us from the African *"Ik"* is the $200+ billion deposited in money market mutual funds!

We were on the same ruinous road at breakneck speed that has already wrecked the *"Ik"* when the Reagan administration put on the brakes and attempted to turn things around. The Carter administration was taking us at an accelerated pace toward economic, political and social oblivion. Reagan, though he hasn't done nearly what needs to be done, attempted a slow turn. Will he succeed? Probably not. The jury is still out, however. The real jury is those depositors who have $200+ billion placed in money market mutual funds. If they vote with their pocketbooks for inflation hedges—gold, silver, antiques, collectibles, commodities, real estate, numismatics, high priced livestock, gems and the like—in their collective minds, they will have determined that we, as a society, have decided to become the American equivalent of the African *"Ik."* If, on the other hand, they vote with their investment dollars for municipal bonds, corporate bonds, U.S. government bonds and stocks, then as a group, they will have determined that American society has turned around. They will have decided, in effect, that we have again taken a long-term view. Collectibles and inflation hedges of all kinds are short-term, destruction-oriented investments. Stocks and bonds are long-term, growth oriented in nature. Over $200 billion in money market funds is waiting on the sidelines. It is the market jury which will stand in judgment of our politicians' decisions, which are nothing more than a reflection of our mass thinking.

Now, let's turn to the concept of a *"panic."* We are at the point in Funk's *"Human Action Cycle"* when a panic is most likely. The mass movement of $200+ billion of investment money from money market funds to a different investment medium, any medium, will precipitate a panic. There is no question about it. A vote of *"no confidence"* for the U.S. dollar, which is effectively a vote of no confidence for U.S. politicians and our way of life, should lead to a *"white-hot"* pace of economic activity resulting in total exhaustion. Investors will scramble into gold, silver, collectibles, commodities, numismatics, gems, antiques, high-priced livestock, real estate, and probably even U.S. stocks as they flee the U.S. dollar. And collectively, investors are at the point where the next time they throw in the towel on the U.S. dollar, it could be for good. They almost did so in the first quarter, 1980!

If a run on the dollar occurs again, the vindictive violence which will be inflicted upon our politicians will be a horror to behold. It will not be a *"pretty panic."* On the other hand, if the economy goes *"cold turkey,"* while we will still have to suffer through a deflationary depression, bonds should do well, as well as stocks in selected industries. This inflation will not be stopped without a painful deflationary depression that breaks the back of the *"extended credit pumped-up price structure."* Fear, real fear, brought about by falling prices and bankruptcies, will be necessary to bust this inflation. For every action, there is an equal and opposite reaction. The booms and busts in economies are no exception. We are in the midst of the painful deflationary interlude I have been writing about since 1979, with hyper-inflation knocking at the door.

Given the pervasive *"soft"* social and political attitudes, the lack of discipline and initiative, the rampant selfishness and present orientation, as well as the economic and political illiteracy of the masses, the weight of evidence forces us to conclude that the panic will be of the *"white hot"* kind, leading to economic exhaustion and prostration. The markets, however, will give us signs as to which scenario is correct. As long as gold does not take off again upside, our social order should hold together. If gold, however, rallies, while interest rates rise, expect a panic run on the U.S. dollar. Such a run should be accompanied by bull markets in commodities generally. By contrast, if commodities continue to slide, and interest rates fall while international currencies weaken, and gold stays soft, the U.S. dollar will be king.

THE 50-YEAR HUMAN ACTION CYCLE

9/4/81

Economist James M. Funk was the author of THE 56-YEAR CYCLE OF PROSPERITY, DEPRESSION AND PRICES, written in 1932. Penned during the depths of The Great Depression, Funk was in touch with human economic reality. The collective arrogance of economic man in the late 1920s had just undergone the sobering experience of 1929-1932. As a result, Funk saw economic human action with more humility than today's pumped-up, myopic economists. So much of Funk's wisdom is applicable today:

> *"Before being long embarked upon our task, we were impressed with the strange phenomena of repeated history. But stranger still, was the similarity of 'chains of events' which culminated in similar capital events. And most strange was the 'same lapse of time' which attended each of these succeeding events. Therefore, the 'effect' of each prior event is the present; the 'present' is the 'cause' of the next event. This seems to substantiate or else is substantiated by the expression: 'The present is a necessary product of all the past and the necessary cause of all the future.'"*

To James M. Funk, writing to us some 50 years ago, history had meaning. In our short-term society, possessed by the evolutionary, humanistic, inflationary bias, history has no meaning. For evolution assumes no constants such as human nature. And, since man is evolving, there is little we can learn from the past. The past has no meaning. Thus, history has no meaning.

Continuing Funk's insights:

> *"History reveals that it takes humanity about 56 years to learn and forget. We must therefore refer to such a lapse of time in experience as a cycle . . .and liken each cycle to a long ride on a merry-go-round, which always returns us, after a definite lapse of time, to the same place or condition from which we started.*
>
> *"It requires about 56 years for humanity 'to revert back' to the same economic conditions, 'like rabbits to the spot from where first pursued' . . . .because we have not profited by experience, history, or have not exercised our faculties of good judgment in diagnosing business situations. In a word, very few people, 'read*

117

and think' for themselves . . . .They are moved by mob psychology, mass emotions. Thus, a few agents sway the mob, manufacture their thoughts and create public opinion. However, these few 'leaders of man' know the 'psychology of the moment,' and 'manufacture accordingly.' These few owe their success to their 'psychological instincts' . . . ."

Two more quick comments harmonious with Funk's observations:

1. Economies and markets are psychological in nature. They are the result of mass human action. This is why Ludwig von Mises named his classic treatise on economics, HUMAN ACTION.

2. These approximate 50-year economic cycles seem to have at least three things in common:

   a. A human action progression, a chain of events,

   b. The creation and contraction of credit accompanied by the expansion and contraction of the production of capital goods,

   c. Weather changes.

Funk focused on collective human folly, the tendency of people, in their ignorance, to go along with the crowd. He also astutely observed how so much foolishness eventually leads to destruction. He wrote:

" 'Humanity does not profit by experience' . . . .We should say: 'Profit by history;' because the life span is too short to permit more than one 'ride.'

"The average mentality is that of a 12 year old child . . . .The average individual has not sufficient ambition to read a book and try to 'think out' its import. He would prefer that knowledge come naturally, and since it doesn't, he becomes socialistic . . . .in cycles . . . .and demands that the government divide equally all the wealth. On account of this predominating lack of ambition, which is known and taken advantage of by a growing number, a group of fraudulent or else ignorant politicians rule this, and every other nation. This very fact accounts for the rise and fall of nations.

"A similar chain of cause and effect events of the past will reflect our future because humans have not changed much throughout history, 'just a change of clothes.'

"Starting with only the necessities of life, then better things, polite culture, refinement; then accumulation, it's security, greed, jealousy, envy. Then the War Spirit, hunger for applause, vanity. Then the awakening, remorse, the shallowness realized. Then blaming, fault finding, repudiation. Then 'wild orgies of wanton waste.' Then exhaustion, panic, prostration; then depression and cool reasoning, the realization that the 'fiddler must be paid,' and the condition of mind which submits to the long siege in bondage."

Regarding economic reality, and where we stand in time in this economic cycle, the following comments by James M. Funk are vital. They help us to clearly discern, not only where we stand in economic time, but also provide us with the perspective necessary to plan our financial future.

> *"Briefly, we found the Cyclic-Order to be: Depression—thrift, Thrift—confidence—investment, Investment—activity—prosperity, Prosperity—easy credit—over-production, Over-production—'pressure' sales—fictitious collateral, Saturation of fictitious collateral—panic, Panic—depression. . . . One is tied to the other; one produces and is produced by the other.*
>
> *"If we start with depression, we will, by natural progressive stages, return to depression: . . .*
>
> *"Depression produces thrift. . . . Thift produces confidence. . . . Confidence produces investment. . . . Investment produces activity. . . . Activity produces prosperity. . . . Prosperity produces easy-credit. . . . Easy-credit produces over-production. . . . Over-production produces fictitious sales, and fictitious collateral. . . . These produce an economic structure of fictitious paper value. . . . When the structure is so recognized, it is abandoned, which is another way of expressing PANIC. . . . Panic produces depression."*

Without question, we are in the time frame when an economic panic could/should occur. We are at the point in the 50-year cycle (Funk's 56-year cycle) when the economy should top out and turn down with a vengeance (a panic). With the election of Ronald Reagan as President, the *"economic structure of fictitious paper value"* was recognized. People became tired of the game.

Speaking of being tired of the game, Funk quoted THE WALL STREET JOURNAL of that time. This short paragraph from THE WALL STREET JOURNAL expresses what, to this writer, is the touchstone of about where the public is now.

> *"With everyone instinctively sensing the situation, everyone sought to withdraw his funds from the banks; the banks sought to collect their loans. Everyone sought cash to pay his debts; credit dried up. The fact is, people were tired, on the verge of breakdown. The pace was too fast; it lasted too long. They wanted to rest, quit the game, sell out. But there were no buyers. In their wild frenzy the mob annihilated their own fortunes and the whole structure by 'running' the banks and by not trusting each other."*[14]

Today the general public instinctively senses and understands the problems with big government and big banks. Investors have withdrawn billions of dollars from the banks and S & Ls and placed them in money market funds. And, the greatest growth in the money market funds has been in those funds which handle strictly government securities, the safest of all paper investments.

Financial institutions are having trouble collecting their loans. Long-term credit has dried up as investment bond houses and mortgage banking firms know all too well. Our people are tired. The inflationary pace has been too fast. It has lasted too long. Our people need a rest. The landslide election of Ronald Reagan was a vote to quit the inflationary game. Buyers are dropping out of the picture right and left, particularly in the real estate markets.

Mankind is still his own greatest enemy. The tendency that all of us have when under undue pressure and/or when exhausted is to self-destruct. Self-destruction occurs far more easily for collective, undisciplined mankind. Economic self-destruction is called a panic. It seems there is a subconscious, psychological mechanism that triggers this self-destruction when people are living contrary to their ethical standards, or when self-destruction near-term is necessary for survival long-term.

The popular slogan during Funk's era, prior to The Great Depression was, *"If you want to be rich, owe somebody."* This slogan applied in spades to our collective economic perspective throughout the 1970s. But, with the highest real interest rates since prior to The Great Depression, the game changed. For now, *"If you want to be rich, owe nobody."* Compound interest has recently been the name of the game.

It is uncanny how Funk's remarks concerning the debt situation, particularly government debt, is applicable to our day and age.

> *"Government debts are, as a whole, taxpayer debts, which means every man, woman and child in the nation. In various ways the burden is carried by every one of them. In time of crisis the government can print money, but the value of the dollar will be lowered as a consequence; it can borrow and can pass on to coming generations a growing debt with compound interest. The depression periods . . . are the result of such action. It can raise the money by taxation, but industry and business cannot then afford to operate; unemployment becomes more acute than ever. The government can feed that nation by going into business after the Communistic system, which means that the individual will lose his liberty and identity. Thus, the human will lose liberties he has fought for since the beginning of time."*

The more things change, the more they remain the same. The debt which James M. Funk identified in 1932 as an unmanageable burden which leads to a panic and crash is with us today.

Debt is a curse for man. It has been decisively shown historically that debt, long-term, is never constructive to the health and well-being of any business or country. Debt was condemned in the Old Testament of the Bible and the New Testament as well. *"Owe no man any thing, . . ."* Debt is the cause of the boom/bust cycle. The expansion of credit, creating good times, results in inflation. Inflation leads to a loss of confidence which results in the contraction of credit. This leads to deflation which creates hard times.

James M. Funk saw clearly that debt was the cause of the economic cycle, a cycle intrinsically unstable. The curse of infinite compounding interest, this abstract, timeless, eternal concept, was never meant for plodding, limited, mistake-prone, finite man. The two, when mixed together, produce an explosive mixture which reeks chaos and havoc all over the economic landscape.

The debt piper is waiting to be paid. The *"established"* investment community ignored the Dow Theory sell signal in the stock market. It disregarded the major long-term sell signal in commodities. It snubbed its nose at the bond market crash, the greatest financial crash since The Great Depression. It has only slightly regarded the dire straits of the real estate and automobile industries, two economic mainstays of our economy. It has indignantly ignored the plight of the American farmer, who has experienced the lowest farm income in a generation on a constant dollar basis. It has shrugged off the non-performing loans (billions of dollars) owed U.S. banks.

Since 1960, the total U.S. personal, business and government debt has grown from $779 billion to $4,652 billion in 1980. Personal debt jumped 576%, business debt 658%, and government debt 330%. And government has guaranteed loans for just about everything but the kitchen sink, and that, too, in some cases.

We hear the debt piper's tune down the street. Meanwhile, our people are tired. They are tired mentally, psychologically, emotionally and financially. They don't have solid financial statements or other assets put away for a rainy economic day. When the debt piper knocks at the door, given this weary state of affairs, the most likely human response will be to panic.

THE 50-YEAR DEBT CYCLE

6/27/80

There are a number of 50-year cycles which have been documented throughout history. In the Old Testament of the Bible, in Leviticus 25, a 50-year debt cycle is revealed. There were seven series of seven years (49 years), plus the year of jubilee. During the year of jubilee, debt was effectively liquidated and the economy was cleansed.

Wheat, the staff of life, runs in a 54-year cycle that has been traced back to 1260 A.D.

R. N. Elliott, in his work, NATURE'S LAW, documented a 55-year Fibonacci number cycle in commodity prices. Commodities peaked in 1864, 1919 and 1973-74.

The Aztecs adhered to a 52-53-year climatic, religious, social, political and economic cycle.

The gold/commodity ratio peaked in 1920 and fifty years later in 1970.

Professor Jay W. Forrester of MIT found a 45-60-year cycle in capital goods. It is Dr. Forrester's conclusion that the capital goods cycle has now peaked. Dr. Forrester, working with the Systems Dynamic Group of the Sloan School of Management at MIT, discovered that approximately every 50 years there is lagging new capital investment and low productivity. The last time this situation existed was in the 1920s.

Capital goods investments are really long-term investments. Therefore, capital goods investments require long-term money. The bond market collapse in late 1979 and early 1980 destroyed the little remaining faith in long-term monetary instruments. Thus, capital goods fell victim to the bond market collapse. One could say, therefore, that capital goods are a function of the debt cycle, too.

Long-term investment is a function of confidence. Why should investors risk their money long-term when the business cycle is so volatile with inflation whipsaws up and down? Stated differently, why plant oats (long-term) when all one can truly count on is cabbages (short-term)? Diminishing confidence correlates directly with shorter-term investments. Diminishing confidence is a direct result of increasing debt.

There also appears to be a technology cycle of nearly 50 years that approximates the 50-year capital goods boom/bust cycle. This was first observed by Joseph Schumpeter. Our technology today is mature. And, there is little incentive for new technological development, given present over-bearing government regulation and taxation. Furthermore, the American people today are too comfortable with the existing level of technology. Necessity is the mother of invention. We have no necessity, yet. Patents granted to U.S. residents have been declining, relative to their 1860-1930 rate of increase, since 1930. Just look at the age of our present technology and its conditions: Television, the interstate highway system, our air transportation system. It is mature. It is over-taxed and over-regulated. Factory capacity is excessive.

The 56-year Human Action Cycle, the 56-year Human Action Progression, which was popularized by James M. Funk in his 1932 work, CYCLES OF PROSPERITY, DEPRESSION and PRICES, runs roughly as follows: Depression, thrift, confidence, investment, activity, prosperity, easy credit, over-production, misuse of credit (poor collateral), over-consumption, inflation, loss of confidence, panic, depression. We are at the point in the cycle when the loss of confidence is becoming so great that the next most likely major financial event is a panic leading to a depression. A century before, in 1837, Lord Overstone of Great Britain observed the same 50-year boom/bust human action cycle. Obviously, human nature did not change significantly during those 100 years. The more things change the more they remain the same. Lord Overstone's 50-year human action cycle: Quiescence, improvement, growing confidence, prosperity, excitement, over-trading, convulsion, pressure, stagnation, distress, quiescence.

We have seen several minipanics, probably shock waves prior to a major panic. In the past two years, the pre-shocks include a stock market crash, a bond market collapse, and a silver market free fall. Potential danger areas for triggering an upcoming panic domestically are the failure of any of a number of major banks or corporations, or a real estate bust, beginning with the housing market. Internationally, defaults by Third World countries, a scramble out of Eurodollars, or loan defaults by Communist-bloc countries could trigger a panic.

Finally, we must review the much maligned Kondratieff Wave. Kondratieff was a Russian economist who, in 1925, published his work on Western Civilization economic cycles. He studied the free world's economies and found that they fluctuated in economic cycles that peak, on average, every 54 years. His research into industrial production, wages, wholesale prices, and interest rates in France, Great Britain, the U.S. and Germany confirmed that the economies of the free world are basically self-correcting. From Kondratieff's perspective, we are at the equivalent of the end of the *"Roaring 20s."* The Kondratieff Wave peaked in 1974. We are completing the plateau period prior to a secondary depression. The secondary depression normally begins with a panic.

It's interesting to observe, that if the U.S. Wholesale Price Index is adjusted as if the U.S. remained on the gold standard all along, and gold prices had been allowed to rise consistently, that wholesale prices, in gold standard dollars, have turned down. Furthermore, the breakdown in the Kondratieff Wave in 1974, evidenced by the severe 1974-75 recession, was, in a technical sense, the first leg of a new bear market. What we saw in the debt-laden recovery from March, 1975 to January, 1980 was, technically speaking, a retest of the high. It was a bull trap. The public was *"suckered in"* by increasing its debt 50%. The masses bought at the top, as usual.

It is important that we realize exactly what debt is. Debt is borrowing from the future, while collateralizing the past. We consume now, at a cost, instead of in the future. This leaves a vacuum in the future. Everything falls in a vacuum. Prices fall and economic activity decreases. When it happens rapidly, it is called a bust, a panic.

Debt has a cost. Its cost is interest, for interest is nothing more than the cost of money. During times of high inflation, the cost of money increases along with all other prices. When a consumer borrows, the amount of interest he pays decreases his ability to consume in the future. The higher the interest, the greater the future decreased consumption. The amount of dollars paid in interest cannot subsequently be used to purchase goods and services. Also, dollars which pay interest cannot be saved by the general public and therefore cannot be borrowed by businessmen from the general public to build factories without creating new money (inflation). So consumption debt results in less capital formation, too, fewer jobs, and ultimately less consumption.

The expanding increase in debt leads inevitably to a shorter and shorter term perspective, particularly when debt is incurred by the consumer. Massive consumer borrowing for the consumption of goods and services bids up the price of those goods. Other consumers, seeing this buying war, hop on the bandwagon and spend, too, before prices rise even higher. This mob psychology borrowing eventually leads to a buying panic. During this time of panic, at the end of the 50-year cycle, consumers exhaust their savings and borrowing capacity.

The consumer has to pay back his loans. This means, for an extended period in the future, he will be unable to buy. Futhermore, because he was in a bidding war with other consumers, he paid more for his home, automobile, or whatever, than he should have. Thus, his total consumption, based upon real value, was substantially reduced. In short, he overpaid, and must pay for his expensive consumption well into the future or he will go bankrupt.

Debt is a form of slavery. Consumers who are in debt, like businessmen, are on a treadmill. And the speed of the treadmill increases with the age of the cycle. The velocity of money increases as the cycle ages. Debtors have no freedom to stop, reflect, take a rest, or do their own thing. They have bills to pay. They must work to pay off their debts. Anxiety results. Eventually, anger and exhaustion set in. But, just before the exhaustion occurs, debtors accelerate their borrowing/buying. It is just like a blow-off in the market. Everyone is scrambling to get theirs as they bid up prices in the marketplace.

There is an action/reaction pattern here. The exhausting fast pace of life during the latter stages of the 50-year business (debt) cycle is compensated for by inactivity (unemployment) (bankruptcy) (debt repayment) during a depression.

Debt is the primary source of inflation. While the federal government is the ultimate source of inflation in that it issues currency, runs deficits, establishes and maintains the banking system, and controls the money supply, the government sector, in a debt sense, is overwhelmed by the private sector. The federal government is, without a doubt, a horrible example of how one should manage one's financial affairs. The interest on our national debt exceeds $85,000 a minute. But, the main source of inflation is debt created through the fractional reserve banking system, where each dollar is multiplied 2.58-7 times. And the private sector is the greatest user of debt. It starts with the Federal Reserve purchasing government bonds and the subsequent increase of deposits at commercial banks. These banks then lend money (credit) to customers. Inflation is an increase in the supply of money. Far and away, the main increase in the supply of money occurs through the assumption of debt by consumers and businesses. The private sector accounts for 70% of all borrowing.

Expanding debt increases the velocity or turnover of money, and thus inflation. It's like an auction which picks up speed. Because consumers borrow from the future, production has to be increased now. But there is a lag time before production can catch up with accelerated demand. So, prices are bid up in the economy, just like they are in any market. People buy now because they expect higher prices tomorrow. With debt they are not limited to the extent of their personal production. The tendency is to over-extend. To meet the near term inflation demand, excess productive capacity, in a long-term sense, comes on stream. This excess production of capital goods prolongs the depression and deepens it.

Money should be a commodity. The fractional reserve banking system is a pyramid game causing the boom/bust cycle. The leverage in the banking system today is only slightly less than in the commodity markets. There is an exact analogy between positions established in the commodity futures market on margin and loans made by businesses and consumers in our fractional reserve banking system. Excesses occur both on the upside and the downside.

Debt should come from savings. Debt should never be used for consumption of goods and services. Consumption debt is short-term gratification, not based upon personal production. Debt should only be used for productive purposes, such as the creation of factories and capital goods—assets which create jobs and result in a long-term increase in the wealth of the society. Debt should always be short-term (less than 7 years).

What serves as money should be freely determined by the marketplace. The creation of money should not be a government monopoly. Money is, after all, a form of energy. This ties money to the laws of thermodynamics. Energy can be neither created nor destroyed. It can only be transferred. Government must be disenfranchised from its ability to create money out of thin air, and, in the process, con the public into believing it has created wealth. Government can only confiscate and redistribute wealth. This is theft. Theft is immoral.

From 1949 to 1953, a 17% increase in bank debt produced $1.00 in GNP. From March, 1978 through March, 1979, it took $1.88 in bank debt to produce $1.00 in GNP. Looked at somewhat differently, prior to World War II, the U.S. economy carried $1.00 of debt for every $1.00 of GNP. Lately it's been $5.00 of debt for $1.00 of GNP. (Is a bigger war in store? Wars destroy wealth.)

Debt to an economy is like hard drugs to an addict. It takes more and more debt to hype up the economy each time around. The economy, like the addict, dies (hyperinflation) or goes cold-turkey (deflation and depression) eventually.

On February 15, 1979, THE WALL STREET JOURNAL released the following table. (See next page.)

It is obvious that the greatest increase in debt has occurred in the consumer and business sectors of the economy. Thus, consumer and business borrowing is confirmed as the primary source of inflation.

In 1946 overall debt was 156% of GNP. In 1979, overall debt was 146% of GNP. Amazing? The federal government debt in 1946 was 103.5% of GNP. In 1979 federal government debt was only 27.1% of GNP. Consumer debt in 1946 was 16% of GNP, but in 1979 it was 53.9% of GNP. Private business debt in 1946 was 29.4% of GNP, but

Table 1

	1950 (billions)	1978 (billions)	% of Increase
Debt Outstanding for Consumers and Households:	$ 67	$1,031	1,400%
Debt Outstanding for Non-Financial Corporations:	$ 71	$ 834	1,070%
Debt Outstanding for State and Local Governments:	$ 22	$ 390	1,220%
Debt Outstanding for the Federal Government	$217	$ 611	180%

in 1979 it was 52% of GNP. State and local government debt in 1946 was 7% of GNP, but in 1979 it was 12.3% of GNP. These debt/GNP levels are remarkably close to those of the late 1920s. Stated flatly, we have done ourselves in. Private sector, consumer and business borrowing is overwhelmingly the main cause of inflation, the primary cause of the boom and the coming bust.

While the federal budget is approximately $600 billion and the federal debt is about $840 billion, the domestic debt is in excess of $4 trillion. Stated simply, the private sector swamps the federal sector. Even if one includes the off-budget items and admits we truly have a $200 billion federal deficit, it is already discounted (absorbed) by the economy.

There is no way, during a panic, that the federal government can bail out all of the private sector. If the economy deteriorates gradually, the federal government has a chance. But, panics (surprises) happen rapidly, just like bear markets. The federal government is slow and inefficient. Just look how much trouble it has had in trying to put together the Chrysler bailout package. And, it has had all the time in the world to do so. Besides, the federal government has been reacting to economic events over the past two years. Governments that react are not in control. Those in control, plan, not react.

At MIT, Professor J. W. Forrester found that changes in monetary and fiscal policy have little effect in counteracting the panics in the economy that occur approximately every 50 years.

Politically, the government will try to save the economy. This will lead to increased federal controls and huge federal deficits due to the fact that 77% of the federal budget is now uncontrollable (locked in by law). It's true also that the U.S. government is fifth in the world in relying on the income taxes of businesses and consumers to finance its operation. This tax intake will assuredly be on the decline during an economic panic and following contraction. And, a 1% increase in unemployment results in a $25 billion federal deficit minimum.

We will have the worst of all worlds. A deflationary depression in the private sector, and increasing federal deficits that will make past deficits look like a Sunday School picnic. But the point is this: The contraction in the private sector will be much greater than the deficits created by the federal sector, at least initially.

Picture a barrel with a small hole in the top and an enormous hole in the bottom. The barrel represents the economy. Federal deficits will be poured through the small hole in the top while water floods out the bottom (the private sector). Private sector collapse will not be offset by federal spending. The result is decreasing water in the barrel, declining economic activity and bankruptcies. The government will have to be careful with its bail-out programs in any case. The government could be checkmated by higher OPEC oil prices, an oil embargo, a run on the banks, a flight to gold, or a Eurodollar collapse. In such a time, expect defaults on loans by Lesser Developed Countries. Forty percent of the debt owed the U.S. banks is owed by these Third World countries. Also, Soviet military adventurism is a threat during this time. The only way the federal government can disguise a panic is by seizing total control of the economy. Such might just happen.

In this analyst's opinion, preparations for a panic are underway. Consumer confidence is the lowest it has been since World War II. If one thing is certain, it is that a debt economy must have confidence in order to prevent a panic and collapse. Businessmen, before they will borrow, must anticipate the expansion of their market and, therefore, an increase in profit. So, confidence is necessary for business, too. This is certainly not the case presently. Some cities and states are technically bankrupt. Many pension plans are unfunded. Confidence is collapsing in all segments of the economy.

The handwriting is on the wall. Get out of debt. Stay liquid. Stay in short-term T-bills. Put some gold and silver coins and cash in a safe deposit box. Stay alert for the opportunity to short the commodity market in a big way.

*   *   *

"Business made the wrong bet on inflation back in the 1970s. Corporate management thought it could just keep borrowing and paying back in cheaper dollars forever. And, because of the huge reliance on excessive debt today, the economy will stay flat on its face until at least the middle of next year."

David M. Jones, G. Aubrey Lanston & Co., Reprinted from the September 20, 1982, issue of BUSINESS WEEK by special permission, © 1982 by McGraw-Hill, Inc., NY, NY 10020. All rights reserved.

INFLATION: BRINKMANSHIP

8/7/81

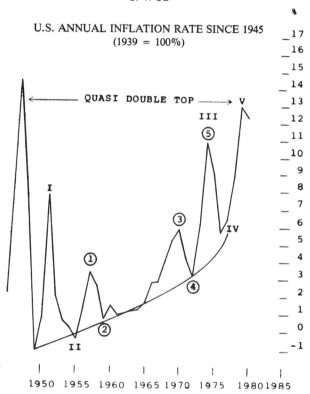

U.S. ANNUAL INFLATION RATE SINCE 1945
(1939 = 100%)

QUASI DOUBLE TOP

For purposes of technical analysis, we have charted the U.S. annual inflation rate since 1945. This date is in the ball park for the beginning of this 50-year economic cycle (Kondratieff Wave), which got off the ground around 1950. As we are in the terminal stages of this 30-year economic upthrust (since 1950), it seemed plausible that the graphed U.S. annual rate of inflation, analyzed technically, would shed some light on what we should expect economically. What the graphed annual rate of U.S. inflation in fact reveals is that we are/were technically at a significant crossroad, a turning point, *"on the brink."*

129

Since the inception of the U.S. inflationary trend in 1949, we have had three drives up. A market normally makes three drives to a top. These three drives are depicted as Roman Numerals I, III, and V. This is solid Elliott Wave theory—five waves, three drives to a top.

Notice, for now, that inflation peaked out on an annual basis in 1979. That the annual inflation rate so far in 1981 is lower is indisputable, lending further credence to the 1979 peak which occurred, interestingly enough, 50 years from the stock market crash of 1929. The year 1979 was when the bond market crashed as well. Copper usage, a primary economic indicator, peaked in 1979 at 3.2 million metric tons, too. And, 1979 is the year when historians could declare that the Second Great U.S. Depression began.

The inflation graph conforms nicely to a four-point uptrend line, which accelerates into a French curve. The accelerating rise, as evidenced by the French curve, shows a market moving to maturity, approaching a final peak or a blow-off.

A quasi double top was also made in 1979, the 1979 peak being just slightly lower than the 1947 inflationary high. Technically, one would expect a consolidation or sell-off as the market approaches the old high, completing the Elliott Wave five wave sequence. Such was the case with the U.S. annual inflation rate. The sell-off began in 1980 and accelerated in 1981.

What's next? Have we seen THE top in inflation? Or, is the U.S. inflation rate selling off technically as would be expected at an old high, prior to exceeding that high, rocketing to even greater rates of inflation? Why guess? The U.S. inflation rate graph, like any market, will tell its own story in due time. For now, as investors, we must hedge against disinflation or deflation, a severe economic recession or worse. This certainly would seem what this chart, and the inflation rates of 1981 so far, indicate is prudent action. The recent precipitous declines in commodities, bonds and stocks support this conclusion, also. But since inflation is a political malady which poisons the economic system, we must stay attuned to political events and legislation as well as our key economic and market indicators to determine if the U.S. annual inflation rate will again turn up and move to new highs, rather than go through the naturally corrective disinflationary then deflationary processes.

We want to stay liquid in cash or cash equivalents—T-Bills primarily, a few greenbacks, some survival gold and silver coins, a few collectors' items, a fully-owned home and business, and no debt! Necessities for business and personal use should also be stockpiled, particularly items difficult to obtain.

The clear risk now is for those who have hedged against more inflation. By being liquid, if disinflation and/or deflation accelerates, as now appears to be the case, we win big. Cash is king. If the inflationary threat again appears, we can move quickly from our liquidity to inflation hedges and gold-real money. By being liquid now, we maintain our options, our flexibility and our maneuverability. Those who are now fully hedged against inflation, loaded up with *"things"* and heavy in debt are suffering during this disinflationary period, and could well be bankrupted if this disinflation accelerates into a deflation. Even if these investors are correct long-term and inflation does totally destroy the U.S. dollar, those investors totally hedged against inflation now will have to suffer through the pain and losses of this disinflationary interlude. They have no options. They are locked in, married to inflation.

The one investment I like best during times such as these is commodity futures. No bias, you understand, just good logic. Commodity positions are liquid which meets our first investment criteria. And, commodity trading can be equally as profitable during inflationary or disinflationary times. We can go long or short, hedge against inflation or disinflation, with total liquidity at all times. It can be the best of all worlds for the disciplined trader who exercises good money management.

One further observation before we leave the graph of the U.S. annual inflation rate and this study.

THE POST-WORLD WAR II U.S. ECONOMY

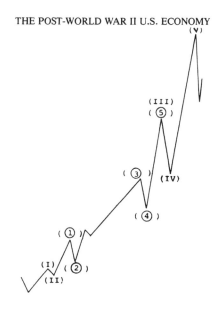

1950 1955 1960 1965 1970 1975 1980 1985

Notice this graph of the post-World War II U.S. economy. The lows on the graph are the exact dates of the recessionary lows. The highs are the exact dates of the recovery highs. The severity of the reactions (the difference between the highs and lows) and the degree of the recoveries (the difference between the lows and highs) were subjectively based upon the psychology of the consuming public during that particular time, and the public's willingness to incur new debt. What is incredible is how accurately this subjective presentation of U.S. economic activity since World War II parallels the U.S. annual inflation rate during the same period. To further illustrate this point, I have taken the key highs and lows marked on the U.S. annual inflation rate graph and placed them on the comparable high and low turning points for the U.S. economy, post-World War II. Notice that the graphs of both the U.S. annual inflation rate and the post-World War II U.S. economy are, for all practical purposes, identical. Do these graphs suggest a relationship, a correlation between inflation, consumer psychology and the assumption of the debt? You bet!

Technically, inflation topped out in 1979. Our conservative investing posture since that time, coupled with speculation in commodities, has proven to be a prudent course of action. We have been on the right side of the economy for two years, and we intend to stay there as long as the trend remains clearly disinflationary. Always thinking like a chess player, or a good market trader, or a psychologist, we will remain alert to the telltale signs suggesting a return of inflation. Those signs include a bottom in gold primarily, and copper and silver secondarily; a weakening U.S. dollar marked by appreciating Swiss Franc prices; declining bond prices (bonds can't win); appreciating spot and futures commodity prices, not due to weather or war scare factors; and political acts of desperation by the President, Congress and/or the Federal Reserve that clearly spell a return of inflation. Until the inflationary signals return, if they do return, we will stand pat with our disinflationary posture.

AN ECONOMIC SQUARING OF PRICE AND TIME

4/17/81

Commodity trading activity, as graphed on a bar chart, is delineated in terms of price and time. The vertical scale is marked off in increments of price; the horizontal scale is surveyed in units of time. The results of the thinking of thousands of men are represented each day (time) on a bar chart of corn, for example, by price—the high, the low, and the closing price.

In a much broader sense, we find *"price and time"* to hold true in history. Price is translated into events; time is represented by both cycles and linear time. So, just as price in time is representative of human action on a bar chart, so also are events in time the footprints of history.

While it can be readily seen that the abstract concept of price becomes concrete when two men strike a contract in a free market, and while historical events are easily acknowledged, by contrast, understanding the time element is not quite so simple.

There are two apparently conflicting theories of time. They are: (1) Time is linear; and (2) Time is cyclical. With reference to history, time moves in a straight line with purpose and meaning, with causes producing effects. So, history is linear. But history also repeats itself, and seems to move in a great eternal circle. So, history can be charted in terms of cyclical time, too. With the cyclical view of time, since man returns to the same starting point over and over again, history has no ultimate meaning.

Which is true, a linear view of history that establishes purpose and meaning, or a cyclical view of history where history and therefore life itself is, in the final analysis, meaningless?

History, in fact, establishes that both concepts of time are true, but neither is complete without the other. It takes unity, or a marriage of both concepts of time to establish the correct, comprehensive view of historical reality.

History does have meaning, for we learn much which is potentially useful from both the achievements and failures of civilizations which

133

have gone before us. Civilizations do rise and fall (cycles) in keeping with cause and effect (linear time). Societies do reap what they sow in a linear sense. But the fact that civilizations rise and fall creates, secondarily, a historical cycle. Since human nature is a constant and has not changed throughout time, civilizations, which are men acting collectively throughout history, tend to repeat themselves in much the same way, over and over again. So, there are cycles of civilizations. It does not have to be so. Men collectively, as a social corporate body, can break out of the fatalistic cyclical rise and fall of civilizations and extend a culture's linear life. Men, so far, have just not chosen to do so. In this sense, men are still slaves. They have not yet decided to liberate themselves from this slavery of the natural order.

On a personal level, each of us is born, lives and dies in linear time. During our linear life span, we go through many yearly cycles, monthly cycles and daily cycles, which are operative until we are called to the grave which is the end of our linear time.

In nature, the sun rises and the sun sets, day after day, month after month, year after year, in a seemingly never-ending cycle. Yet, due to entropy, the second law of thermodynamics, we know our sun at some point in linear time will burn out, and the cycle of the rising and setting of the sun will cease. Linear time thus calls the sun's cycle to its conclusion.

Here's one more example of the working of linear and cyclical time. As a woman moves from birth into her teenage years her fertility cycle begins. As she moves into late middle age her fertility cycle ends. Linear time (old age) calls an end to the fertility cycle.

Linear time and cyclical time are integrated. They work together. Cyclical time, however, is subordinate to linear time. When linear time is up, the cycle ceases. So, linear time calls the ultimate shots.

Just as the key in understanding commodity price action is the understanding of price in time, so, too, is the understanding of history dependent upon discerning events which occur in time. The key to understanding the future of price action in the market rests with the squaring of price and time. The key to understanding the future of history is dependent upon the squaring of events with time. Historical events are confirmed by cycles in linear time. The event occurs when the cycle falls due. And, while the squaring of price and time in markets, or in history, seems to emphasize cycles, which is appropriate since we are focusing on a particular point in a market or in history, it also integrates with superior, linear time. For, each cyclic high or low in a market, or in history, as the case may be, combines and meshes in cause and effect harmonious linear fashion with preceding cyclic turning points in orchestrating what the next cyclic turning point will be.

As different notes make up chords on a piano, so do different cyclic turning points combine in progressive, and therefore linear harmonious fashion, to predict future turning points in markets or history.

We speak of having come full circle, 360 degrees, a complete cycle. The very concept of having come full circle is the idea of a completed event, the working out of linear cause and effect.

A circle is 360 degrees. When a circle is divided by one-half, a critical divisor, the quotient is 180 degrees. This is the natural division between night and day, too.

When 360 degrees—a circle—is divided by 4, the quotient is 90 degrees. Ninety degrees is one-quarter of a circle, a right angle geometrically, and one-quarter of a year. It's interesting to observe that in terms of the four 90-degree divisions of a circle, that there are four seasons in a year—spring, summer, fall, and winter. There are also four elements—earth, air, fire and water. Man's existence is ultimately divided in four categories—theology, ecology, politics and economics. We even speak of four divisions of the day—morning, afternoon, evening and night. With the movement from 90 degrees, one-quarter of a circle and a right angle geometrically, to one quarter of a year, we have accomplished the mathematical and geometric fusion of the abstract with the concrete.

It's interesting to speculate if perhaps prior to the time of the universal flood, which legends in at least sixty-four societies scattered throughout the world confirm, the earth completed its year in 360 days, the number of degrees in a circle. Who knows? Perhaps our globe even sat upright on its axis. (Readers of Immanuel Velikovsky take note.) Is the concept of a perfect 360-day year, being the concrete equivalent of the abstract 360 degrees in a circle, so farfetched? Let's reflect for a minute. The ancient world operated under a lunar calendar consisting of twelve 30-day lunar months, 360 days, equaling 360 degrees.

The oldest civilization that we know the most about is the Egyptian civilization. Quoting from the ENCYCLOPAEDIA BRITANNICA, *"The Egyptians appeared to have begun with a lunar calendar."* If there is one thing we know about the Egyptians, it is that they were mathematically exact, for example, in their construction of the pyramids. The Great Pyramid of Gizeh is a precise mathematical structure, based upon the mathematical ratio of Phi and Pi. (Phi is an unending ratio as is Pi. The natural summation series, which is found in such things as a leaf's distribution, commonly called the Fibonacci series, produces the ratio of Phi.) The temperature inside the King's Chamber of the Great Pyramid is 68 degrees F., the perfect temperature for health and long life. The Great Pyramid is located on a line perpendicular to True North. The Great Pyramid is situated exactly on meridians which, if extended, exactly divide the land masses of the earth into equal areas.

The point is that the Egyptians knew exactly what they were doing. So, why the lunar calendar? Error, when so precise otherwise? Unlikely. Later, the Egyptians corrected their 360-day calendar.

Another example? Again, quoting from the ENCYCLOPAEDIA BRITANNICA:

> *"The Babylonian calendar imposed by the kings under the first Dynasty of Babylon, on all the cities immediately under their rule, was adopted by the Assyrians at the end of the Second Millennium, B.C., was used by the Jews on their return from exile, and was widely used in the Christian era. This calendar was equated with the Sumerian calendar in use at Nippur at the time of the Third Dynasty of Ur (about 2300-2150 B.C.) . . . These were lunar months, and in general their length was 30 days; . . ."*[15]

Three hundred and sixty degrees divided by two is one hundred and eighty degrees, divided by three is one hundred and twenty degrees, divided by four is ninety degrees, divided by six is sixty degrees, and divided by eight is forty-five degrees. Each of these degrees—180 degrees, 120 degrees, 90 degrees, 60 degrees and 45 degrees—can be translated into days—180 days, 120 days, 90 days, 60 days and 45 days. These key division points mark the turning points in history and markets in terms of days, months or years for cultures that choose to be slaves to the natural order. And, furthermore, each of these cyclical turning points acts as a cause which must be blended with all the preceding cyclical turning points in order to produce the next cyclical turning point—the effect. Thus, each turning point in a market or in history is a function of all that went before it. Cause and effect, as earlier discussed, is a linear concept of time. So, cyclical time and linear time are in harmony with the squaring of price and time in markets, and in the squaring of events with time in history. This is heavenly symmetry. Furthermore, multiples of these key division numbers are also significant in the harmonics of markets or history. Additionally, natural numbers of support or resistance, along a linear numerical continuum, such as 25, 50, 75, 100, 1/3 and 2/3s are significant points of demarcation.

Finally, we need to discuss the number 144. W. D. Gann's Master Time and Price Calculator was the *"Square of 144."* There are 144 solar systems with planets. The first Fibonacci number which is also a square (12×12) is 144. (The Fibonacci ratio permeates the natural order.) In Revelation 14 of the Bible, 144,000 are *"Redeemed."*

It would seem that all of time, whether in terms of markets or history, is orchestrated by an Unseen Hand which calls the tune, as it were, to the turning points of history, particularly if man sees himself as an animal, evolved or otherwise. It was Johannes Kepler, the 17th century German Christian astronomer, whose three great laws formed the basis of modern astronomy, who saw geometry and the Hand of God as being one and the same.

The greatest market analyst of all time, W. D. Gann, wrote,

> *"I figure things by mathematics. There is nothing mysterious about any of my predictions. If I have the data, I can use algebra and geometry and tell exactly by the theory of cycles when a certain thing is going to occur again.*
>
> *"If we wish to avert failure in speculation, we must deal with causes. Everything in existence is based on exact proportion and perfect relationship. There is no chance in nature because mathematic principles of the highest order lie at the foundation of all things."*

Now, let's turn to economic harmonics, the squaring of economic events with time, to see where we find ourselves today in light of past economic history.

The 1973 recession, the worst since the Great Depression of the 1930s, occurred **180 years** from the Depression of 1793. It was a key turning point.

The United States experienced a panic in 1873. That panic was exactly **100 years** prior to the Mini-panic of 1973. The number 100 is a number of completion and a natural number of resistance.

It was **60 years** from the Panic of 1913 to the 1973 recession. Sixty is 1/6 of a circle.

Interestingly enough, 1973 was also the peak of the 54-year Kondratieff Wave cycle. The 1973 economic decline was the initial break following an unpopular war (Vietnam). The 1973-75 recession, in keeping with Kondratieff theory, was followed by a plateau period of from 6 to 10 years. During this time, there was the appearance of affluence and good times. This plateau period is followed by a panic and a crash, which then begins a secondary depression. So, based upon Kondratieff Wave theory, we should expect a panic and a crash, ushering in a secondary depression, to commence by 1984.

Wheat, the staff of life, which runs in a 54-year cycle that has been documented as far back as 1260 A.D., peaked in 1974 during the middle of the 1973-75 recession.

The trough of the 1973-75 recession occurred in March, 1975. The year 1975 is **150 years** removed from the Depression of 1825. The number 150 is a number of natural resistance and, therefore, a significant turning point as a multiple of 50.

It was 50 years from the Crash of 1929 to the Bond Market Crash of 1979. The Bond market crash in late 1979 was the worst market crash since the stock market crash in 1929. The 1979 Bond market crash almost collapsed our financial system.

The trough of the 1949 recession occurred in November. November, 1979 was 30 years from November, 1949, or **360 months.** So, the year of the 50th anniversary of the Great Depression squared with **360 months** from a significant post-World War II recession trough and triggered the late 1979 Bond market crash.

Prior to the Depression of 1825, the Panic of 1819 occurred, **six years** earlier. The 1973-75 recession occurred very quickly, and some economists considered it a panic. In any case, it's interesting to observe that from the middle of the 1973-75 recession, the year 1974, to the year 1980 was also **six years.** We had literally an economic panic downside in first quarter, 1980, which again threatened to repeat in 4th quarter, 1980, when the prime rate soared above 20 percent.

The Panic of 1873 was preceded by the Recession of 1866. Therefore, it was **seven years** from the Recession of 1866 to the Panic of 1873. The year of 1980 was **seven years** from the beginning of the Mini-panic and Recession of 1973.

The Western land boom collapsed in 1836. It should come as no surprise that **144 years** later, in the year 1980, real estate was also hard hit in both the first and fourth quarters of 1980. Skyrocketing interest rates, in both cases better than 20 percent, literally dried up the real estate market. In 1980 and early 1981, the greatest number of bankruptcies being filed were by real estate agents and small contractors.

The Recession of 1920 was **60 years** from the year 1980. Here again, we find harmony. Hutner's Cycles of Optimism and Pessimism turned down in 1980, too.

The year 1980 was **120 months** (10 years) removed from the Recession of 1970. The depression which began in 1930 was **120 months** (10 years) removed from the Recession and Mini-depression of 1920.

The trough of the Recession of 1958 occurred in April. From April, 1958 to October, 1980 was **270 months,** a multiple of 90. So, we were three times 90, three-quarters of a circle removed from the April, 1958 recession in October, 1980, when interest rates started higher, sending the economy into a slump.

The trough of the 1973-75 recession occurred in March, 1975. From March, 1975 to October, 1980 is **67 months,** or two-thirds.

The trough of the 1970 recession occurred in November. From November, 1970 to November, 1980 was 10 years or **120 months.** No wonder we had all the fireworks in October and November, 1980.

It's interesting to observe that the commodity bull market began in 1970-71, 10 years ago. COMMODITIES magazine (Oct., 1980) discussed how the 5.7-year cycle in corn, the 9.1-year cycle in wheat, the 3.2-year cycle in soybeans, the 4.5-year cycle in cotton, the 7.2-year cycle in cattle, and the 6.2-year cycle in gold were projected to top in late 1980 or early 1981. The commodity markets, of course, topped in November, 1980. When commodities subsequently crashed in early December, 1980, that four-day loss was the largest in the 25-year history of the CRB Futures Price Index.

The Panic of 1837 which followed the Western land collapse of 1836 is **144 years** removed from the year 1981.

It is **120 years** from the Panic of 1861 to 1981. One hundred twenty is one third of a circle and a significant turning point.

The year 1983 is **90 years** removed from the Panic of 1893. Ninety years is one-half of 180 and one-quarter of 360. Ninety degrees, 90 years, 90 months, 90 days, one-quarter of a year, is very significant as a turning point. The year 1983 being removed 90 years from the Panic of 1893 suggests we are very close to a financial debacle.

The 5.58-year silver cycle should bottom in late 1982-83, according to CYCLES. Elliott Wave expert, A. J. Frost, predicts a stock market peak for 1983. The rate of change of energy consumption per capita prediction worldwide peaks and then crashes in 1983. Energy consumption, as Norman Alcock has noted in CYCLES, parallels economic activity.

Dr. H. A. Merklein, Director of the International Institute of the University of Dallas, has predicted that the interest on the federal debt will exceed the net capital generating capacity of the economy between mid-1982 and the end of 1983. At that point of time the federal government is bankrupt.

In summary, expect a panic and a crash by 1983, beginning the secondary depression of the Kondratieff Wave. This depression should continue until 1996 or 2004. (These dates are in keeping with the termination of the cold/dry era.) Expect a runaway, inflationary depression long-term, preceded by a severe deflationary interlude. Needless to say, the fallout from the Panic and Crash of 1981-1983 could lead to a Democratic political landslide in 1984, which should be followed by widespread civil unrest, particularly in the cities, in 1985 and 1986, as the economy disintegrates.

The year 1970, the years 1973-75, and the years 1979, 1980, 1981 and 1983 were and are years of major turning points in economic history. The corrections that we should have experienced economically, but did not experience completely in 1970, 1973-75, and

1979-80, due to interference with the economy by the Federal Reserve, the U.S. Treasury, and the Executive Branch, will be vindicated. In other words, we have not experienced the natural adjustments to the extent necessary when they came due cyclically. In any market, as in the silver market debacle during 1980, unnatural input leads to far more severe reactions, the natural response to excessive actions. Expect the panic and crash that begins in 1981-1983, that triggers a worldwide depression lasting 13 to 21 years, to result in the total destruction of the U.S. dollar long-term, since man has not yet chosen to take the spiritual high road which frees him from the slavery of such cycles.

An Economic Squaring of Price and Time

1. The 1973 Recession was **180 years** from the Depression of 1793.
2. It was **100 years** from the Panic of 1873 to the 1973 Recession.
3. It was **60 years** from the Panic of 1913 to the 1973 Recession.
4. It was **150 years** from the Depression of 1825 to the year 1975, the trough of the Recession.
5. It was **50 years** from the Crash of 1929 to the Bond Market Crash of 1979.
6. The trough of the 1949 Recession occurred in November. From November, 1949 to November, 1979, when the Bond Market crashed, was **360 months.**
7. It was **144 years** from the Western land boom collapse in 1836 to the 1980 Recession and real estate fall off.
8. It was **67 years** from the Panic of 1913 to the 1980 Recession.
9. It was **60 years** from the Recession of 1920 to the 1980 Recession.
10. It was **120 months** from the Recession of 1970 to the Recession of 1980. (It was **120 months** from the Recession of 1920 to the Depression of 1930.)
11. The trough of the Recession of 1958 occurred in April. From April, 1958 to October, 1980 was **270 months.** Bonds collapsed.
12. The trough of the 1973-75 Recession occurred in March, 1975. From March, 1975 to October, 1980 was **67 months.** Currencies collapsed.
13. The trough of the 1970 Recession occurred in November. From November, 1970 to November, 1980 was **120 months.** Commodities peaked.
14. It is **144 years** from the Panic of 1837 to 1981.
15. It is **120 years** from the Panic of 1861 to 1981.
16. It is **90 years** from the Panic of 1893 to 1983.

THE OPM DEBT METHOD:
A CATALYST FOR CLASS WARFARE

4/2/82

Natural harmony should exist between labor, management and ownership in a free enterprise-oriented, free market economy. Without the fractional reserve banking system, without debt capitalism, labor would have a financial stake in investments by way of stocks, joint ventures and partnerships. All involved parties would pull together in the work process. It is only with the delegation of authority and responsibility of one's funds, usually by wage earners' deposits in financial institutions, that distance builds between entrepreneurs, management and labor. Thus, debt with accompanying interest, created bank loans, are an instrument of economic class warfare. The situation is aggravated with the Fed's monetizing of Treasury debt and the inflationary fractional reserve banking system.

At the culmination of the upleg of a 50-year cycle, where we are now, we find this stacked debt deck adds insult to injury for the working man. The rich get richer while the poor get poorer. Working men's real wages are at 25-year lows.

The January 14, 1982 WALL STREET JOURNAL had a front-page feature article on *"Ace Developer."* The headlines read, *"Donald Trump Builds a Real-Estate Empire Using Loans, Contacts." "Flashy New York Promoter Sells Prestige, Glamour Along With His Buildings."*[16] Notice from the headlines alone that this real-estate empire was built with loans, OPM (Other People's Money) and contacts. Also notice that the wealth was created by promotion, prestige and glamour according to THE WALL STREET JOURNAL. Not exactly the grass roots, humble production process in the traditional American sense. According to the WSJ, loans, who you know, status, hype and fluff built the wealth of this empire.

THE WALL STREET JOURNAL went on to relate how Donald John Trump's riches are another example of how the rich get richer. The elderly Mr. Trump (76 years of age), Donald Trump's father, is still working behind the scenes. The family empire is estimated to be

141

worth $250 million. Not bad. Actually, it's great that a father and son are working together. Roots!

Should we, or any American for that matter, be envious of an honest success story? Heavens, no! What we must question though is whether or not Mr. Trump, along with other super-rich American entrepreneurs, has worked in line with the principle that *"Self-interest is best served by service to others long-term."* We must also see if the financial/economic system with which Mr. Trump was/is involved was/is one of equal opportunity and fair play. *"Loans," "contacts," "flash," "promotion," "prestige"* and *"glamour"* suggest not.

Now some of us, and I know this was my tendency for a number of years, will start to feel the hairs on the back of our necks stand straight up at this type of criticism of an American entrepreneur who *"made it."* But did he really benefit society while he *"made it?"* Did he *"make it"* in the sense that he assumed risk, put forth productive effort, used his personal funds exclusively or those of his partners or stockholders who shared in the risk **and** the rewards, which is the classic American way? Or did it all happen some other way? Let's look.

THE WALL STREET JOURNAL told us how Trump played his cards in one nice, neat paragraph:

> *"Behind the flash and glitter, Mr. Trump had substantial backing from conservative financial institutions led by Equitable, which financed $25 million of the Grand Hyatt, and Chase Manhattan Bank, which led a group in making all $150 million in loans on Trump Tower. With their help he has added about $80 million, by one informal estimate, to the net worth of Trump Organization, his family's business, with the Grand Hyatt and Trump Tower alone.* ***He did this without putting any of his family's housing assets on the line, because his share of each project was financed by loans against the project itself."*** [17] (Emphasis added.)

This paragraph says it all and makes this writer's point very clearly. Let's examine it. First of all, **Mr. Trump had nothing at stake personally in terms of financial risk in a project that netted him $80 million.** Objectively, should he have received some compensation for putting the project together? Of course. A man should be paid for his labor. To the extent of $80 million? With no financial risk? Not hardly. Now who took the risk? Equitable and Chase Manhattan. And, undoubtedly, they got a healthy interest rate for the **loans** they made. We all know that $175 million isn't peanuts. But did Chase and Equitable really take the risk? Were the individual officers who made the loan decisions at Chase and Equitable accountable, on the line, for that $175 million? Of course not. Then who really did take the risk?

The stockholders of Chase and Equitable? Sort of. But who really provided the $175 million to make the Grand Hyatt and Trump Tower a success? Wasn't it the depositors in those *"banks?"* Shouldn't they have shared in that $80 million windfall that Mr. Trump received? Should not risk be commensurate with reward?

Wouldn't an economic system that outlawed the fractional reserve banking system, that was generally antagonistic to debt and interest, that stressed individual responsibility, lead to more joint ventures, partnerships and stock issues and result rightfully in greater wealth for a greater number of individuals more equitably distributed than what we saw here by way of an $80 million windfall to Mr. Trump? Isn't it time we had a financial system with rules that encouraged a long-term view, and protected the ignorant from the rapacious? How much happier would the residents of New York City have been if that $80 million had been split by contract among all those *"depositors"* in Chase Manhattan and Equitable with, of course, a negotiated fee paid to Mr. Trump? They would have been a lot happier! And Mr. Trump still would have done his job. And he still would have made a bundle. Mr. Trump just took advantage of an economic and financial system (which ours is) that encourages financial irresponsibility on the part of the general public. Our financial institutions encourage the abuse of the common man's productivity.

Now let's go for the throat of this matter. How about the money that you and I deposit in Chase Manhattan, with the U.S. Treasury by way of T-Bills, in Citibank or in the Bank of America? How many multinational banks draw funds from our local correspondent bank? How do you and I feel about $80 billion of our money being loaned to the Soviet Union, $28 billion to Poland and $500 billion to Zaire, Brazil and the other Third World countries? How do you and I feel about us subsidizing the Export-Import Bank, the Federal Financing Bank, the boondoggles the federal government legislates, and all the wealth transfer programs? Would we make those loans ourselves? By no stretch of the imagination would we! But, by the delegation of our financial responsibility, we have become financially irresponsible and have thus contributed to the tremendous extant evils in our social, economic and political order. We have sold out for a little compound interest. Interest (usury) was formerly condemned in our Christian culture.

What do we do? We can do nothing and continue to support a financial system that promotes our own self-destruction long-term. We can limit our investments to sole proprietorships, partnerships, stocks and joint ventures which avoid debt. We can keep our wealth tied up in *"things,"* fully owned, including gold and silver or cash. Remember, however, that Federal Reserve Notes are debt. You haven't been paid when you hold cash. We can avoid financial institutions all together. Such action by all Americans would have prevented Harold Smith and Sammie Marshall from embezzling $21 million from Wells Fargo Bank recently. Your bank? Your money?

RICH MAN/POOR MAN

4/2/82

A big chunk of the Great American Dream is to *"get rich."* The secret of maintaining an important part of the Great American Dream is to *"stay rich."* Part and parcel of the time honored formula of how to *"get rich"* is to *"buy low and sell high."* This is a *"contrary opinion"* approach which requires an investor to stand alone and go against the investing prejudices of the masses—buy what no one else wants when it's out of favor, and sell what everyone else wants when it's in favor.

The long-term success *"fundamental"* involves *"anticipating and meeting a future economic need."* An equally valid perspective, however, which seldom receives much attention, is the fact that throughout history there is only one difference between the rich and the poor: *"The rich own the assets; the poor rent them."* Owning assets is a long-term, upper class, delayed gratification perspective. Renting assets is a short-term, lower class, conspicuous consumption viewpoint. The trick, thus, becomes which assets to own when.

For purposes of this discussion, there are only two assets an investor should hold: tangible assets and monetary assets. Tangible assets are such assets as businesses, income-producing real estate, farms, ranches, gold, silver, commodities, collectibles and the like. Monetary assets include cash, C.D.'s, money market mutual funds, T-Bills and bonds. Again, the key is which assets to own when, and when to rent. The timing of a particular asset ownership is everything.

Generally, we want to own tangible assets (real goods) when the rate of inflation is above the interest rate after tax consideration and the debt economy is expanding. These days are over for now and probably until George Bush or a Democrat becomes president, or until the Fed again monetizes the Treasury debt. Timing the ownership of tangible assets is everything. It's best to move into tangible assets in anticipation of these conditions. (During hyperinflation, the interest rate exceeds the inflation rate.)

Monetary assets (Money Market Mutual Funds, bonds, C.D.'s and T-Bills), generally speaking, should be held when their rate of return

145

after tax considerations is above the rate of inflation and the economy is contracting. Stated somewhat differently, we want to own monetary assets when compound interest is working for us in a real sense.

The general public has little understanding of compound interest. Let's take the IRA accounts which are now billed to the general public as a way to become a millionaire in 30 years. If the advertising was true, than all bond holders would be rich today, which they obviously are not. Nevertheless, $2,000 invested yearly in an IRA account, compounded daily over 30 years at 5 percent interest earns approximately $150,000, at 10 percent about $400,000, but at 15 percent over $1,300,000. Notice the substantial difference in earnings with the same $2,000 with interest compounded daily over the 30-year period when the interest rates of 5 and 15 percent are compared. There is in excess of $1 million difference! The compound interest spread runs all the way from $150,000 to over $1,300,000, so great is the difference between 5 and 15 percent compound interest.

Now let's take this simple example and apply it to our $1 trillion plus federal debt. It becomes obvious why debt and compound interest are eating the U.S. economy alive; why interest on the federal debt is the third largest item in the federal budget; why the federal government is consuming 80 percent and up to possibly 100 percent of the national savings pool; why the overwhelming fundamental crisis in our economic system, which cannot be resolved easily, is the destruction of the foundation of our economic system—the collapse of the long-term bond market.

The only tangible assets we want to own while we hold monetary assets are survival-oriented assets and those income-producing assets whose net rate of return after all costs and tax and social considerations is higher than the net rate of return received from monetary assets. Thus, basically we want to hold only real money making tangible assets at a time when monetary assets are the preferred investment.

We have been dealing with the highest real interest rates in 50 years—about 9 percent (3 percent is the norm). It is a sad commentary on the American public's financial illiteracy that the general public was totally in debt at a time when smart money was liquid and enjoying the highest real rate of return in modern history.

Contrary opinion works in nearly all markets most of the time. Anticipation of a trend change is an important key. Thus, contrary opinion for timing purposes, in this sense, is everything. Contrary opinion applies to debt in the 1980's.

It's important for an investor to realize that in moving from tangible assets to monetary assets and back again, it takes far more lead time to move from tangible assets to liquid, monetary assets, than it takes to move from liquid, monetary assets to tangible assets. Thus, we must be more careful to anticipate and prepare for disinflation or deflation than inflation. It generally takes more time and effort to sell tangible assets in order to get liquid than it does to buy tangible assets with liquidity. A good rule of thumb, in not only investing but in all areas of life, is that it's very easy to get into a deal or a relationship, but it is usually more difficult and time consuming to get out of one.

(There are other more *"traditional"* criteria which are always of timeless importance in evaluating any investment opportunity: Risk vs. reward potential, tax consequences, liquidity, flexibility and other options connected with the investment, the ability to manage or monitor the investment at various chronological times and at different geographic locations, and the effect of the investment on one's personal life-style.)

From all of the foregoing, it should be painfully obvious that it is not easy to invest today. In fact, evaluating and choosing an investment is downright difficult. Planning is not totally impossible; it is just next to impossible. There is no long-term. Because timing is everything, everyone today is a speculator, much like a commodity speculator. And as Wall Street loves to point out, approximately 85 percent of all commodity speculators lose.

Since every investor today is effectively a commodity speculator, nearly every investment's ultimate success is determined by the timing of entry and exit into the investment. If we dig even deeper, we find that every investment is leveraged, just like a commodity futures contract. Even if a tangible asset is fully owned, with no debt, it is still leveraged. How? Because that tangible asset is established and owned on the unstable base of the fractional reserve banking system, which is a leveraged system, just like the commodity futures market. So, the environment in which an asset is owned today is both leveraged and volatile. Thus, investing is a stacked deck in favor of the flexible speculator.

Slowly, but surely, the investing public is realizing that we have a long-term detrimental, basically dishonest financial system. The central bank, the Federal Reserve, is the creator of inflation, when it monetizes the U.S. Treasury's debt. The fractional reserve banking system is the engine of inflation, as loans are created through the system. Thus, the real workings of our banking and financial system, which are understood by only a few, benefit primarily banks, insiders and speculators.

It is possible and even feasible to have an honest, stable, long-term financial system that promotes *"Wealth for All"* with stable or falling prices over time, if there are no wars, tragedies or climatic upsets. All that is required is for commodities to be monetized at the local level (free market money), for the Federal Reserve and the fractional reserve banking system to be outlawed, to restrict and preferably discourage or eliminate consumer loans, to encourage stock issues, joint ventures and partnerships, to make interest no longer tax deductible, and to limit loans and interest to the extent of a specific investment project (less than 7 years), along with the political outlawing of legalized theft—the abolition of the welfare state. Doing away with graduated income taxes, property taxes and estate taxes would help immeasurably also. Then *"Wealth for All,"* the *"trickle down"* economics, would work. *"Wealth for All"* would be cumulative due to free solar energy, inheritance, cumulative technology and the natural harmony that results from the specialization and division of labor in a free economy. Free market commodity money would grease the economic skids.

Our entire financial system today works against us long-term. It promotes and encourages debt, speculation and irresponsibility. This should not be particularly surprising at the end of a 510-year civilization cycle and a 200-year national cycle. The political system and the financial system are both closely interrelated. Both are frozen and irresponsive, set in their tracks, acting against the interest of the common man.

One reason why investors have such difficulty dealing with today's financial environment is that it is antogonistic to their most basic spiritual need—*"the need for security."* In the investing realm, because we cling to security, we resist change, fear the unknown, and hate to admit when we are wrong. Thus, in investing, we tend to freeze and not make a decision; once we have made a decision we tend not to implement it; we tend to stay with what we know best and have an inclination to become rigid. In today's investing environment, where timing is everything, however, rigidity is suicidal. Flexibility is mandatory. Therefore, we now painfully see the psychological bottom line as to why investing today requires us to swim against the tide of our own human instincts, to literally fly in the face of our own human nature. Successful investing today requires flexibility and precise timing. Yet both of these attributes are contrary to our basic security need.

WHY YOU CAN'T GET AND STAY RICH

7/23/82

Another appropriate title for this chapter, borrowed from the Rolling Stones, is, *"I Can't Get No Satisfaction."* And yet another is, *"How Our Institutions Frustrate Us."* Let's state our position right up front: It's now impossible to get really rich in this country except through illegal means, except by doing financial harm to your fellow man, except through luck (short-term), except by complicated offshore and other tax planning, or except by engaging in socially unproductive speculation. Stated differently, the long-held Great American Dream of working hard, saving, investing and prospering long-term is a blatant, vicious, disarming lie! All of our institutions are geared to snare, cripple and discourage the hard-working, thrifty, honest, long-term oriented, creative, and productive members of our society.

First of all, let's recognize that the entire economic environment is rampantly speculative—one big crap shoot—a big commodity futures market if you will. With the economic roller coaster ride dictated by the Fed's decision to monetize the deficit, by the Fed's expansion and contraction of the money supply today, with the effects of these Fed actions leading to a 2.58 to 7 times expansion of that money (credit) through the fractional reserve banking system, every business transaction and every investment is, by the very nature of this fractional reserve system, high-risk, speculative, leveraged and unstable. This instability is compounded by the velocity (turnover) of money, a function of economic psychology. Thus, you have to be lucky and/or marked by exceptional skill, discipline and endurance to succeed today.

Now, let's assume that you head out to pursue the Great American Dream. Let's assume that you're an entrepreneur who starts a business with a product or service that you anticipate will meet future demand. Let's further assume that you are successful in this enterprise, that you correctly anticipated and met the public's demand, and that you capitalized your business from personal savings, the issuance of stock, a general or limited partnership, or a joint venture. In other words, you have not assumed any debt. So far, so good. The Great American Dream presumably is realized. But, wait a minute. The fruits of your labor are quickly confiscated via taxation. Not only is your corporation's income taxed, your dividend income taxed, but your personal salary, if married and filing jointly, for all amounts over $85,600 in 1982, subject to a 50% income tax. With inflation and the real costs of things these days, we can't seriously talk about getting rich at $85,600 a year, taxed at 50%, can we? Comfortable, yes, but not rich, not the fulfillment of the Great American Dream. The total tax burden is 81.6% of your corporate net income flowing through to you. So, following the ropes dictated by the American success ethic, we quickly find that you, our young, budding successful American entrepreneur, who has diligently met the needs of the consuming public, not only is accountable to stockholders, partners, or folks with whom you jointed ventured, but that you are also subject to the brutal and inflexible demands of your partner, Uncle Sam, to the tune of an astounding 81.6% (federal and state taxes). Why be efficient? Why be thrifty? The entire tax system encourages waste, corruption, laziness and unproductive activity. The likelihood is that once this Reagan reprieve is over, the tax system will get even worse. It already has.

Let's say that you, our bright businessman, have found some *"tax shelters"* to defer your income. Just what is a deferral? A deferral is nothing more than putting off paying the tax piper. And, most tax shelter gimmicks backfire. What's your risk? Have your poured your money down a rat hole? Can you be sure in today's unstable economic and political environment that your cash will be there down the road to meet the tax requirement when the deferred tax comes due? Will the investment hold up over time? Can you be certain, in today's volatile tax environment, that the tax law will not change between now and then, rendering this now legal deferral subject to some penalty or disallowance years down the road? After all, everything is relative and subject to change these days. There is no way to be positively sure, particularly in the hazy tax area. The penalty and 20% interest charges up the risk of tax shelters immeasurably. (At 20% interest, compounded, money doubles in 3½ years).

Now, let's turn the tables and assume that you, our brilliant entrepreneur, took the path followed by most entrepreneurs in this day and age. Let's assume you became successful with the all-too-popular OPM method (other people's money). What have you in fact done? In reality, you have used, without permission, money deposited by irresponsible folks in financial institutions. You have supported the inflationary fractional reserve banking system, which has enabled you to leverage your investment, profit from inflation, all at the expense of your irresponsible fellow man. True, folks who deposit their money in financial institutions get what they deserve—ripped off. These *"banks,"* in turn, loan out the deposits, in fact, many, many times the original deposit amount. This is inflationary.

Instead of assuming the responsibility and accountability for the use of their own money and then investing it wisely, most folks, if they're not up to their ears in hock and have money to save, funnel it off to a middleman (a bank, credit union, or savings and loan normally), who then pays them a pittance (a low rate of interest), and then turns around and takes a healthy cut from you, the entrepreneur, who borrows the money.

Did the original depositors have anything to say about how they felt about their money being loaned to you for your business? No. Did the *"bank"* only loan to you in the first place because you had some wealth to collateralize or because the government guaranteed the loan with someone else's wealth? And, to make matters worse, through the system of loans and redeposits, the original dollar of deposit can be multiplied (created out of thin air) 2.58 to 7 times (inflationary), these irresponsible depositors have contributed to their own financial demise. When the original *"bank"* deposit is multiplied 2.58 times to 7 times, what has in fact been done is to gear up the engines of inflation in the fractional reserve banking system, so you, the entrepreneur, can profit on assets which appreciate during inflationary times, while the depositors suffer and lose real wealth because the rate of interest paid them by the financial institution does not keep up with the rate of inflation (not to mention the fact that interest income is taxed). The irresponsible depositors in established financial institutions always lose—always! They lose during inflation because their rate of return (interest) does not keep up with the rate of inflation, and they own no hard assets. (Taxes compound the loss.) They lose during disinflation because seldom do interest rates, even during disinflation, yield real rates of return above the rate of inflation, particularly after tax consequences are considered, even with the new tax law. (Today's high real interest rates are so unique, we haven't seen them for 50 years.) It's a lose-lose situation for depositors in financial institutions. It's a win-win situation short-term for the *"bank,"* which charges a healthy premium (interest) for money borrowed each time the original dollar is again loaned out. Legal counterfeiting by *"banks"* is very profitable. Money market mutual funds gave the thrifty saver some long-deserved relief.

The entrepreneur wins big during inflation as the value of his assets explode. He gets caught on the downside, during the economic contraction, if he's illiquid and in debt.

You, as the entrepreneur who borrowed money, even if you pay taxes and do not defer income, are taking one heck of a risk, particularly when the game changes from boom to bust, from inflationary good times to disinflationary tight money times. (The real estate speculators of the 1970s have learned this painful lesson all too well recently.) Leverage can work for you or against you. When cash flow declines, ceases to come in, and/or when market prices drop, the interest rate clock keeps right on ticking and the debt service remains constant. The difference between the two, the loss, has to be made up by you, the entrepreneur, in the same hard, heavy dollars on the downside, as with the light, fluffy, profitable inflationary dollars on the upside. Turnabout is fair play. Now, if you, the entrepreneur, were bright enough, if you, as a businessman, were a sharp enough speculator, you would sell out at the inflationary peak and buy back at the disinflation low. But, here comes the kicker. Can you pick tops and bottoms? Here's the real reason why few businessmen really become rich and stay that way down through the generations now. Few and far between are the businessmen who understand markets, or who understand the nature of the fractional reserve banking system and the Fed. Few and far between are the businessmen who understand market psychology, the human action side of a market economy. Few in number are the businessmen who understand cyclical economics at all. Fewer indeed are the businessmen who have the make-up and ability to change at a moment's notice. About all businessmen know how to do or have time to do is to work hard and pump out a product or service at a profit in the present environment. They seldom anticipate the future. They prosper for awhile, but get caught short and/or go belly up during the turning points which they neither anticipate nor understand. How could they comprehend it all, without the economic, cyclical or psychological basis to do so? They eventually literally run off a cliff.

In a nutshell, most businessmen succeed because they are lucky for awhile. They ride a trend to the hilt and then miss the turning point. There is a whole unwritten story about the number of men who have succeeded for a time and then failed miserably. In fact, the *"failed miserably"* chapter is a chapter we are seeing written now by thousands of small businessmen, thousands of real estate speculators, thousands of farmers, and even major corporations and banks.

It takes a genius, a flexible, hardy, disciplined, lucky genius to steer his financial craft through all these stormy waters today and survive. But, even a genius has to *"sleep"* occasionally because he is a human being. And when he shuts down, the crosscurrents catch him, too.

This is why you (we) cannot get and stay rich. And we are seeing why next to no one can get rich and stay that way long-term now without violating the Great American Dream recipe.

Of course, a few will get lucky and sell out at the top of an economic cycle, just like at the top of a commodity bull market. But, there is no assurance, and very little probability, that these few will do anything other than lose ground on the subsequent downside of the business cycle and/or miss the next move up. They, too, will get ground under or suffer the slow attrition of their wealth.

But, you may rightfully argue, some do get rich today, don't they? In real estate? Yes, using OPM and leverage, **if** they know when to sell and buy. In commodities? Yes, using margin (money that they don't have) **if** they buy and sell at the right time. In oil and gas? Yes, **if** they sell at the right time, **or** the civilization doesn't self-destruct, **or** if a better energy source is not created. In inventions which lead to new business? Yes, but taxes eat them alive, too, long-term. Service businesses? Yes, until the consumer stops spending. Honestly now, how many inventors, real estate developers, oil and gas men, and/or businessmen have made their fortunes without borrowing money, and thus without financially depriving (unintentionally) their fellow man? How much richer should this *"natural aristocracy"* be if it was not burdened with excessive taxes and regulations? How much richer would we all be if the free market were free and men were responsible long-term? How much greater harmony would exist in our society if the economic rules were changed so that money was a commodity, so that labor, management and ownership had a stake, by contract, in economic ventures, so that economic activity was *"win-win"* as a result of free enterprise contracts.

Some lucky soul may win a raffle occasionally, or hit the jackpot at Las Vegas, or ride the big wave in the commodity futures market. But, these folks are few and far between. An increasing number are making their own road to riches through barter, the underground economy, tax evasion, the black market, crime, go-for-broke leveraged speculation, and questionable, highly-complex offshore corporations and trusts. Of course, for the already established wealthy, there are the long-standing foundations and trusts, the expensive, well-connected attorneys and CPAs, who, for handsome fee, can see that your wealth is *"sheltered."* (Sheltered from what? Maybe sheltered from a real rate of return, after tax planning fees, tax preparation fees, audit defense fees, interest and penalties.) BUT THIS IS NOT THE GREAT AMERICAN DREAM, WHEREBY ONE MAN'S PROSPERITY IS A BY-PRODUCT OF SERVING HIS FELLOW MAN ECONOMICALLY!

Inheritance to our children for what's left? Better now. Thank you

Mr. Reagan. The miracle of compound interest? It's a loser most of the time after inflation and taxes. Just look at what's happened to bonds in recent years. Common stocks? The DJIA went nowhere for 18 years. Only traders (speculators) make it today.

Do you want to know the real reason why this writer settled upon the commodity futures market as a *"reasonable"* place to earn a living in these trying times? Because, simply put, the commodity futures market is the most honest, open, liquid and flexible of the speculative environments in which investments and businesses exist today. It is the lesser of the evils. Wins and losses just take place faster in the commodity futures market than they do in the economy-at-large. The pace is quicker, but the realities are the same. Men have less time to live with their illusions in the futures markets. The world's entire economic system today is an unstable, leveraged, boom/bust, commodity market-type crap shoot. At least, in the commodity futures markets, the cards are pretty much on the table. Sure there are scandals, and the brokerage system is inefficient and costly. But the rules are pretty well known. The multinational grain companies have the inside track, a stacked deck, but traders know it. By contrast, few even recognize the rules, much less understand them, in our fractional reserve banking economy.

The commodity futures market is just a leveraged speculation on top of a leveraged speculation. We enjoy 90 to 95% leverage in a commodity futures position on top the 2.58 to 6-7 times leverage in the fractional reserve banking system. No wonder we see booms and busts in the commodity futures markets. And now we have commodity options on top of it. Wow! What a financial circus! Step right up ladies and gentlemen and place your bets!

In addition to the up-front nature of the commodity speculation, the ability to make money in good times or bad times (up or down markets), the instant liquidity available with the option to open or close a position on a moment's notice, and the flexibility to trade when you want to trade from wherever you want to trade worldwide are real bonuses. For now we have an added boost—favorable tax treatment. Where else in our spastic economy can we realize a 32% maximum tax rate on profits, regardless if we buy or sell, or stay with the position one minute or one year? The 32% maximum tax rate in commodity futures trading today may be the greatest chance we have at getting rich in this spastic economic system. Our politicians had to have made a mistake to give us a 32% maximum tax rate on commodity trading profits. Politicians don't understand the commodity futures market. This writer knows they don't understand the economic and financial system. I've spent time in Washington. And, they probably figured that since only 15% make money trading commodities, what the heck. *"They Shoot Horses, Don't They?"*

We are all becoming progressively poorer! Some of us may prosper for awhile, but the sum and substance of it all is that as a nation, we are going down the tubes financially. At some point (next 20 years?), we'll probably have a revolution, and if history is any guide, the few remaining innovative rich will be eliminated and mass misery will be the result. The fires of revolution are just like the fires that burn down a home or a business. All that's left when the fire is out is rubble. No mythical phoenix ever arises.

We have done, and are doing, nearly everything possible in this country to destroy wealth. Those who shepherd the real new wealth created by the sun by way of crops, timber, fish and animals are being discouraged from being productive. These primary producers cannot turn a profit. The primary producers are thus rightfully discouraged. The harder these folks work, the deeper in debt and the poorer they get. Timber, crops, animals and sea resources are not produced at anywhere near their maximum, long-term productive capacities now in this country.

Human resources, human capabilities and talents are being misused, miseducated and squandered in this country. Through the draining off of incentive via confiscatory economics (taxation), bureaucracy, make work generated by needless regulations which contribute nothing to productivity, the wasted hours spent by millions of citizens in our nation who work for government which creates nothing by the way of new goods and services but bleeds income from the production of productive others, the thousands of hours spent avoiding taxes and wasted in the public schools on subjects which emphasize envy—and conformity—all these discourage human physical and mental efforts to produce. Our greatest loss today is wasted human talent.

It is only productivity that leads to real, increasing, new wealth for all, whether it's from increased human productivity via physical or mental labor, technology, the division of labor, or from real new wealth created as a by-product or the free energy input from the sun.

The hundreds of thousands of CPAs and attorneys, who guide us (?) through the paperwork maze, the unproductive social services which have arisen from our complicated political system, our unfair tax system, our fractured families, which have left distraught lives and a bewildered population—all sharply detract from productivity. There is no wealth without freedom, productivity and the cooperative division of labor. The teaching of envy in public schools and universities destroys the cooperation necessary for the division of labor to exist. The delegation of productivity (money) through our banking system exacerbates the problem. Bureaucracies devour wealth.

Our entrenched rigid institutions, which promote security and maintenance of the status quo, put up barrier after barrier to stop the entrepreneur who has a creative idea, which can lead to a higher and better use of a human or natural resource. Institutions, by their very nature, resist change. We see the epitome of the poor use of natural and human resources in the Soviet Union, the collectivist society, where the *"group,"* and particularly the *"power elite,"* are maintained lavishly at the expense of the individual. And yet we, thanks to our unyielding institutions, are headed down that same road (as Tip O'Neill's limousine). It's insane. We will not collectively face or deal with economic reality. We hide from, minimize, excuse away, ignore or play patsy with the problems that we recognize. Just look at Reagan's tax and budget cuts. What a joke.

Our solutions are irrational. And, perhaps the greatest insanity of all is that our productivity, the wealth we do create, we then export to the most *"insane of the insane"* economically, the Soviet Union and other communist countries. We give the Soviet Union and its satellites our wealth by way of loans, proteins and technology. We have been rushing madly to prop up this communist economic insanity. We have also given away over $200 billion in foreign aid. It's crazy. We're committing economic suicide.

Loans to communist countries, of which the Soviet Union is the prime example, are nothing more than the transfer of wealth. When the working men and women of America make their wealth deposits in established financial institutions, they cop out on assuming responsibility for their own money. When they do so, they suffer a commensurate loss of financial freedom. Freedom always goes with responsibility. The financial institutions, then working with their correspondent banks, make frivolous loans to bankrupt economies, like the Soviet Union and Third World countries, which effectively transfers our wealth abroad. This money, our wealth (thanks to the financial irresponsibility of the American general public), is then used inefficiently in the Soviet and like economies to produce goods and services (utilizing slave labor), which are then exported back to Western civilization to compete with American-made goods and services. This forces Americans out of jobs and into unemployment lines. So, the ultimate, vicious cyclical truth is that American workers' deposits in financial institutions, in a round robin way, finance their own unemployment. We pay a very high price for being individually irresponsible financially in this country. Each $1 billion U.S. multinational banks and corporations invest abroad costs 25,000 U.S. jobs, according to M.I.T.

The desire to earn interest, to make money the *"easy way,"* is the culprit. A lack of sense of responsibility to produce and to be a *"good steward"* of our wealth equals no freedom to consume, and ultimately, poverty. *"Free enterprise results in the unequal distribution of earned wealth. Socialism results in the equal distribution of poverty."*

One thing we can now say for sure. There should be no profit motive in debt. Debt should be charitable. It's no longer a mystery as to why you (we) can't get and stay rich. The whole rotten economic system works for the benefit of a few, to the detriment of you and me, who want to pursue this Great American Dream.

*   *   *

"A country that taxes interest and dividend income at almost punitive rates . . . that taxes capital gains resulting solely from inflation . . . and that taxes corporate profits twice when paid out as dividends is saying to its citizens in unmistakable terms— 'spend, don't save.' "

Edward R. Telling, Chairman and Chief Executive Officer, Sears, Roebuck & Co.

*   *   *

"It's hard to realize now that the United States got along for over a century and a quarter without an income tax. Then one was proposed in 1894 but the Supreme Court held it unconstitutional."

Vermont Royster, THE WALL STREET JOURNAL, July 28, 1982.
(Reprinted by permission of THE WALL STREET JOURNAL, copyright Dow Jones & Company, Inc., 1982. All rights reserved.)

*   *   *

"Who do you think the Republican Party is accountable to? Do you think it's accountable to registered Republicans? Garbage. They don't give a damn what registered Republicans think. They care about what their contributors think."

John T. Dolan, NCPAC National Chairman
July 12, 1982

THOUGHTS ON CONSPIRACIES

12/19/80

It would seem that there is a banking conspiracy aimed at improving the lot of the bankers to the detriment of everyone else. Banking links with government have been noted at least as far back as the Napoleonic wars. In this country, financial interests have recently organized and influenced such infamous organizations as The Trilateral Commission and The Council on Foreign Relations, also known as the Eastern Establishment. Money is power, political power.

It seems to be a bit hasty, however, to conclude that such *"conspiracies"* are the result of clandestine, midnight meetings by men who all think alike, and who plot deviously against the rest of us. So many big egos couldn't possibly get along.

It seems more true to state that there exists conspiracies of self-interest. This reality has been noted in history since at least the time of Adam Smith. He warned that businessmen who connive together for the betterment of their own self-interest do not enhance the welfare of the general public.

Adam Smith (THE WEALTH OF NATIONS) was a keen observer of human nature. This *"Adam"* of economics knew that men were typically greedy and lusted for power. (*"The love of money is the root of all evil."*) If they could enhance their financial worth and increase their power at the expense of the public interest, they would do so. But, their motivation was not conspiracy just for the sake of conspiracy. Rather, their motivation was short-term self-interest, the enlargement and embellishment of their own narrow objectives.

The evolutionary *"robber barons"* of the late 1800s and early 1900s believed that self-interest was best served by selfishness. This new thinking was contrary to the traditional, pre-Darwin, American perspective that self-interest was best served by service.

Banks and bankers control the money of the people. The Federal Reserve is the banker's bank. Money is power. Money is absolute in our economic system. Therefore, it stands to reason that those who control money will have maximum influence over financial, economic and political events, and sadly, military misadventures, too. Bankers

158

are following a very logical plan of action, which simply furthers their own self-interest. It was the international bankers who benefited from the giveaway of the Panama Canal. Panama, with the ownership of the canal, can pay its debts to the international bankers. And, Panama is the world's newest international banking center.

Multinational bankers prefer dictatorships to democracies. Under socialistic dictatorships, multinational banks only have to deal with one leader or a small bureaucracy. By contrast, democracies tend to be extensively bureacratic, as well as unstable. Democracies' leadership and financial policies are constantly changing, inhibiting the planning and schemes of multinational bankers. Democratic leaders are accountable to the people. Dictators can be bribed and bought.

It is difficult to believe that many bankers, or groups of bankers, go to bed every night rejoicing in all the evil and pain they have caused their fellow man during the day. Of course, the Marquis de Sade will find a few followers, here and there. But, by and large, men, and this includes even hard-core criminals, believe they are basically good and just in their actions. Any civilized, rational ego that sees itself as evil for very long self-destructs.

Men do a tremendous job of justifying their actions in terms of truth, justice, right, God, liberty, country, freedom, fraternity, brotherhood, whatever. This is why strong principles and firm standards of right and wrong are important for a society (Biblical law). Unyielding, fair, ethical laws give men a *"fix,"* a standard, other than their own. Relative standards by contrast, are altered, manipulated and justified to suit the whims of the party involved. Relative standards justify action taken before or after the fact.

Excessive influence leads to legislated monopolies. Such is the case with banking in this country, and also internationally (BIS, IMF). We do **not** have a free market in money and banking. This prevents competition and precludes checks and balances against corruption and monetary abuse. Rather, we have our monopoly central bank, called The Federal Reserve. Money is power. Power corrupts, and absolute power corrupts absolutely. We should at least suspect, with human nature being what it is, that there is some corruption in The Federal Reserve. How often do we hear any negative press on the banking industry? Who audits The Federal Reserve? Who discusses abolishing the fractional reserve banking system? We certainly don't see such discussions on the TV nightly news, do we?

The banking industry is the most powerful, most influential, and most well-financed special interest group in this country. But, bankers are evil only to the extent that the pursuit of their own self-interest is contrary to law, fair play, and the best interest of the common man.

Unfortunately, such pursuit is widely manifest.

Throughout history, freedom has been very rare. Those in power have regularly been contemptuous of the masses. As one elitist Eastern liberal social planner put it, *"The masses are no better than maggots in a flour sack."* With this view of man, it is no wonder that the likes of Brookings and the Aspen Institute for Humanistic Studies, financed by international bankers, plan, manipulate, direct and control history. They do it, they believe, for our own good.

It takes an informed and enlightened citizenry to fight this natural tendency toward a concentration of power in the hands of a few. It takes a willingness, by individuals, not to accept bribes, which is exactly what government transfer payments are. Men have to be willing to stand on principle and believe in fair play, rather than sell out cheap to Social Security, welfare, government contracts and the like. Such is not the trend in this country, where over 81 million people are dependent upon government for their income. We are progressively becoming economic slaves. Remember, slaves don't own property.

Freedom is like a garden. It will prosper and flourish only if the appointed caretakers give it tender loving care,—water it, weed it, and protect it from abuse. Left to itself, freedom, like a neglected garden, will be subject to the encroachment of parasitic weeds until, through the passing of time, it no longer exists.

*   *   *

"It is the Western bankers who are keeping the overdrawn Polish economy afloat with about $19 billion in Western loans. Contrary to normal East-West logic, the Western bankers have a vested interest in supporting Poland's Communist government and in resisting the more extreme economic demands of the strikers."

Murray Marder, Washington Post correspondent, in GOLD STANDARD NEWS,
1127-1131 West 41st St., Kansas City, Missouri 64111

SLAVE STATE ECONOMICS

9/3/82

We have really bungled things badly over the years to become the economic and political slaves we are today. We have done the equivalent of drive through three road blocks, each a mile apart, in order to plunge over the cliff into the pit of slavery.

On the material level, the difference between a slave and a free man is that a slave owns nothing. On the abstract level, there is effectively only one word that separates free men from slaves—*responsibility!* Responsible men are independent, free. Irresponsible men are dependent and thus slaves. The lack of responsibility by free men leads to slavery. Responsibility is, therefore, basic long-term to the ownership of property since slaves own nothing. Thus, personal responsibility, freedom and ownership of property are all related.

It's no different in the animal kingdom. Animals that run *"wild"* are free and independent, and responsibly look after their own economic welfare. Domesticated animals, by contrast, are dependent upon people for their economic welfare (food, water, health care, shelter) and thus are slaves. They are irresponsible and *"own"* nothing. Is this *"slavery"* of dependent animals any different than the slavery of people who depend upon government doles and subsidies? No!

In terms of our political freedom, the local family used to take responsibility for all the spiritual and material needs of its members. If the local family failed in any area, the local church filled the gap. Where the local church slipped up, this vacuum was filled at the local community level (towns, cities and counties). Thus, irresponsibility had to be manifest on three levels (the three road blocks to slavery)—the local family, the local church, and the local community—before slavery could be enacted by the bureaucratic planners at the federal level.

Big government always fills the vacuum of irresponsibility. Personal responsibility, decentralization and property rights all run together. Personal irresponsibility, centralization and slavery all run together. Take your pick. It's one or the other. It always has been. It is no different today, and it holds true in all institutions.

Economically, each of us should be falling all over ourselves with potential free time, doing work which is productive and self-satisfying, making responsible maximum use of our individual talents, and cooperatively exchanging goods and services desired by our fellow man. Each of us are potential geniuses in our God-given talented areas, which, if developed, leads to wealth. When free men develop their talents through work and produce needed goods and services, they cooperate with other men naturally in the exchange of these goods and services. Thus, the very efficient specialization and division of labor is a naturally-flowing economic function among free men. Freedom and prosperity come with the dependence of the specialization and division of labor in the free market, where men fulfill their self-interest by service to each other long-term.

Each responsible generation should be passing a greater inheritance on to the next generation. Thus, wealth should be cumulative in families, with each generation having a higher economic starting point than the one which preceded it.

Technology in a civilization is at least cumulative. Through savings and research, men can and do responsibly develop better ways of utilizing human and natural resources. This further adds to economic wealth.

Finally, because the free new solar energy which graces us every day is converted into economically usable matter (commodities), which can be stored over time, this real new solar produced wealth can also be added to the economic jackpot. So, we have had to work hard at not becoming filthy rich, given all these wealth-producing factors.

We are still living in economic infancy. Natural gas plants have been manufactured which convert natural gas into protein that can feed the entire world. A strain of barley has been developed that will flourish in 100% seawater, along with a wheat strain which grows abundantly in 50% seawater. Science has discovered that there are carbohydrates and complex proteins available in the air we breathe. Some people have been able to convert solar energy into usable energy, living on sunlight, water and air. There are millions of acres of land on this earth begging to be reclaimed and put again to productive use. Most of the world's deserts are the result of the short-term use and abuse of that land by decadent civilizations. Soviet technology has advanced to the point that it can profitably alter the weather for the benefit of all mankind. We already *"control"* the climate in a limited way in that we exercise dominion over the seasons through *"air conditioning"* our homes year-round. If we had our value structure straight, all these basic and technological economic variables, which naturally move toward making us all filthy rich, would do exactly that—move us into the age of *"Wealth for All."* But, no, rather than take the beneficial long-term view where everyone wins, rather than let the free market determine what serves as money (moral commodity money), rather than having real new wealth monetized at the local level, we instead let the most worthless of all commodities (paper) and credit which is created out of thin air, serve as money. Then, we borrow from the future, while collateralizing the past, to consume in the present (short-term), all the while our loans and borrowing compete against other borrowers, which *"drives up the price of eggs"* to unreasonable levels, leading to booms and subsequent painful busts. (A tip of the hat here to our leveraged fractional reserve banking system for making inflation and booms and busts possible. A second tip of the hat, of course, to the Federal Reserve, the *"central"* bank in this country which controls the money supply, as the creator of inflation when it monetizes the federal deficit.)

In slave-like obedience, we deposit our hard-earned productivity, our money, in financial institutions as *"savings,"* which not only lose value after taxes and inflation are considered, but are used to:

1. Spur inflation through pyramiding loans in the fractional reserve banking system,

2. Finance projects conceived or ill-conceived by aggressive OPM entrepreneurs who get rich while we get poor, thus promoting economic class warfare,

3. Loan to Third World countries and communist powers who either (a) build competing factories that eventually result in the production of goods which lead to our unemployment, (b) waste our money, resulting in the effective squandering and loss of our hard-earned productivity, (c) produce military hardware to destroy us. Next, we allow ourselves to be taxed on better than 50% of our income (all taxes considered), an amount far greater than any economic slave in history has been taxed, with the exception of what occurs in a pure slave state, such as the Soviet Union.

We obediently go to work and do the task we have been programmed to perform as nice little humanoids, and then we go home and watch television to reinforce this indoctrination first instilled in the public schools and universities.

As economic slaves, we enjoy the illusion of a high economic lifestyle, due to debt. Debt, however, simply enables our slave masters to steal our productivity throughout our lifetimes. As slaves, we enjoy the good life only because over all these centuries it has been next to impossible to destroy all the abundance of wealth flowing from the above-discussed positive factors in the free market. But, wars come along every now and then which destroy all this wealth so that the sick rapacious process can begin all over again. And, we keep trying like the dickens to kill the golden goose—ourselves. We love to self-destruct.

Establishment economists keep telling us that man has an unlimited desire for goods and services. Hogwash! This is an evil, twisted slice of Marxist *"dialectic materialism,"* which effectively states that man's condition is determined by his economic environment, that man is a slave to endless economic needs and his environment, rather than man rising above his condition, changing it and exercising dominion over it. Only a man who sees himself as an undisciplined, evolved humanistic animal has an unlimited desire for goods and services. A man who sees himself as a created *"spiritual being with an animal nature"* can exercise self-discipline and effectively say, *"Enough is enough. I have enough goods and services to meet my consumer needs. I require no more. All else I require to consume is for maintenance functions only, or for the further development of my talents."*

The old adage, *"Every man has his price,"* is based on the assumption that a man will always act, when push comes to shove, like an evolved humanistic, evolutionary animal. That is to say, when the chips are down, men will seek the gratification of their creature (animal) comforts first and foremost, satisfying their animalistic instincts, thus sacrificing moral principle. Greed is the greatest stumbling block for most men. This is why greed makes *"The love of money is the root of all evil"* true. When, *"Every man has his price,"* then effectively every man is a whore at some price level, and there is no moral standard which cannot be breached, and so everything can be compromised. Thus, morals do not exist. Everything is relative. Conflict is inevitable. So, effectively, the statement that *"Every man has his price"* claims that every man, at some price, will sell out and become a slave.

Political slavery is closely tied to economic slavery because government is an economic parasite that strives to control the productivity of men. Free men do not sacrifice abstract political principle any more than they sell out for economic reasons. By contrast, there is nothing for which a slave is willing to die. This is why a slave is a slave. Free men take a stand and say, effectively, at some point, *"No one may transgress these personal or property rights except over my dead body."* Stated differently, free men, who see themselves as spiritual beings who rule over and discipline their animal natures, decide that a principle is more important than life itself. Animalistic economic survival is subordinate to doing the right thing.

Until men decide what they are willing to die for, they do not know for what reasons they live. Nor do they maximize their economic development. In fact, throughout history, it has been the conviction to stand, fight and die for principle, the ultimate human sacrifice, which has both preserved and allowed human freedom and the economic free market to exist and flourish. Free men do not compromise on political or economic principle. This is why they are free. Slaves compromise on both counts. Free men draw their strength from above and from within. Slaves draw their psuedo-strength from without, from material things. This is satanic Marxism. We have become a nation and a world of compromisers. We have, and are increasingly becoming, both a nation and a world of slaves.

Jesus Christ set the standard for free men. He neither compromised with Satan when tempted (his first temptation was economic), nor with the Jewish religious leaders, nor with the representative of the Roman Empire. He stood fast on principle, both political and economic. Because he did so, he not only set the standard for us, but in fact enabled us to be both free and prosperous men, politically and economically in time.

* * *

"If you do not fight for what is right when you can easily win without out bloodshed, if you do not fight when the victory will be easy and not too costly, the moment may come when you will have to fight with all the odds against you and with only a precarious chance of survival . . . You may even have to fight when there is no hope of victory, for it is better to perish than to live as slaves."

Winston Churchill

* * *

"The destiny of mankind is not decided by material computation. When great causes are on the move in the world . . . we learn we are spirits, not animals, and that something is going on in space and time, which, whether we like it or not, spells duty."

Winston Churchill

* * *

"The renewal of civilization has nothing to do with movements which bear the character of experiences of the crowd; these are never anything but reactions to extended happenings. But civilization can only revive when there shall come into being in a number of in-

dividuals a new tone of mind independent of the one prevalent among the crowd and in opposition to it, a tone of mind which will gradually win influence over the collective one, and in the end determine its character. It is only an ethical movement which can rescue us from the slough of barbarism, and the ethical comes into existence only in individuals."

Albert Schweitzer

*   *   *

"But underlying Thomas' needling of the finance industry is a deeper, cynical view of men for whom the making of money is a 'raison d'etre.' In the author's view, devotees of dollars for their own sake are a distasteful breed indeed.

"Thomas laments that breeding and the code of honor that once went with it have all but disappeared, to be replaced by new moral imperatives: expediency and self-gratification. For proof, he looks no further than today's money churners—the banks and institutions of Wall Street, . . . They seduce their customers into greed purely to satiate their own money lust. And the winners in the high-stakes game are the gunslingers whose personal ethics are as impoverished as their pockets are full."

"A Balanced Budget: A Balanced Budget By Law?"

Public Law 95-435, which the 95th Congress approved October 10, 1978, reads, *"Sec. 7 Beginning with the fiscal year 1981, the total budget outlays of the Federal Government shall not exceed its receipts."*

Should this law be enforced? Who will enforce it? No one. Law today is power, pure and simple, the rule of men.

*   *   *

"Since 1972, work with the Biodynamic/French Intensive Method has reaped enormous returns: the vegetable yield potential is in the range of 2 to 16+ times U.S. commercial mechanized levels (with an average of four times) and wheat harvests have been as high as five times the national average."

Ecology Action

"At Tenneco I worked on developing protein from a derivative of natural gas. And it did satisfy human metabolism. We found we could indeed make a very nutritional protein concentrate from natural gas, and if we had ten plants scattered around the United States, each covering one square mile, we could produce all of the protein, vitamins and minerals that all of the American people needed for year-round consumption . . . I have the patents in my own name because the Tenneco Corporation stopped development of this product. They said that if they had a mountain of protein they wouldn't know what to do with it. They fired our whole team after we discovered this process."

Paul Stitt, Biochemist, author of
FIGHTING THE FOOD GIANTS
in ACRES, U.S.A., December 27, 1981

THE SOLAR ECONOMY

1/18/80

We live in a Grade A, certified, nearly 100% solar economy right now! We always have. We always will. And it's high time the rest of the pygmies along the Potomac began to realize exactly what that means. And what it means is this:

Everything that everyone touches or uses or does every day and every night is—either directly or indirectly—almost 100% solar powered. ("Almost" because there are a few other forces in the universe which do influence life on earth . . . such as the mass of the moon which can—for instance—affect the globe's tides, starlight that also strikes our planet's surface, random meteorites and space dust which add a certain amount of mass to the world each year, etc.)

For all practical purposes, however, everything that we need and want and use every day and night of our lives either directly or indirectly comes from the sun . . . is purified by the sun . . . is renewed by the sun . . . is powered by the sun . . . is changed from a form that we cannot use into a form that we can use by solar energy.

The sun's rays drive the whole hydrological cycle which distills water from the earth's oceans, transports that vapor to the planet's land masses, and condenses it into cool rains. Rains which slowly transform rock into soil, refresh the earth's vegetation and animals, and carry nutrients down into the oceans for the use of aquatic life before—once again—endlessly repeating the same vital solar-powered cycle.

That's the biggie. And while it's going on, myriad forms of plant life—supported by solar-created soil—are busily collecting ol' Sol's rays and turning them into biomass (roots, stems, branches, leaves, blossoms, fruit, seeds, etc.). Which—in turn—feeds animals, birds, and humans . . . houses us, clothes us, warms us when we burn it . . . sometimes turns into petroleum, natural gas, and coal for our later use . . . serves us in countless other ways . . . or simply falls over and decomposes into soil which eventually supports new vegetation that just as faithfully feeds us, houses us, clothes us, etc., the next time around.

168

And all the while, that same solar-powered plant life is shading us in the summer and then automatically dropping its leaves during the winter so that more of the sun's rays will reach us just when we need them most. And that vegetation is constantly using solar radiation to purify our air and our water for us. And to regulate our micro-climate while—on a planetary scale—another portion of the sun's rays which strike the earth's atmosphere is powering the winds which distribute the pollen that fertilize our crops . . . and turn the blades of our windmills . . . and push our sailing vessels across the oceans . . . and distribute those cooling rains . . . and do so much more to make human life and commerce possible.

In short: We live in a solar economy now, we always have, and we always will. And our intricately interrelated, solar-powered web of life operates—and can only operate—on a decentralized, planet-wide, all-inclusive basis. The cooling of the shaded side of the globe exactly balances the warming of the planet's sunlight face . . . what goes up over the oceans must eventually come down on the land . . . the pack rat which scampers along the spine of the Rocky Mountains is indeed distantly related to the sea slug burrowing into the bottom of the Pacific.

Furthermore, you can't tear a hole in that solar-driven web of life anywhere on the earth's surface . . . without making the web tremble—albeit ever so slightly—everywhere on the face of the globe. Little rips, of course, send very small shock waves across the mesh of life. But large rents—the overgrazing of the Sahel in Africa, the bulldozing away of the Amazon Basin, or the pulverizing of our western states' shale into oil—can visibly alter our planet's weather patterns, change rich valleys into barren deserts, and pit brother against brother 10,000 miles away.

It is obvious, then, that the way of life which is best for our society is that way which most nearly parallels the natural lines of force . . . that way which does the least damage to our delicate solar-powered web of life . . . that way which is most evenly spread out and balanced and decentralized. Decentralization. That's the key.

Reprinted with permission from "Economic Outlook,"
THE MOTHER EARTH NEWS, Sept./Oct. 1979,
105 Stoney Mountain Road, Hendersonville, NC 28739.

BREAD IS BASIC

11/7/80

When we talk about economics these days, the words and phrases which quickly fill the air are: *"supply side economics," "marginal utility," "Chicago vs. Keynesian economics," "monetary and fiscal policy," "inflation," "petrodollar recycling,"* and so forth. All these buzz words are evidence of the frames of reference from which they spring, that of urban intellectuals. They are products of a culturally sophisticated age, marked by mathematical complexity and computer technology. Collectively, economists focus on money as an absolute in the financial/economic system. Money is king, and calls all the shots. Money is the measure of wealth and worth, both net and personal. We are dealing here with a mind set that saturates our society.

In a few moments of fleeting fantasy, let's assume that we are the remnant of a boatload of people. We are shipwrecked and marooned upon an island in the Pacific. All we have are the clothes on our backs and the resources of the island, in terms of economic goods. With no hope of rescue, we start to build an economy. We begin with the basis of economic production—land and labor. These two must work in harmony for there to be economic progress and production. (Notice that there has to be production before there can be consumption. Our economic order today often gets the cart before the horse.)

Assuming that our island is located in a moderate climate, receives ample rainfall and sunshine, is blessed with lush vegetation, trees, fertile valleys, streams, and an abundance of animals, we have the foundation necessary for producing economic wealth. Certainly, we should be thankful that we weren't marooned on a desert island. The resources available on an arid island wasteland make the production of economic wealth far more difficult, if not impossible.

Next, let us assume that the men and women who were shipwrecked with us are of strong, hard-working stock. So, our labor resource is the best possible, too. If we had been marooned with a group of elderly people, or young children, or sick or lazy individuals, we would have quickly learned that our labor force was marginally productive. So, it becomes readily apparent that high quality land and labor are the raw materials of maximum economic productivity, and that both somewhat depend upon the *"luck of the draw."* Climate, natural flora and fauna, water, and minerals are real environmental assets. Good physical condition, moderate age, and a positive mental attitude toward work are also the *"luck of the draw"* in the case of our shipwrecked passengers. (This is also true when a new government comes to power in a nation.)

With favorable land and labor, we begin to produce capital—houses, fishing gear, canoes, bows and arrows, cooking and eating utensils, etc. Notice that land and labor, are the raw materials for the production of capital, and subsequently, goods and services. What goods will be produced? The goods most desired. Only if a good or service is desired, will it have value. It is questionable, particularly initially on the island, if gold would be viewed as being very valuable. Fish, fruits, a horse, a milk cow, shelter, boats and bows and arrows would probably be in the greatest demand initially. These items have value. Only after our new culture is established would we then view gold as having value. Then, and only then, would gold serve, as it has always served, as a medium of exchange, which holds its value as a store of wealth and is easily divisible, recognized and non-destructible. Gold only becomes valuable after the basic biological needs of our group are met.

We were lucky enough to establish a gold mine on our island after the first three years of civilization. Some members of our work force mined the yellow metal and produced gold coins. The gold coins had value, because they represented actual productivity—toil and sweat. Our rice farmer was willing to trade "x" number of bushels of rice for "x" number of gold coins, because he recognized he was receiving value for value. Both rice and gold are the result of productivity. All productivity on our island, all goods and services, stemmed from the earth. They were made possible by labor. *This is also true today in our society. We just fail to recognize it!*

All goods and services, as well as real money, gold and silver, are the result of work, the expenditure of energy. Recall the first and second laws of thermodynamics. Energy is neither created nor destroyed. It is only transferred, and something is always lost in the transfer. Economics operates in harmony with these laws. This is just plain, good old country economics. It is a far cry from city-centered, fictional, debt-created wealth.

On our island (in the rural country, too) goods, services and money are *produced* into being. The Federal Reserve, on the other hand, simply creates money out of thin air when it monetizes the debt or bails out banks and corporations. The Fed lends money into circulation.

This is what inflation is all about, the creation of something (money) (debt) out of nothing.

Why did we go to all the trouble of creating this fantasy? Primarily, to reprogram our thinking. We no longer think in terms of who and what creates true economic prosperity. The land is the ultimate source of all wealth. The labor of men produces the wealth which is latent in the land. From this observation, we should see that when the land is unfruitful, such as during times of drought, the net result for the economy-at-large will be decreasing economic prosperity, less wealth. This is why drought and depressions go hand-in-hand. The land is less productive, so less wealth is produced, and hard times hit.

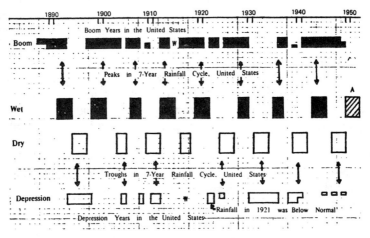

The 7-Year Rainfall Cycle in the United States
in Relation to Boom and Depression Years

Source: Foundation for the Study of Cycles,
124 South Highland Ave., Pittsburgh, PA 15206

Tractors have to be produced. Gold has to be produced. Wheat has to be produced. Thus, equipment, money and food are all produced by the sweat of men's brows. Wheat and tractors cannot be created out of nothing. Neither should money. When money is earned into circulation rather than created out of thin air and borrowed into circulation, not only does inflation not exist, but, with the concomitant elimination of the fractional reserve banking system, the boom/bust cycle, is eliminated, too. Remember that a cycle is, by its very nature, unstable. Men desire stability, for with it comes a sense of security, well-being, and a long-term view. Eliminating the interest earned by the banks which own the Federal Reserve on money which is created out of thin air, plus outlawing the fractional reserve banking system, would go a long way toward providing us with a sound, stable, and long-term secure economy. True, our economy would not grow as fast, but growth would come in real terms, not in terms of illusionary, debt-created wealth that is liquidated in the bust which follows the inflationary boom.

With all this in mind, let's look at a study entitled, *"The Implications of an International Gold Based Economic System to Raw Materials Prices,"* prepared by Peter L. Brandt and Daniel Markey at the Chicago Board of Trade (9/7/79). They looked at the relationship between gold and other raw materials (commodities). (By the way, what we have been discussing above in terms of real economic exchange is nothing more or less than barter. Barter today can be quite efficient when computers are utilized.)

Brandt and Markey stated, *"While all raw material prices will continue to be traded in currency terms, the currency expression of that raw material's value will be in relationship to gold and silver over the long-term."* Brandt and Markey are relating to economic reality (barter) in a society that thinks in terms of computerized banking illusion.

Based upon $350 gold, it was these gentlemen's conclusion that the price of corn should be $4.65 a bushel, wheat $7.00, soybean $11.65, oats $2.48, cotton $1.03 per pound, hogs $.65, cattle $1.13, bellies $.81, broilers $.67, cocoa $1.94, sugar $.16, and copper $1.52, production shortfalls aside.

Let's assume, just for the sake of argument, that Brandt and Markey's analysis is roughly accurate. What conclusions can we draw with relative confidence? Basic commodities, collectively, have not moved up substantially, at all. In fact, these basic commodities are, for the most part, still selling for less than they should have when gold was at $350 an ounce!

What's wrong?. . . .There is a political/fear/anxiety factor built into the price of gold, which distorts its relationship to other commodities. Gold is real money, and the stampede to gold and the distortion of the ratios is, in fact, evidence of an invisible depression. During a depression, people seek money, real money, which is, historically, gold. Commodities are cheap in a depression, and we have been through an inflationary depression in terms of gold vs. commodities in the late 1970s.

This warped gold/commodity relationship also suggests that eventually the price of commodities may have, long-term, a lot higher to go, particularly if the price of gold maintains its present lofty levels or soars higher.

In terms of real money, gold, the price of raw materials have deflated drastically. If they stay low in terms of gold, or if the price of gold declines and these raw material prices hold steady or decline further, the implications should be obvious for the economy-at-large. We will have a tremendous shake-out. Commodities ultimately are real wealth.

If commodity prices rise sharply, and realign with gold, the cost of basics for the American consumer will send the Misery Index through the roof. Commodities are the real anchor, the reality to which all economic activity ultimately returns. Bread is basic.

*   *   *

"Man—despite his artistic pretensions, his sophistication, and his many accomplishments—owes his existence to a six-inch layer of topsoil and the fact that it rains."

Anonymous

COMMODITIES AND CHAOS IN THE 1980s

11/2/79

Until two years ago, commodity analysts and traders were relegated to commodity workshop presentations at major investment seminars. This was not without justification. After all, anyone who works in a *pit* or in a *ring*, instead of on a stock trading *floor*, has to be second class. The commodity trading *pit* reminds us of snakes, just as the commodity trading *ring* reminds us of the circus.

Commodity traders are called *speculators*, instead of *investors*. Some commodity traders are *scalpers*, reminding us of the not so pleasant Indian confrontations of the previous two centuries. And what about the *hedgers* in the commodity market? Don't politicians *hedge* their statements, and gamblers *hedge* their bets? Obviously, the language of the commodity industry is verbage from the *"other side of the tracks."*

But, the lack of respect for the commodity industry goes much deeper than spurious linguistics. The alienation is basically cultural.

As a civilization matures into old age, becomes sterile, frozen, and resists change, the *cities* of that civilization *dominate* the culture. The towering edifices, the skyscrapers, which delineate the pulse of the city, are the ultimate in separation from the land and its produce. The glass, concrete, steel, plastic and asphalt of the cities are different from Nature and Nature's commodities. The cities want to be above the natural world. The farmer, the rancher, the man who works with his hands and sweats, is held in low esteem.

In the investment sphere, commodities have been, and are, the target of this misplaced arrogance. The world cities (in a mature civilization) which rule over the culture act as a vacuum cleaner, draw to themselves all the resources, commodities, if you will, and attempt to bankrupt the rural country.

It is the city, after all, with its artificial environment and its intellectual power, that gives rise to money as an absolute. Money becomes an end unto itself, distinct from goods and services. The city, the apex of the civilization, reaches the point of total domination when money becomes fully abstract. This is the harbinger of the age of inflation

175

and the ultimate destruction of the currency and the city, as well as the civilization. Money, at this point of total abstraction, has totally alienated itself from the soil, and the man of the soil. This strain between the unnatural and the natural, between the artificial and the real, can only be stretched so far before reality brings the city to its knees. This collapse occurs when the country says, *"No more! Enough!"* and cuts the resource umbilical cord to the city. Inflation begets the barter system which ultimately leaves the city dwellers with nothing to trade.

With this historical perspective on the rise and fall of all city-states, Western Civilization *included*, we can start to see why commodities are again becoming popular. True, the *"devil may care"* nature of the American public, the urge to eat, drink, and be merry, the rampant, reckless speculation—all contribute to the surging interest in the highly leveraged, fast-moving, commodity markets. But, subconsciously, and in truth, the rediscovery of commodities is the beginning of a return to reality, to the seeds of our civilization, to our roots.

Many of us recognize this immediately in the flight from paper money to gold. The decay of confidence in paper money, and the subsequent reestablishment of gold as money, is a return to natural reality. The U.S. gold medallions, the South African Kruggerand, the People's Republic of China's one-half ounce gold coin, Australia's plan to mint its first gold coin in over 50 years, Canada's new *"Maple Leaf"* gold bullion coin, the Arab gold purchases, the gold hoarding by European central banks—all represent a flight from the illusion of paper money and its get rich quick debt-created wealth. The day of *conservative* reality, which is *liberal* in the classical sense of the word, is again dawning. Commodities are basic to this truth. They are tangible. They are the first fruits of the good earth! Man is being brought back to the question of ultimacy. He is again facing the issue that the creation of paper money is the act of a god, the act of a government playing *creator*. But government is, in fact, a *parasite* which draws its power to spend from *taxing* people and *inflating* the currency. What a tremendous paradox! A *civilization* is on the verge of *collapse* when its *government* is fully developed. How could it be otherwise? The ultimate in conflict exists when government, the parasite, plays the role of God! The movement toward gold and commodities is a clear turn from governmental monetary fiction toward truth and reality. Truth and reality are, as always, inseparable.

Inescapably, chaos will result, most probably in the 1980s, as the entrenched Washington establishment and their tyrannical paper money *vie* with the truth of gold and commodities. The battle is between a world in the grip of a false idea, the crippling *myth* of state *sovereignty,* and, by contrast, the world of truth and individual freedom based in gold and commodities. The theological undercurrents, which run to the source of truth, echo the words of an American statesman, *"Men must be governed by God or they will be ruled by tyrants."* Tyranny is the foe that men who relish freedom face today, a tyranny which we have allowed, through negligence, to mushroom. The working out of this struggle will result in volatility in the commodity markets unlike that which we have witnessed to date. This volatility will present a tremendous, once in a lifetime opportunity for profits for the quick. One must be quick, or one will be dead in the financial sense of the word.

The contemporary social, political and economic events are the *"squaring of price and time."* Events are confirming cycles! For example, the mid-year review of the economy by the Joint Economic Committee stated that unless there is a radical shift which stimulates capital formation and increases productivity *"the American economy faces a bleak future."* Our standard of living will sharply decline.

George Gallup, Jr., wrote that the United States is headed into *"a period of severe dislocations in society,"* and that the 1980s *"may not be a very pleasant decade in which to live."* This was Mr. Gallup's conclusion in his 105-page report entitled, *"Religion in America— 1979-1980."* Even the ever optimistic guru of the establishment business community, Herman Khan, Director of the Hudson Institute, has admitted that the 1980s could well be the *"sobering 80s."*

These fundamental forecasts square or, in other words, confirm the time projections by the Foundation for the Study of Cycles, which call for a lower stock market through the end of the decade. These fundamental forecasts confirm the timing of Elliott Wave, which projects the end of the Western Civilization super-cycle in the mid-late 1980s. They concur with the timing of the Kondratieff Wave, which calls for a secondary depression in this country beginning in the 1980s.

Unstable weather in the upcoming decade will add to the volatility of commodities. This instability will provide an opportunity for the financially supple. The weather during the past 50 years has been the best it has been for food production in the past 5,000. The decade of the 1980s is predicted to have the most variable and severe weather in the history of this country. The freezing of the Great Lakes, snow in Florida, vicious tornados, and grapefruit-size hail mark just the beginning of this time of climatic trouble.

Over the last decade there has been greater than a 780% increase in the number of earthquakes over that of the decade of the 1930s—a 780% leap in 40-50 years. The Mayan civilization of Central America, which was obsessed with the precise measurement of time astronomically, predicted that beginning in 1987 we would enter the *"hell period"* of our civilization. It is forecast to be a time when earthquakes will literally rip the earth apart. Volcanoes will also be active.

We also have a sunspot peak. Following these peaks, the earth normally becomes colder and drier. Some climatologists are predicting a mini ice age during the 1980s, much like the earth experienced between 1655 and 1720.

Volcanos have suddenly come to life in the Eastern Pacific, approximately 900 miles Southwest of San Diego. As we are at the peak of the 99-year, 6-month volcano cycle, we should expect an increase in volcanic activity. Violent eruptions, like the one in the Virgin Islands, are a forerunner of what is to come.

Volcanic eruptions pump vast quantities of dust containing sulphur dioxide crystals high into the atmosphere. These crystals reflect solar radiation back into space. The result is a cooler planet and less favorable growing conditions.

As if all of this was not enough, the arch enemy of man, the insects, are on the warpath again. Insects presently consume 42% of the world's food supply. Two hundred twenty-three agricultural pests have become resistant to pesticides. In the past few years, we have had to deal with the menace of swarms of grasshoppers in the Western rangelands, with tobacco budworms in California, rootworms in the Midwest, and seed corn beetles in the nation's corn belt. These tormentors from the natural order will aggravate commodity price volatility as we enter the age of *"protein gold."* These forecast climatic and natural disasters are confirmed by cycles. So, again, we have the *"squaring* of *price* and *time"* as Professor Raymond H. Wheeler's Drought and Civil War Clock marks the intersection of the 510-year cycle with the 170-year cycle in 1980.

The emerging, worldwide, cold, dry, chaotic condition has historically been accompanied by global revolution. Wheeler stated, back in the late 40s and the early 50s, that 1980 would be THE turning point for Western Civilization. This is just what Solzhenitsyn said, too. The Iranian and Nicaraguan revolutions, as well as the insurrections in Africa, are heralding the entry of this revolutionary age.

It is indeed alarming that our vital commodities—oil, chromium, copper, antimony, cobalt, magnesium and the like—are provided from areas which are ravaged by revolution. It is indeed sobering that the survival of this vulnerable commodity lifeline has prevented our own revolution. We have no cause for comfort. When a civilization has matured to the point that its lifestyle is dependent upon imported commodities, which it can no longer afford, it is on the brink of collapse.

Today, better than 83% of the people in our country believe the U.S. government and its laws are irrelevant. The *silent* revolution is already underway. Witness the barter system and the tax revolt. All it will take is severe economic distress to trigger, and then transform, this silence into violence. Those who cry for unlicensed, irresponsible freedom, those who claim the world is moving toward greater democracy miss the truth of history. We are moving toward anarchy, not greater democracy. The cycle is from the rule by one (a monarchy or dictatorship), to the rule by a few (a republic or aristocracy), to the rule by many (a democracy), to anarchy (lawlessness), then back again to the rule by one. Those who say we are moving toward greater democracy are working from the same erroneous social evolutionary base as those who sold us the hideous, evil, and inaccurate concept of the sovereignty of government with its tyranny of paper money. In this *Alice in Wonderland* social/political environment, commodities will gyrate violently as they reestablish their kingship. The *"aware"* will have the opportunity to profit.

Back in 1978, I first alerted the world to the threat of an upcoming world war in my book, CYCLES OF WAR: THE NEXT SIX YEARS. I was considered an alarmist. But now, we see a stampede of books warning of the danger of World War III. Books such as THE BEAR AT THE BACK DOOR, WORLD WAR III, THE ELEVENTH HOUR, THE THIRD WORLD WAR, and THE WARMONGERS are just a few examples. In CYCLES OF WAR, I also predicted a tax revolt, worsening inflation, more extreme weather, a swing toward the political right, trouble in Nicaragua and South Africa, and increasing Soviet military aggression in the face of a continuing unstable Carter administration. These predictions were right on! They have come to pass. . . . Remember the adage, *"Those who live close to the truth are seldom surprised by the future."*

From 1980 through 1984, this nation will be on *"red alert"* for its survival. Those who point to the decadence and inefficiency of the Soviet Union ignore the fact that our technology has made Soviet military might their strong suit. Those who point correctly to corruption and waste in the military/industry complex, and those who note that bankers are the ultimate beneficiaries of war, do us a service. But they lead us into harm's way and miss a lesson of history when they call for disarmament. Political power still ultimately comes from the barrel of a gun. Because human nature is a constant, war is a constant! Needless to say, during the turmoil of war, commodity prices explode.

The 1980s' whirlwind of monetary and economic distress, climatic instability, social and political upheavals, and war will result in the greatest volatility ever seen in the history of the commodity markets. The lurches in such an environment will make the concept of trading long-term obsolete, virtually impossible. Stability will be the exception rather than the rule. It is the swing trader who will survive and become wealthy.

I have grown up in the commodity business during the past nine years. Since 1973, the level of sophistication of commodity traders who have entered the markets has declined sharply as the reckless, the emotional, and the greedy have entered the markets in droves. In my studies, I have never found recklessness, greed, and unbridled emotion to be an asset in accomplishing anything worthwhile, long-term. In the upcoming years, the greedy, the reckless and the emotional will suffer their financial demise. The humble, the responsive, and the disciplined will survive and prosper. Old wealth will die. New wealth will emerge. Money management and trading technique may be far more important than the ability to correctly forecast the future.

We have before us a tremendous challenge. We, who have been in the philosophical minority in this country for the past 100 years, will again have an opportunity to triumph. Courage and truth are on our side. The trend is turning in our favor.

We have been deluded into believing that what we do doesn't matter, that we are a Social Security number of little importance. It's untrue. It's a myth. We are among the most intelligent, powerful, and resourceful people in the world. All we have to do is flex our muscles to break the mythical chain of insignificance.

In times of radical change, like the 1980s, not only will commodities become king, but new leaders will emerge, at first locally and then nationally. It is always thus during times of rapid change. The bureaucracy is slow, inefficient, and dedicated to the maintenance of the status quo. It will fail under the pressure. In its vacuum, we must stand responsibly. We must keep faith with our ancestors. We must live up to our heritage. If we do not, then we will live and die in a slave state.

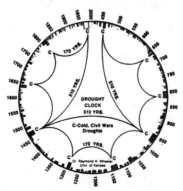

Source: Mainsprings of Civilization—1945

THE BEST COLLECTIBLE AND INVESTMENT

New

After years of research, this writer may have settled upon the best collectible/investment for this uncertain age. It's not perfect. No investment ever is. But all things considered, it could be the best. What comes closest to the *"Holy Grail?"* Quality, well-bred livestock/exotic animals. Such is the ultimate in compounding-portable *"protein gold."* We are moving back to ultimate reality. Cows were the first monetary unit. Later, impressions of cows were stamped on coins.

A major problem with most investments today is that they are either paper, which has no end utility value in and of itself, or that most investments are *represented* by paper, which is subject to theft, fire, default, confiscation or other loss. The hard assets that paper represents today are, in most cases, illiquid and immovable (farmland, factories, machinery, etc.). They also can and do depreciate.

The problem with collectibles, aside from the usual storage, theft, insurance, illiquidity, fire and vandalism problems, not to mention the fact that many are stored in the heart of the enemy camp (the fractional reserve bank), is that collectibles are dead-end investments. Once you buy a collectible, such as a diamond, postage stamp, U.S. gold double eagle, a painting, a bronze, a comic book or a baseball card—once this collectible is purchased—the investor is then forced to live with the *"hope"* of increased inflation/demand, which is necessary if the collectible's value is to appreciate. Collectibles produce no real new wealth.

Quality, well-bred livestock/exotic animals are not only an investment and a collectible, they are also a source of real new wealth! Each year the sun shines; the grass grows; the female animal eats the grass and throws off an offspring. Bingo! Your collectible/investment has just doubled. And, if you work it right, with a little land and a little labor, and not all that much trouble, your investment/collectible will increase your real new wealth year in and year out and turn into a source of lucrative business income. Side benefits may include food, barter, transportation, clothing and fertilizer, as well as liquidity,

181

mobility, and family fun. The tax benefits also accruing to such farm/ranch operations, when carried on for legitimate business purposes, as opposed to a hobby, are far-reaching and quite excellent.

A sad commentary on our society, as *"Wealth For All"* discussed, is that it's next to impossible today to make a profit in *"regular"* agriculture. Commercial livestock (cattle and hogs) and commercial farming (corn, wheat and soybeans) not only have been unable to turn a buck regularly recently, but farmers and ranchers are facing a flood of red ink, which is worse. As an illustration of how deflated basic agriculture prices have become relative to real money (gold), an ounce of gold would have to sell for $131 an ounce to be at *"parity"* with $2.60 corn.

To the best of our research, from all we can determine, the only area where it has been/is possible to make real money in the agricultural arena today consistently is in the area of quality, well-bred livestock/exotic animals.

In our spastic economy, with its boom/bust whipsaws, the only people who have easily prospered are the quick, accurate, flexible speculators. The whipsaw recessions and recoveries and inflations/disinflations, in our fractional reserve banking system's environment, make business decisions and investments the equivalent of those of a commodity futures trader. Few win big, but those who do get rich. The rich get richer and the poor get poorer. The rich then, seeking to reduce their exposure, risk and financial vulnerability, seek a wide spectrum of investments. These include quality, well-bred livestock/exotic animals. Thus, a ready-made market exists if you have the *"stock."* The customers are liquid. They are affluent investors/speculators. The suppliers, few and far between, are professional businessmen, who are shrewd in tax matters, genetics, conformation and scientific agricultural practices. Remember, the world is slowly, but surely, returning to real wealth—commodities. Thus, with quality, well-bred livestock/exotic animals, we are looking at a growth industry over the next two decades. Good breeders will always have a market for sophisticated investors/collectors, and to meet the necessary commercial breeding and consumer demand.

Now, before you conclude that we have found the *"Holy Grail,"* let us hasten to add a few caveats. You have probably heard someone say something to the effect of, *"Be careful in dealing with old Joe Blow. He's a real horse trader."* Truer words were never spoken. You have never been taken, really taken, until you have been taken by a real live *"horse trader."* Nothing in tax shelters, investment seminar booths or inflation hedge salesmen can match it. If you don't know what you are doing with animals, you will wind up poor, quick.

Now, naturally, there is an entry price to be paid, the cost of inefficiency and ignorance during the early stages of the learning curve (in any field). Expect to pay that cost; expect to pay too much, as you learn. Just don't get killed or plunge.

Like any other business, there are some start-up costs by way of the purchases of books and equipment, paying for good counsel (remember the low cost of good advice is always the way to go long-term), and other heavy first-year expenses (capital outlays), involved with getting established to secure a business profit down the road. The recent tax law changes, in terms of investment tax credit and depreciation, however, make these investments attractive if you are serious about doing the work necessary to make your operation a viable business.

An investment in quality, well-bred livestock/exotic animals must be just that, an investment, which is intended to turn a profit down the road. The *"hobby"* approach just won't cut it. The doctor/dentist/lawyer syndrome of buying a house in the country, where you piddle around on a weekend, while maintaining a mansion in the city, will probably not stand up to IRS attack and most probably will not turn a profit. It takes a big operation and a lot of dollars to be able to afford a manager to take proper care of quality, well-bred livestock/exotic animals, if you don't live on the land and do it yourself. If the animals are not properly cared for (which assumes some learning, responsibility and maintenance on your part), they will get sick, die, not produce offspring and/or be stolen.

While diamonds don't produce baby diamonds, and by contrast, llamas produce baby llamas, adding real new wealth, it is not an automatic thing. In other words, a diamond in the hand may be worth two llamas in the bush unless some personal responsibility is assumed for the llamas. What we are coming down to is a fundamental of all good invesments: If you intend for your investment to pay off, you must do your homework. The beauty of exotic animals is that many of them can be raised profitably on a few acres of land.

Another warning. Just like all markets go through periods of rampant optimism and desperate pessimism, leading to overpriced and underpriced conditions, the quality, well-bred livestock/exotic animal market is not any different. Such overpricing usually takes place, however, in certain geographical locations (thoroughbreds in Kentucky for example), and is marked by the influx of *"promoters"* into the field, seeking a fast buck.

While quality, well-bred livestock/exotic animals have become the most well-respected and trusted *"international currency,"* these *"live"* currencies, which could be overpriced at the present time, are thoroughbred horses (Kentucky), quarter horses (Oklahoma and Texas), Arabian horses (California, Oregon and Arizona), and Suffolk sheep (black-faced sheep), if you buy them from a promoter (California, Oregon).

Like any business, you need to look at your local market, see where a void exists, see what the market will bear by way of price, supply and demand, and meet it exclusively if possible. For example, who am I going to sell thoroughbred race horses to up here in Montana? I would have to have the best thoroughbreds in the country to have people travel this far to buy them. So, this writer has not invested in thoroughbreds. How can this writer compete here in Montana with Oregon-raised Suffolk sheep that can graze year-round, when we have to feed hay and shepherd the flock up to six months of the year in Montana? The market for thoroughbreds is in Kentucky. The geography and climate are appropriate there. The market for Suffolk sheep, and sheep in general, is in Oregon. The climate and geography are right, and the facilities to handle the end product (meat and wool) are developing there as they are in the Midwest (Illinois). Get the picture?

Now, don't get me wrong. I'm okay. Sheep are okay. We have passed the bottom of the 8.7-year cycle in sheep. Sheep are more efficient protein producers than cattle, too. But, they also require a great deal more care in terms of worming, shearing and lambing, not to mention requiring protection against the wily old coyotes (who are expanding in number).

A large number of people are getting into raising Rex rabbits in California and Oregon. Fine. It is an emerging market. But with China exporting rabbit meat to this country, and with the Rex rabbit fur pelts just getting off the ground in the fur coat market, while Rex rabbit breeders may be getting in on the ground floor, they may have to wait years, particularly in this economic environment, to realize a real handsome return on their investment. It's downright *"hare"* raising.

Just as it is unprofitable to sit with a commodity position during a trading range for many months (foregoing the interest you could have earned on your money during that period of time), so it is unprofitable to be in on the ground floor in any livestock business if it's not ready to break out upside, or already in an established bull market.

An added danger in the breeder business is that it gets top-heavy, somewhat like the *"greater fool theory."* You remember the greater fool theory? That's the theory that you can make money by paying too much for an investment if you can find a *"greater fool"* who will pay more for it when he buys it from you. Such may be close to being the case presently in the rich, tax-shelter sensitive, family-farm oriented Oregon, California and Utah areas, where Rex rabbits, Arabian horses and Suffolk sheep breeders make money by selling their high-priced livestock to new breeders who they bring into the business. It's sort of like a chain letter or the Amway business. Everyone becomes a distributor, a breeder. However, unlike Amway, where the end product is consumed, when you have a bunch of breeders at the top of a livestock industry, but no commercial end users below, the inverted pyramid has a real strong tendency to collapse, particularly when the economy turns weak. It's hard to find new recruits.

True, the Rex rabbit and Suffolk sheep, for example, both have tremendous end use value. Mutton and rabbit are good protein sources. The Rex rabbit fur makes a luxurious fur coat. Wool is transformed into wool clothing. But, unless the commercial and consumer market is well developed for these items, which it is not at present, the breeders are forced to find another breeder (a greater fool?) to buy their high-priced livestock.

Where can you learn more about getting into quality, well-bred livestock/exotic animals? There are a few men who hold seminars in these areas. A word of warning. There are a lot of promoters moving into this field and most of *"them"* are holding seminars.

Have you ever met a promoter who wasn't personable and a fine talker? That's why these folks are promoters. But with promoters, you want to pay the fee for the seminar, learn as much as you can, ask questions, but be careful about buying any of *"their"* overpriced, quality, well-bred livestock/exotic animals. For most promoters, the crown jewel of the seminar is to have you buy, at inflated prices, their quality, well-bred livestock/exotic animals.

After attending a seminar, go home and sit on it awhile. Let the fires of impulse buying cool down. Do some research of your own regarding the market needs in your own area and then set out to meet them.

Raising quality, well-bred livestock/exotic animals is both work and a business. But it is also fun. Animals are real. Every time after this writer returns from Washington, D.C., he spends a lot of time with his animals. It's good therapy. The animals are real here in Montana. Not so with the beasts back in Washington, D.C.

THE BEST INVESTMENT/COLLECTIBLE
IN EXOTIC ANIMALS—LLAMAS

New

After having investigated the spectrum of well-bred livestock/exotic animals, including all types of cattle, (Texas Longhorns and Chianina cattle included), horses (Arabians, Thoroughbreds, Quarter Horses, Appaloosas, Missouri Fox Trotters, American Fox Trotters), Rex rabbits, buffalo, milk goats, Suffolk sheep, and the whole spectrum of exotic livestock, and going to school on my agriculture investor friends, this analyst has concluded that the best long-term investment for upside appreciation with minimal downside risk is the llama.

Let's look at llamas from both a fundamental and market perspective, including considerations of supply and demand, and also examine the characteristics of the llama itself. In terms of animal characteristics, we shall evaluate utility value, maintenance requirements and aesthetic considerations.

Llamas are related to alpacas, guanacos and the vicunas, all of South America. All four of these species are camelids, South American relatives of the camel family. Only llamas are domesticated to any great extent.

While there are several million llamas in the South American countries of Bolivia, Argentina and Peru, there are at most only 7,000 llamas in the United States, and possibly as few as 3,500. (It's impossible to get an exact count due to the dispersed nature of this prized exotic.)

Here's the beauty of the supply side picture. Since the 1930s, it has been impossible to import llamas from South America into the U.S. due to U.S.D.A. regulations. Furthermore, there is a four-country treaty in South America that prevents the export of these valued animals. There, llamas are viewed as those countries' primary natural resource.

In this country, from investment considerations alone, llamas are in incredibly strong hands. One wealthy exotic cattle breeder, who consistently wins championships at major livestock shows in Denver, Houston and San Antonio, has combed the country looking for

186

llamas. He was only able to pick up half a dozen. Two years ago, a California attorney, who advised and consulted for an investor with $100 million in liquid assets, spent two years rounding up all the llamas he could from all across the land. He ended up with only 50. This writer sent out letters to over 115 llama breeders and raisers across the country and was able to garner only three females. (There were only three must/will sell opportunities.) Put simply, getting hold of llamas, particularly female llamas, is like pulling hens' teeth. They're scarce. There are just not that many llamas available to buy. They are simply not for sale, in many cases, at any price. So, it's impossible for a large investor to come into this market and *"buy them all up."*

Presently, males sell for $500 to $1,500 each. Females sell from $3,500 at birth to $5,000 each. (Llamas give birth to more males than females, which is the reason for the disparity of price between sexes.)

If the American investing public ever wakes to all the positive attributes of these animals, the price of llamas will explode, and probably at least triple.

The best investment opportunities are always those which are not yet generally recognized, and in industries in their infancy. This is the situation with llamas today. Just compare 3,500-7,000 llamas in the United States today (the total supply, 1,000 of which are in zoos) to the 7 million recreational horses which graze across the land. Talk about tight supply and strong handed holders. This writer has never seen anything else like the supply shortage that exists in llamas.

There are approximately 350 llama breeders across the country. If you can meet border crossing restrictions, Canadians will pay you $5,000 for a female llama, sight unseen. Such is the demand in Canada. Demand has started to explode from the U.S. private sector, too.

As a utility animal, llamas have become very popular for backpacking. They can carry 90-110 pounds, 25 to 30 miles per day. The U.S. Forest Service is using llamas to carry food and equipment for trail maintenance crews. Because llamas put the *"run"* on dogs and coyotes, they are being used to intermingle with sheep flocks, sort of a llama protectorate.

Llamas are becoming increasingly popular as pets. Llamas are the closest thing possible to having *"Bambi"* as a pet. Children can ride them. (Male pets should be castrated.) Llamas pull carts. They are a relatively safe animal. Their natural astuteness makes them excellent *"watchdogs."* They will see and hear nearly everything that moves or makes noise in the neighborhood.

Llamas are also in demand as animal breeding investments, with positive tax planning implications. Usually four females and a male (a $15,000-$20,000 investment) is needed to qualify as a llama breeder. Llamas normally are depreciated over a 5 year period. Investment tax credit is allowed on breeding stock the year of purchase. All normal expenses, including feed, utilities, labor and transportation are deductible. Buildings, fences, equipment and machinery utilized for their care and maintenance can be depreciated.

Llamas seldom challenge fences, rail or wire. Fences of 40 to 48 inches high are usually adequate. Llamas are not destructive. Although native to the South American Andes of 6,000-12,000 feet elevation, they are a hardy animal, adaptable to almost any climate and altitude. They readily take all extremes of weather and need little protection. But, this just brushes the surface of llamas' low maintenance requirements.

Llamas can be transported in the back of a pickup or under a camper shell. They can go for several days without food or water. They are very seldom ill and require next to no shots, worming or other health care. They are virtually disease free.

Llamas exhibit very interesting social behavior. They congregate in a herd and are a delight to observe. They are docile animals generally, with calm dispositions. They bed down at night together. Their communication with their ears and tails is fascinating. They make no noise, save for a soft "hum." They are extremely clean, have no odor, and defecate in one place. Their manure, a cold manure, does not readily attract flies and can be used immediately on gardens as fertilizer, being high in nitrogen content.

Llama wool is in great demand, 3-8 inches in length, and is presently selling for over $2.00 an ounce. The demand far exceeds the supply for this, one of the highest quality of all wools. It comes in all colors. The llama fleece contains no lanolin, is spun *"dirty,"* and matures every two years when it may be shorn. The normal llama will yield 3-8 pounds of wool. Mature llamas grow to be 3-4 feet tall at the shoulder and will weigh between 250-500 pounds.

The milk of llamas is fit for human consumption. Llamas live to be 15-20 years of age. They chew a cud and have front teeth only on the lower jaw. Llamas have split hooves. The unique cloven hoof has a hard nail on each toe and a large, soft pad on the heel.

Baby llamas may be the most beautiful, playful, graceful and entertaining of all babies in the animal kingdom. Curious and affectionate, as well as incredibly cute, they are a delight to watch for hours on end. I have never chuckled so much at an animal's behavior in my life.

In terms of conformation, females tend to be taller and more rangy, while males are shorter and more blocky. By blessing of destiny, this writer was able to acquire the most famous and perhaps the best *"conformed"* llama male in the whole country—*"Fortune."* (See back cover.) In keeping with *"Wealth For All,"* some day we hope that *"Fortune Line Llamas"* has its own *"Fortune 500,"* the real thing!

What makes for good conformation in a male llama? A description of *"Fortune"* will pretty much cover it:

1. Attractive, striking color. (While our children literally hug *"Fortune"* and feed him oats by hand, they affectionately refer to him as *"Darth Vader"* of *"Star Wars"* fame.

2. Long, and attractive wool,

3. A flat, level back,

4. A wide chest with a smooth, strong, sloping neck, rising up to erect, curved *"banana"* ears with nice, large, wideset, doe-like eyes, with an attractive cleft upper lip and a lower lip that covers the front teeth on the lower jaw,

5. Strong, broad hips and well muscled legs,

6. A heavy boned, well-muscled, attractively proportioned body, of medium height and weight.

Although technically not a point of conformation, a regal, stately appearance, complimented by a calm, pleasant disposition and personality are part of the hallmarks of a great llama. In *"Fortune's"* case, his powerful, *"Darth Vader"* appearance and color perfectly compliment his high level of awareness, alertness, intelligence, power and dominance, that he displays as he reigns supreme over our modest llama herd. No dog or other male llama dare challenge this *"Darth Vader"* of the llama world. All other males who have confronted *"Fortune"* immediately move into a *"submissive crouch."* And yet, *"Fortune,"* in his regal wisdom, has always exhibited the patience and calm temperament to accommodate children as young as four years old, who stroke his neck and feed him oats. He is a rare combination of power, beauty and even temperament. I hope you are lucky enough to find such superb balance in a llama. *"Fortune"* is living art.

To illustrate how intelligent these animals are and easy to train, this writer has been able to halter break llamas in 30 minutes, and teach them to *"kush"* (kneel) and carry a pack in another half an hour. Once they have learned a lesson, they never forget it, either.

Gestation period for a llama is eleven months. They will breed back within the first month after giving birth. Young female llamas are capable of breeding between a year and a year and a half of age. Females give birth only during daylight hours, in a standing position, the whole process taking approximately a half an hour, and seldom requiring human assistance. At birth, the average llama stands about 28 inches high and weighs approximately 28 pounds.

Consuming far less protein (hay) than horses or cows, and requiring far less maintenance than goats or sheep, llamas do very nicely on a diet of 10 pounds of grass/alfalfa hay a day. Additionally, they require free choice mineral, a salt block and readily available water. Llamas come in all colors.

Are there any negatives to these quiet, adorable animals? They do spit and kick if excessively harassed. However, in over a year, no member of my family has been splattered or kicked. The odds of such occurring is no greater than being kicked by the family horse or bitten by the family dog. Quite frankly, from looking at all the angles—the supply/demand situation, good or bad economic times, maintenance considerations and utility value, there is not a more unique, undervalued exotic animal available in the United States today. And, because llamas are in strong hands and widely distributed among breeders around the country (350 breeders), the foundation for an explosive long-term bull market in llamas exists.

As an analyst, although difficult, it's important that I maintain my objectivity in analyzing any investment. Nevertheless, I can quite honestly say, that my personal experience with llamas has been the most stimulating, interesting and rewarding endeavor with animals I have ever undertaken. The llama is the decathlon champion of exotics.

THOUGHTS ON INFLATION, DEFLATION, AND GOLD

9/14/79

It is the nature of man to think in terms of absolutes—black vs. white, good vs. evil, conservative vs. liberal, etc. Yet, we consider men educated who think through the shades of gray. A man who is able to integrate complex and sometimes seemingly conflicting information is wise.

The natural order has its complexities and apparent contradictions. The double helix is an example from the scientific realm. Another is, if you and I both jump out of an airplane and freefall in exactly the same way, we fall all right (are in motion), but relative to each other, we are at rest (still). Thus, motion and rest coexist simultaneously.

The coexistence of apparent opposites is troubling many investors today. Investors struggle to cope, to maintain their purchasing power and wealth in an *inflationary* environment which is marked by pockets of deflation or disinflation.

Unquestionably, the lessons of history, with their underlying assumption that human nature is a constant, favor our currency being inflated to worthlessness long term. There has never been a fiat currency in history which has survived. If you believe in social evolution, then you believe our currency has a chance to survive. Our money is getting better. Right? If you believe man's nature is a constant, the dollar will eventually be worth zero. Even our monetary view of the future depends upon our ultimate presuppositions, our theological base.

This writer believes that if the U.S. government is left to its own vices, without any *outside* checks and balances, it will inflate the dollar into oblivion, eventually. In every mature democracy, as ours is, the tendency has been to spend more on social services and less on national defense. Based on the lessons of history, this is suicidal because national defense has always been a government's most basic responsibility. Also, eventually, the demand for social services bankrupts the treasury.

The cycle of a civilization is from a monarchy, to an aristocracy, to a democracy, to anarchy, and then back again to a monarchy. Infla-

191

tion and democracy go hand in hand. The act of inflating is the act of destroying the currency, which results in economic chaos, followed by the fall of the government and the ruin of the nation. The result is anarchy. The road to anarchy is clearly the road that the United States and Western Civilization have been traveling. The inflation of the currency is partially the result of the borrowing of the mob—the democratic masses.

The willingness of the public to borrow at historically high rates of interest was just another sign of their low regard for the dollar. The public was following the example set by business and government.

Labor rightfully demands higher wages when inflation becomes intense. Labor never benefits until near the end of the inflationary cycle. Therefore labor, particularly unorganized labor, bears the brunt of inflation along with those who save and those who depend on fixed incomes.

The U.S. government is in a box. The citizens of the United States, for the most part, look to the government to provide for all their needs, to be a security blanket. The clarity with which this is revealed is evidenced by the fact that it was cheaper for the U.S. government to loan Chrysler a billion dollars than it was to pay all the unemployment benefits and lose the tax income which would result due to the layoff of 500,000 Chrysler employees with all its ramifications throughout the economy.

Social Security liabilities will continue to be paid, even though Social Security actuarial liabilities are now greater than what everyone in this entire country owns. Disaster relief continues to flood us (no pun intended). Fifty-six percent of the people in this country depend upon the government for their livelihood. The budget of the Department of Health, Education, and Welfare was larger than the budget of all 50 states combined. Does anyone really believe this major trend will be turned around voluntarily by politicians? History argues, *"No Way!"*

In this writer's opinion, the return to monetary sanity will only take place after some cataclysmic event (panic), or perhaps a series of such events, which will result in a massive change of mind, a return to the gold standard, or the death of the dollar.

Recall Rene Thom's work on discontinuous events, the basis of catastrophe theory. Remember, too, Funk's 50-year cycle of prosperity, depression and prices. We are at the point in the cycle where a panic should most probably occur. A natural catastrophe, the surprise bankruptcy of a major corporation or bank, major defaults by Third World developing countries, withdrawal of Arab funds from U.S.

banks, a panic out of the dollar by Eurodollar holders—all qualify as candidates for catastrophe/panic. These events, though, in and of themselves, may not produce monetary deflation long-term. In fact, they may produce increased inflation long-term as federal deficits will soar to compensate for the lack of tax income. Remember that during the 1974 recession, federal expenditures increased while revenues declined. This resulted in a breath-taking deficit. The greatest threat we face in any recession is even greater deficits, which trigger a panic out of dollars eventually.

Certainly, any of the foregoing economic catastrophes will produce isolated price declines and price deflation. If a corporation like Chrysler goes bankrupt, there will be a lot of cheap real estate surrounding Chrysler's plants. Likewise, bargain prices will be seen for cars, boats, homes, you name it, as desperate former Chrysler employees scramble for liquidity. Even without a catastrophic event, price deflation can be expected to be found in isolated instances where individuals or companies have leveraged themselves so greatly that they are no longer able to meet their debt service and bankruptcy results. Bankruptcy sales are the places to pick up bargains in used and sometimes new goods (in the case of manufacturing firms). This is why this writer has consistently recommended holding some cash, as well as inflation chaos hedges, such as gold. Cash is king during fire or bankruptcy sales. We should expect an increase in these ruinous situations, where individuals and corporations become insolvent. Recognize, too, that the apparent contradiction is, in fact, not a conflict—both cash and gold could simultaneously be king.

Obviously, it will be the non-government sector, the private sector, which will experience these distressing situations. The alienation between non-government workers and government workers will increase. The tension, hostility and antagonism that we are feeling now is just the tip of the iceberg.

It *is* possible that we could go into a net price and monetary deflation temporarily. Remember, the primary source of inflation is the creation of credit through the fractional reserve system, whereby bank deposits are multiplied up to 7 times (excluding Eurodollar borrowing). From 1950 to 1978, consumer debt increased 1,444%, non-bank corporate debt soared 1,070%, state and local government debt exploded 1,220%, while the federal government debt increased just 180%. If the money supply contracts, if the velocity of money decreases, if borrowing decreases, if loan repayment exceeds borrowing, deflation (monetary and price) will occur. The deflation, however, could only be temporary due to increasing government spending. The economic ignorance of the general public, coupled with the desire to avoid pain, could result in public pressure to increase government spending then. And the politicians will respond.

With $950 billion Eurodollars overshadowing $400 billion plus domestic dollars, our destiny is no longer in our hands. The Eurodollar holders demand that the dollar remain strong, or they will flee from it, and thereby destroy it. This international interest is in irreconcilable conflict with the political trend of this country, particularly during a recession.

Discipline could also be imposed upon this country by the Arabs. If the Arabs again embargo oil, or reduce the amount of oil shipped to this country, or withdraw their deposits from U.S. banks, they force economic retrenchment. Debt would decline due to loan payoffs, bankruptcy, and the lack of incentive to borrow. If the U.S. government became a spendthrift during such declining economic activity, the Arabs could threaten to further reduce the oil supply to this country. Obviously, it is unlikely that emotional, irrational Americans would stand for such an event. Military reprisals, possibly the invasion of the Arab oil fields, could result in World War III. Here we are, back to war again as the ultimate solution. Such it has ever been.

While the purchase of gold is viewed by most as a hedge against inflation, it is, in fact, deflationary. Here again, we see the supposed coexistence of opposites. Those who opt for gold are opting for real money and ultimate liquidity. They are foregoing interest income, and thereby are exercising their vote against the debt/banking system. The movement by the avant-garde thinkers, the wealthy, and the general public toward gold is economic action which conflicts with the interest of establishment banking, corporate and government institutions. It is antagonistic to those who rely upon government for their livelihood. An economic eruption is the most likely result when these forces finally square off. (To date, the government is still popular since we are not in a revolution.)

What does a free man do? A free man must reconcile himself to the fact that he will eventually involuntarily break establishment law. He must resign himself to the validity of a higher law (God's law), and that of the U.S. Constitution. Even now, nearly all of us are in violation of some law. We could hardly be otherwise. Fifty thousand pages a year are added to the Federal Register, the law of the land. There are all the *"alphabet agency"* rules and regulations. The number of laws created in the last 2½ years (approximately) are greater than the number of laws created from the beginning of this country up until the past few years.

What does one do? Geographical separation from the cities is of considerable help. Absence makes the government's heart grow fonder for someone else's pocket book, assets and freedom. Diversity of assets internationally is recommended. Diversity of assets domestically into gold, cash, income-producing real estate, farms, animals, commodities, homes, and important retail businesses, such as hardware stores is helpful. These should be in different geographic locations, preferably out of the major cities.

Gold and silver are survival money. They should be held for such use. Home self sufficiency, by way of solar or wood heating, a garden, a greenhouse, livestock and food storage also make sense. One must hedge one's bets. We live in the age of uncertainty. There is no other way to survive with peace of mind intact.

THINKING CLEARLY

9/8/78

It used to be that the mark of an educated man was his ability to: a. Define his terms and, b. Think in terms of categories that crossed various fields of knowledge. A man who could define his terms and think in an integrated manner was respected as a wise man. Now, we no longer define our terms. It is, therefore, no coincidence that men today march toward slavery, all in the name of freedom. Howard K. Smith forecast this sad state of affairs correctly in the Jan. 8, 1955 SATURDAY REVIEW where he stated that, due to exploding knowledge and increased complexity of society, each generation would know less as an individual of the total cultural heritage than the generation that went before it.

One of the problems in our economic sphere today can be traced to our failure to define our terms. Let's look at a couple of examples. Inflation could be defined as an increase in the supply of money. Deflation, contrarily, could be defined as a decrease in the supply of money. If we simply define an economic recovery as an increase in business activity, and an economic recession as a decrease in business activity, then we can see that there are clear distinctions between the terms inflation, deflation, recovery and recession. Furthermore, we could define depression as a severe decline in business activity. Naturally, these terms have relationships to one another, but it is erroneous thinking, in fact, uneducated, to use deflation and depression synonymously.

Depending on how you look at it, we have been through 20-30 years of robust economic activity, a business *"recovery"* in one sense of the word. Likewise, during the latter part of this positive economic cycle, we have had accompanying inflation. We could be about to enter a period of protracted business recession, maybe even a depression. The arguments that are heard most frequently are whether or not this coming recession or depression will be an inflationary one or a deflationary one. During a depression, one would normally expect the purchasing power of money to increase, given that the money is *"sound."* It is only the instability of a fiat currency that makes the question so difficult. Real money, historically, is gold. Therefore, the price of gold could continue to increase as economic activity diminishes, particularly if the general public is frightened because gold is, in fact, real money. Reality (real money) can be ignored during the good times due to the *"hypo"* effect of the multiplier as it takes its toll in increasing the supply of money through the fractional reserve banking system. This is the creation of credit. The natural result of the *liquidation* of the tremendous credit malaise is *balanced* by the *increasing* value of money—perhaps even real money—gold! Therefore, it is this analyst's opinion that we should see higher prices for gold, irregularly higher in the upcoming years, higher in terms of purchasing power. (During the initial stages of a panic and depression, gold should drop since gold is held on margin by many investors.)

A close friend, a primary producer (farmer), mentioned a few weeks back that it doesn't pay to produce items that are necessary for life. His statement hit like a load of bricks. What he said was that if anyone produces the basics necessary for man to live, he will not profit. His statement is true, as can be easily ascertained from observing the low price level of world-wide farm commodity prices and farm bankruptcies. This situation is unrealistic. It is out of tune with natural law. A fiat currency and a leveraged credit system has made it all possible. Those who have observed that we are at the point where we either inflate or die are noting that we are approaching the point of the great readjustment.

INTRINSIC VALUE

4/6/78

Gold has no intrinsic value. Nothing on earth, from an economic point of view, has intrinsic value. Only if people value something does it have value. If something is not valued by people, it simply has no value. Gold has historic value.

The logical extension of the argument that nothing has intrinsic value, but only historic value, slams Marx's theory of the value of labor to the canvas. Marx held that labor had intrinsic value. Not so. The value of labor is derivative; it stems from the value of labor's product.

Let's take an example. Let's say I work my fingers to the bone raising thistles. (Apologies to Scotland—Thistles are their national flower.) I'm up at dawn every day, fertilizing, watering and talking to my thistles. They respond in bristling fashion, and turn out to be the best thistles in the neighborhood. Proud of my labor, I offer my thistles for sale. But no one will buy them. In fact, all the neighbors are mad at me for raising thistles. The neighbors are spending their time digging up the thistles in their own yards and destroying them. The result is that I sell no thistles. None! My labor was wasted. My product (thistles) had no economic value. There was no intrinsic value to my labor. I wasted my time. The moral of this story? Gold has value if it is valued by people.

GOLD PLUS

9/22/78

Men believe in gold because it is historically real money! It is valued by rational and free men as real money. It meets the criteria of real money. It is a store of value, a medium of exchange and a standard of comparative value. Additionally, it conforms with the laws of thermodynamics, which state that energy is neither created nor destroyed, only transferred. The transfer requires the use of some energy and therefore *"productive energy"* is lost in the process. Gold is therefore real, not representative, as is paper money. It took some sweat to bring that gold out of the ground.

But holding gold is no panacea. No investment is void of risk. Gold can be stolen. Gold can be outlawed and confiscated by the government. According to nuclear physicist, Stan Swinney, gold can be created from lead by changing the nucleus during a nuclear reaction.

Now, Stan Swinney is no slouch. He has been involved at the highest level in nuclear physics research. No one is sure (among the general public) that gold has not already been created, the fulfillment of the ancient alchemist's dream. It may not be done regularly because it is too expensive. But if the price of gold goes high enough, we had all best believe that gold will come out of the woodwork (laboratory).

Additionally, there is no guarantee that during the next recession gold will not go down in price. It did during 1975 when the federal deficit soared!

Why be contrary? After all, the expression *"Good as gold"* does have its basis in fact and history just as recently as Vietnam. The only Vietnamese who escaped on the last boats out bought their way on board with gold. But, there is also truth to the caveat, *"Don't have all your eggs in one basket."* It is the simple restatement of the law of probability. Own a home. Store some food. A few extra shovels, a wood stove and a large supply of aspirin make sense, too. After all, when one owns gold, one is preparing for a storm. There is no guarantee that the storm will be only financial. So, why not build a complete ark, or at least, reasonably equip a rowboat. It is the sensible thing to do and surely would comply with the *"prudent man"* rule. In this world, a man needs all kinds of insurance.

GOLD: COMMODITY OR CURRENCY?

1/4/80

Milo Hamilton is [was] the managing editor of COMMODITIES magazine.

You'd have to know Milo to appreciate him. And, Milo's not that easy to get to know. Possessed of an extremely quick and perceptive mind, Milo is also *"tight."* I've often wished I could pour a stiff drink down his throat to loosen him up a bit. In any case, Milo and I both have been thrashing around about whether gold is a commodity or a currency. This has been a fascination for both of us over the past several years.

Gold, in terms of the price of other commodities, should be pegged at $200 an ounce, perhaps less. But, as a reserve asset, as money, the fair price for gold is $700 an ounce or higher. Is gold a commodity ($200 an ounce) or a reserve asset ($700 an ounce)?

At this time in history, when men are caught between the historical reality of gold as money, and yet are indoctrinated by computer entry banking as the means of payment for goods and services, this conflict is not easily resolved. Undoubtedly, the marketplace will work it out before the 1980s is over.

In the November, 1979 issue of COMMODITIES magazine, Milo authored an article entitled, *"Will Gold Hold Its Edge?"* Milo observed that after a severe economic crisis, usually a depression, commodities regain their value relative to the price of gold. *"Put another way, inflation begins to erode the purchasing power of gold. The long cycle in gold's purchasing power runs in a 40-to-60 year span, from low to low."*

Forty to sixty years, eh? Does that sound familiar? Here we are again, up against that master 50-year debt, psychological and capital expenditure cycle. Wheat prices, the Kondratieff Wave, the 55-year Fibonacci number commodity cycle, the 52-year Aztec cycle, and the 50-year cycle in Leviticus 25—all are neon signs illuminating our road through life. Each reminds us, in its own way, of how man repeats himself over and over again. More importantly perhaps, they aid us in our economic planning because through their use, we can make better

200

economic decisions.

Milo continues, *"Inspection of the relationship of gold to the Wholesale Price Index since 1800 suggests that we are moving through and possibly out of, a low of this long cycle."* Apparently so because Milo speaks of a *low*. He further states, *"Drawing on past experience, most commentators who trust in long cycles call for a severe break in the actual price of commodities. That will send us into a 'garden variety' depression, marked by declining prices and a stronger dollar.*

"Traditionally, this mammoth commodity price break comes in the wake of a one-to-one ratio of gold to commodities. That 1.0 peak in the ratio occurred in 1970. The previous peak came in 1920. Since then, commodity prices have dropped sharply in gold terms to the .5 to .4 area. The previous low came in 1933 at similar levels. In October, an ounce of gold bought twice the amount of raw materials it could command in 1970."

Hold it! Some important observations. Are we about to have a severe break in the price of commodities? It is certainly possible! We are entering a recession at minimum. The case for deflation has never been stronger. After a possible run up in 1980, commodities could fall like a rock. But, Milo correctly noted that the mammoth commodity price break historically comes in the *wake* of (after) a 1 to 1 ratio of gold to commodities. That 1.0 peak in the ratio occurred in 1970, and occurred previously . . . guess when? 1920, 50 years prior to the 1970 peak. That 50-year cycle hits us smack in the face again. The up wave of the economic cycle ends in a sharp recession, such as 1970, followed by a 7- to 10-year plateau period, bringing us theoretically to 1980. What's next? A panic followed by a secondary depression? Is this where we are now? But, perhaps we have seen an invisible crash in commodity prices, because as Milo pointed out, in terms of gold or real money, commodities have dropped to the .5 and .4 area, *a level that has not been seen since 1933*, the pits of the Great Depression.

The 1970s have been wracked by economic crises and a depression as far as the real purchasing power of commodities goes. Perhaps they are about to retrieve some of their purchasing power relative to gold. That would certainly substantiate my theory that we are entering the age of *"protein gold."*

Milo goes on to say, *"History also tells us that the recent lows in commodity prices relative to gold last but a brief time of perhaps 3 to 8 years. It is high time for raw materials to launch a full-scale attack on gold's purchasing power."*

Milo builds an impressive case: *"The ratio of COMMODITIES Magazine Index (CMI), a basket of futures markets, to gold suggests commodities refuse to give further ground to gold. In the last twelve* *months, the CMI/gold ratio declined 3 points on a $230 rise in the gold price. During the $100 move in 1976-78, the same ratio moved 41 points in favor of gold.*

"Put another way, commodities appear to have struck major bottoms in real or barter terms."

Back to our original argument, *"Is gold a commodity or a currency?"* Will it rise to $700 or fall to $200? If gold is real money, as I suspect before this whole 1980 financial/economic debacle is over it will be, since every fiat currency in history has always inflated to total worthlessness, gold may not only go to $700 per ounce, but to infinity. But, assuming a modest case for gold at $700 per ounce, the catch-up move by commodities could be breathtaking. Milo envisions a move that will bring the barter relationship back to 1.0, the 1970 level. *"That would suggest $18 wheat, $12 corn, $330 cattle, $178 hogs and $3 cotton."* That's worth whistling Dixie for, isn't it, boys? If commodities blow to those lofty price levels, no longer will the silk shirted Wall Streeters be able to sit on their duffs, look out their windows, chuckle at the commodity traders, and sneer, *"Those old hayseeds sit on tractors from dawn to dusk bellowing out verses of, 'The old cow died and the pigs went crazy, but oh that cornbread sopped in gravy.' "*

I agree with Milo that grains are the key commodity to watch. This is why this analyst is primarily keeping his eye on corn and wheat. Without the above logic (commodities to gold), who would believe it is possible for commodities to go to the moon?

Milo concludes, *"In early October, gold commanded a 1100% premium over its 1967 price while the grain index traded at a mere 250% above 1967 levels. The ratio of the grain index to gold stood at .23 this October vs. .60 at the top of gold's bull market in late 1974. In barter exchange terms, grains have devalued to one-third of their 1974 levels during this year."*

Based on Milo's analysis, it's a *"can't lose"* situation for primary producers of commodities, particularly grains, long-term. If gold goes up, commodities skyrocket because the gold to commodity ratio is at rock bottom. If gold holds steady, commodities should do some catching up because the ratio is still at rock bottom. If gold drops, commodities should hold relatively steady in order to return the gold/commodity ratio to a more historically equitable level.

Boy, isn't it nice to have a sure thing again in this *"catch-as-catch-can"* world? The nagging questions that must be asked are, *"Why are we so smart?" "Why are we the only ones who have noticed this aberration?" "Why hasn't all the smart money in the world seen our 'sure thing' and hopped on board?"* Perhaps it's a little *"Catch 22"* called debt. Perhaps it is the 510-year civilization cycle.

The great worldwide inflation of the 1970s was a dollar based, bank credit inflation. It was thus, a 5-7-to-1 leveraged inflation, similar to the commodity markets. Debt and prices have pyramided sharply in the 1970s. They could decrease just as sharply in the 1980s. (They could contract three times more rapidly.)

Contrary to popular opinion, ⅔ of our bank credit debt structure has been incurred by the consuming public and business, not by the government. And farmers? The poor farmers? They could be about to have it *"socked to 'em"* again. They are the epitome of speculators in equipment, machinery and agricultural land. If the credit crunch and collapse of the debt pyramid occurs *before* commodity prices improve, we could see a tragedy of tragedies, possibly culminating in the nationalization of agriculture or its confiscation by multinational debt capitalism. For, if such a scenario unfolds, farmers will be forced to liquidate and/or go into bankruptcy when their loans are called, regardless of what commodity prices are doing. Lending agencies may be forced to pull the rug out from under farmers to save their own lending skins.

The American farmer has a way of having it *"stuck to him."* I would not be surprised to see it happen. American agriculture is the most important industry in this country, not only because food is basic, but also because of the tremendous clout it gives the United States in world markets.

THE CORPORATION: A FAMILY IN DISGUISE

4/20/78

An article in December, 1977 PSYCHOLOGY TODAY entitled, *"Oedipus in the Board Room"* turned on all kinds of lights for this writer. The thrust of the article was how *"All organizations are run like families . . ."* It focused on the work of Harry Levinson, the head of the Levinson Institute in Cambridge, Massachusetts. Levinson is a clinical psychologist. He stated,

> *"All organizations recapitulate the basic family structure in a culture. Our earliest experiences with our parents are repeated in our subsequent relationships with authority. Early family life determines our assumptions of how power is distributed, and as we grow up we form groups on the same model. Organizations encourage this by acting 'in loco parentis.' If everyone knows what the rules are, things run smoothly. Since a business and a family share similar psychodynamics, you find the same sorts of problems in business—or in any organization—that you uncover in therapy."* [18]

Two years ago I spent time with a top industrial psychologist in order to learn what my blind spots were, where I was likely to protect myself from unfavorable information and nurture myths. This psychologist told me that organizations do the same thing, confirming Levinson's observations. I learned that it is important to work with *"like-minded people,"* family-type people. It is vital for success.

Corporations have their own distinctive styles, viewpoints and personalities, as do families. This orientation is, quite naturally, set by the companies' top executives who, in turn, draw people to the organization who *"fit"* with its viewpoints. Psychological contracts are drawn and violation of these unstated taboos leads to much unhappiness.

Two quick examples of this come to mind. In the U.S. Air Force, the standard was *"never rock the boat."* Stay quiet, do the job, and don't question the superior officer. *"Change will come in time, but it will not be initiated by you."* Second example. A major real estate development firm in this country has risen from the working roots of a kind and benevolent entrepreneur. He is literally the *"father"* of the

204

company. The bright young executives who have been attracted to him (Harvard MBA's and the like) are uniquely in need of a solid father image. Amazingly, unknown to them, they have substituted the head of the company for their own inadequate, unloving father. It is the ideal mixture of the natural inclination for entrepreneurship with the supportive all-knowing father. One chief executive caustically remarked, *"These boys just live for a pat on the head from _____."* These *"boys"* are 25-40 years old! The company provides them with psychological support, hard work and fair wages. Should any of them moonlight or show the slightest lack of total loyalty to the company, however, they are ruthlessly cut (fired) from the *"family."*

Levinson comments,

> *"Organizations' personalities are partly a product of the ego ideal of the founder or head who holds up a certain standard of behavior and sets up a particular kind of structure, thereby attracting certain kinds of people. They, in turn, attract more of their own kind. As you build in policies and practices with which these people are comfortable, the corporate personality endures. By the time they are in place for a couple of generations, you have extruded from the system people who don't fit, and a personality type has become well established."* [19]

An employee is just a child in the corporation's family. The best executives respond like good parents, fulfilling the needs of the children. Perhaps this is why there is no best management style, and why management is situational. In each *"family"* the needs are different.

Levinson recommended Harold Searles' COLLECTED PAPERS ON SCHIZOPHRENIA AND RELATED SUBJECTS as the very best book to read in order to gain an understanding of what goes on in corporations. He likes the chapter *"On Driving the Other Person Crazy"* best.

We can learn some important lessons from viewing the corporation as a *"family."* All of us work for a living. Our job should be consistent with our needs. The corporation should share a *"commonality"* with our needs and personality. If is does not, then we are likely to be consistently unhappy regardless of *"job benefits."*

What does this imply for the government bureaucracies? No wonder there is such a problem with alcohol and inefficiency in the military service, the government alphabet agencies, and all the rest of the departments. They are not likely to change and, in fact, it will probably take a radical and painful change initiated from the outside environment to cause alteration. Is this why historically institutions die? Because they cannot respond? What does this say for the country? The White House? The Soviet Union? Is there a similarity here between organizations and the primary trends in markets, where it finally takes a painful panic to disillusion the bulls? Probably so.

For those of you who trade stocks, you now have an additional tool to use in evaluating your stock investments. Will a company, based upon its *"family"* values, be able to change in the future, to alter its style consistent with your view of the future? If you visit a company before you invest, be sure to be sensitive to your **initial** impressions of the *"family."* Write them down. They could prove invaluable as an input to your investment decisions. Families are basic to human, social, government and business success. And the character of the men who head the families determine their destiny long-term.

PEDIGREE

8/6/82

This analyst has been jousting with the commodity markets for over a decade. It seems like several lifetimes. And, in a way, it has been. In some ten years plus, I have seen the birth, maturing, old age and death of innumerable bull and bear markets. I have watched the rise and fall, the coming and going, of countless numbers of commodity traders. This experience has enabled me to come as near as possible to living a countless number of lifetimes. Each bull or bear market, each commodity trader, has something in common with those that went before. And yet, each experience is, in its own way, unique. I continue to learn and grow.

I remember the early 1970s, when *"commodities"* were not even in the vocabulary of most investors, and when *"commodity markets"* were a subject which raised eyebrows, denoting disapproval. Then came the explosion of the 1972-73 commodity bull markets, which spun investors around and sparked widespread public interest. The lifting of wage and price controls and the Russian grain sales hitting the headlines, both contributed to the *"commodity rush for riches,"* the *"California gold rush"* equivalent a century later. And, I remember the black eyes of that period, too—the scandal in the potato market with all the aspersions cast at Simplot; the Goldstein-Samuelson commodity options scandal, where the investing public lost millions. Yes, what interesting years those were. And profitable ones, also.

The commodity markets matured as a respectable speculation medium during the last half of the 1970s and early 1980s. Respectability for gold and interest rate futures enhanced the status of commodity trading. More significantly, as our society became increasingly short-term oriented and people were pressured to make ends meet, squeezed by inflation on one hand and high taxes on the other, folks viewed commodity trading as a high risk way out. With inflation, men increasingly take a short-term view. Long-term investments and orientation disappear. So, commodity trading filled the bill of the pervasive, national, short-term perspective.

207

It logically followed that the gambling craze would become extensive. This get-rich-quick/easy-money bit resulted in booming times for
for Las Vegas and later, Atlantic City. The zero-sum game of commodity trading fit very nicely with this *"devil-may-care"* syndrome.

Next came the headline-grabbing fundamental of national and
world-wide drought. With the media hype came a record number of
contracts traded in the commodity markets in 1980. Men were provided with yet another excuse to flee from the responsibility, pain,
frustration and the limitations of all-encompassing government regulations, high taxes, inflation, crime, pollution and political incompetence. They maintained their sanity through entertaining
escapism. Drugs, booze, movies, television and particularly professional sports provided a welcome break from reality also. The rush
was on to any distraction where men could identify with anything
other than themselves and their problems. In this *"Alice In Wonderland"* environment, commodity trading found a natural niche. Big investors, under the strain of unstable financial conditions, easily
became speculators. Small investors saw the commodity markets as
the last mystical *"road to riches."* Even the unsophisticated public
caught this *"rags-to-riches"* commodity trading bug, clinging to a
straw passing by on the winds of desperate hope. Walter Mittys by the
thousands were captured by the fantasy of instant wealth via commodity trading. The stimulating opportunity to *"ride the big wave,"*
to escape from the dull routine of one's life's work and a dreary life-
style was another promise held out to the gleeful newcomers.

One would think that men who attempt to get rich winning other
men's money would see that the promise of the commodity market, a
golden flight from an insecure, increasingly insane world to a Tahiti
paradise, was a come-on. But, desperation grasps at straws. And the
hands reached out. Never mind that better than 85 percent or more
lose due to the leverage in commodity trading which, in turn, demands
critical timing of entry and exit of commodity positions. Never mind
that this well-timed entry and exit with close stops generates brokerage
commissions of 50% to 100% of a commodity trader's account each
year before he pays himself. *"Never mind all this. It's my shot at 'The
Great Escape' and I want it, now!"* Reason is long lost in the exhilarating emotional furor of the trading moment. The financial
hangover comes later.

Long ago I concluded that the successful commodity trader could
have been successful at most anything he chose to do in life. The successful commodity trader is disciplined, organized, rational, patient,
and hardworking. He approaches commodity trading just like any
successful businessman approaches his business. This does not mean,

however, that all successful men will be successful trading commodities. Not by a long shot! One thing I have learned for certain in
these ten plus years is that many, if not most, successful men are *not*
successful trading commodities. Why? Most successful men, along the
road to becoming prosperous, develop a great deal of confidence and
pride. The latter, pride, will gut a commodity trader quickly. Leverage
and fast market moves will clean out the financial house of traders
who believe they can fight the market. Proud men invariably try to
"fight the tape." Also, many successful men have achieved their fame
and fortune by focusing exclusively on their job, by becoming compe-
tent at just what they do at work. This success has not required them
to deal first and foremost with their personal weaknesses, the chinks
in their armor. This is not the case in the commodity markets. Money
is so closely tied to man's sense of security that all the personal
weaknesses, including greed, fear and hope, immediately come to the
surface to ensnare the commodity trader. Perhaps this is why commodity trading is a more difficult way to make money than nearly any
other way. Not only does a trader have to contend with leverage, timing of trades, high commission costs, hard work and attention to
detail in a fast-moving, stressful environment, he must also have it all
together personally, mentally, emotionally and psychologically. Not
many do. And not many are successful . . . The market is a great
teacher for those willing to listen and learn. It is one of the best
around.

I am continually amazed, ever astonished at the number of novice
commodity traders who fancy themselves as master escape artists,
seeking to accomplish *"The Great Escape"* from their status as *"wage
slaves."* Captured by the belief that the *"Great Pie in the Sky"* is
theirs, not by and by, but here and now, commodity trading for too
many becomes a narcotic, a drug to flee from the drudgery of their
Walter Mitty-type jobs. Even now, 24 million Americans, 25 percent
of all U.S. workers, are unhappy with their work. Most, who seek
refuge in the commodity markets, in their heart of hearts, know they
will lose. Their odds of success are less than 15%. They know that
67% of all new businesses fail by the fifth year. They are aware that
only 7% of today's work force is self-employed. Yet, in Las Vegas-
fashion, they believe they will be the *"one"* that *"hits the jackpot."*
They are *"closet"* entrepreneurs seeking the *"breakout."*

We have explored the environment which has given rise to the
tremendous interest in commodity trading. By next moving on to examine the *"nature of the beast,"* the entrepreneur, his role in society,
what motivates him, his characteristics, his strengths and weaknesses,
his contribution to society and his prospects for the future, we will

plow new ground. Some of what follows may cut to the quick, but such pain is always necessary for growth. And it is understanding and growth we should all be after. For, when we take this necessary growth path, we enhance our probability of long-term rewards.

I have long been fascinated with the human being who calls himself, or is considered by others to be, an entrepreneur. He is increasingly a vanishing breed in our security-oriented society. He is a *"rare breed of cat"* (7 percent of the work force). I belong to that den. You may, too, either by intellectual association, business or life-style, or as a commodity trader. I have yet to meet my first commodity trader who was not, at a minimum, a *"closet"* entrepreneur. I have written many times how critical it is that we have a handle on ourselves if we are to be successful trading commodities. We must understand ourselves better, not only so we have a chance of being successful in the commodity markets, but so that we can be more *"real,"* more rational, more patient, more discerning and more productive. We, thus, must understand our entrepreneurial spirit if we are to *"get it all together."*

Back in November, 1975, Albert Shapero wrote an enlightening piece, *"The Displaced, Uncomfortable Entrepreneur"* for PSYCHOLOGY TODAY. He made some interesting and helpful observations about the entrepreneurial *"breed of cat."* As a rule, entrepreneurs are displaced persons; they don't fit. They are, by and large, the rejects of an old establishment society, the dropouts, antisocial misfits, who could care less about what the masses of people think. They are almost rabid in their desire to be independent, autonomous, self-reliant and free from the control of others. Entrepreneurs have usually been failures in ventures earlier in life. They often do not catch fire until their late 30s and early 40s.

In their drive for the illusion of total freedom, entrepreneurs are, more often than not, blind to risk or view risk as minimal. (How many times have I seen this with commodity traders!) Because their motivational drive is primarily for independence, they tend to care little about money, and are basically indifferent about what money can buy. Money is a means to an end; the destination is absolute freedom.

Money is, however, a standard by which entrepreneurs gauge themselves against everyone else, the way they establish their self-worth.

Entrepreneurs usually have to borrow money. Nearly 90 percent of the financial resources utilized by entrepreneurs come from family and friends. (This is consistent with my observation of commodity traders' capital sources.) It is logical that entrepreneurs who care little about money, or are blind to risk, borrow money from others. Remember, too, they are not discouraged by earlier failures, either. Once we focus strongly on the reality that the primary drive of the entrepreneur is to be totally independent, we can readily see that money is simply a tool and a status symbol.

The entrepreneur is possessed by the desire to control the course of his own life, to be totally free from the control of others. As such, however, he must be individually responsible and dedicated. Entrepreneurs are not clock watchers. They work 14 hours a day, seven days a week. And they love it. Their work is their escape *and* their life. Their total freedom is their slavery to their work. This quickly distinguishes the commodity trading *"closet"* entrepreneur from the dilettante who is simply moving with the trading masses, flowing with the crowd, much like the mob in a casino.

There is tremendous irony; it is a remarkable paradox that entrepreneurs, the antisocial dropouts and rejects of society, are, in fact, the most creative members of society. It is they who bring changes, adaptations and seize the opportunities which allow society-at-large to progress. Richard Cornuelle, author of DE-MANAGING AMERICA, THE FINAL REVOLUTION (Random House) wrote *". . . society may be kept moving by its misfits—people who fail to respond to the expensive housebreaking procedures educators call 'socialization.'"*[20]

Entrepreneurs are misfits, exhibiting characteristics common to revolutionaries, musicians and poets. Because they are in many ways unemployable, they become self-employed. And, while being alienated from society, they are the creative engine that keeps society rolling. As Cornuelle also wrote, *". . . a society stays alive when it stays adaptable, and not because people learn to repeat established procedures with increasing efficiency."*[21]

Let's reflect a minute. With only 7 percent of our working force now self-employed, and with our society increasingly emphasizing security and *"established procedures with increasing efficiency,"* we must at least tentatively acknowledge that these circumstances are consistent with the end of a 510-year civilization cycle. At the end of this cycle, security is emphasized. Entrepreneurs and change are discouraged. History and cycles are square. They are in harmony.

Psychologist David McClelland who, along with Cornuelle, was cited in the November, 1975 PSYCHOLOGY TODAY, *". . . has shown that entire civilizations expand and contract, rise or fall, as a function of the 'entrepreneurial motive . . .'"*[22]

Because men are imperfect, men's view of the future is imperfect. Bureaucrats and civil servants in stuffy corporations and government agencies value security most of all. They avoid risk, promote the preservation of the status quo and consistently provide society with just more of the same goods and services. By contrast, the entrepreneur is creative. Only free men are creative. The entrepreneur rebuffs security and embraces risk. (A *"healthy"* entrepreneur will derive his sense of security from a positive father image or a *"heavenly"* Father.) He is future oriented and concentrates on outfoxing other entrepreneurs in anticipating the demand for the future goods and services which will be most desired. This is what entrepreneurial profit is all about—the correct anticipation of future needs. This is also what profit is all about in commodity futures trading—the accurate projection of commodity price movement in days to come. Both the entrepreneur and the commodity trader, in this sense, are one and the same. They are forced to deal with, and make assessments about, an uncertain future. This requires flexibility and a willingness to change as input and data become available which alters futuristic assessments.

A gambler at a casino and a *"flippant"* commodity trader have much in common, also. Neither calculates the cost of his actions. Both take excessive and unreasonable risks. By contrast, both entrepreneurs and professional commodity speculators attempt to reduce their exposure to the greatest degree possible so that future success may be assured.

If there is one thing history has taught us, it is that it is nearly impossible to guess from what source or sources creativity will spring in response to human needs. This is why government planning and control is so devastating to the welfare of a people long-term. Government stifles creative thinking, freedom, independent action and personal use of property. Government is primarily made up of people who desire security first and foremost. Security is the opposite of, and therefore antagonistic to, creative risk taking. So, government encourages stagnation which, in an ever-changing world that demands continual adaptation, is the death knell for society. This is why all great civilizations fall when their governments become fully developed.

Government is contrary to natural law. The entrepreneur is in harmony with natural law. In this country, we are just now coming back to the truth of Say's Law of Markets which states effectively that supply creates its own demand. Man has unknown wants and desires. Because the majority of people are uncreative, how will they know what they really want and/or need by way of goods and services unless a large variety is offered to them by the marketplace? An undifferentiated, pervasive, non-homogenous, all-encompassing supply of goods and services become available to consumers under free market conditions. Such variety demands innovation and creativity by entrepreneurs. Government vies with the entrepreneur for resources. With the growth of government comes increased taxation, controls and inflation, all of which rob the entrepreneur of resources which could have been more efficiently used in supplying innumerable goods and services for society.

Just look at the Soviet Union. There we find the same old *"sixes and sevens,"* the same standard, dull consumer goods. No new products, no new services are offered. Just economic stagnation. And, as we well know, we find few entrepreneurs in the U.S.S.R. either. They steal their technology from us. Say is correct; supply creates demand.

Entrepreneurs, in the process of providing goods and services, hire employees who then use their wages, their purchasing power, to buy the infinite variety of goods and services. This process, left unrestricted, leads to widespread wealth and prosperity. The ultimate sources of all wealth, raw materials and human creativity, are allowed to find their highest and best use in the free market. And, men are forced, by contract, to act responsibly for the best interest of all parties involved. The smaller companies, organized by entrepreneurs, create 80 percent of all new jobs in our society. They also account for 80 percent of all the major new innovations.

Entrepreneurs, operating in the free market, are forced, long-term, to be moral, to operate consistent with long-term principles. Many times I have written that the key to business success long-term is found by embracing the principle, *"Self-interest is best served by service."* In his recent best seller, WEALTH AND POVERTY, George Gilder wrote that capitalism was based upon giving and generosity. Free enterprise is others-oriented. This is exactly what I have been saying and writing for years. It is, furthermore, consistent with the Christian business ethics upon which our society was founded: *"Give, and it shall be given unto you; . . ."* (Luke 6:38) *"It is more blessed to give than to receive."* (Acts 20:35) Perhaps now we can better understand why the United States of America is unique in history. In this country, long-term, abstract, true religious principles were historically consistent with short-term, concrete actions of men. American free enterprise economics was the outworking of Christian free enterprise principles. Men gave in order to receive.

It is no accident that with the demise of religious principles, there has been the compensating growth of government. Government regulations fill the vacuum of former moral, self-regulation and free enterprise *"win-win"* contracting. And, as business has increasingly taken on an irresponsible, short-term, selfish perspective, so it has built for itself the prison of government regulations and controls, with all that goes along with it—decreasing freedom, stifled creativity, higher costs, diminished wealth, and economic stagnation.

A society can get by, even if it has a substandard physical resource base. History has documented this truth many times for us. But, when a country stifles, subdues and squashes its creative and inventive entrepreneurs, it has chosen the road to ruin regardless of its wealth of natural resources. Human ingenuity must put these resources to good use. And this is exactly what entrepreneurs do. Bad weather and negative climatic changes aggravate a poor economic situation in a society. This is a part of the problem we face presently. Thus, we now need entrepreneurs more than ever before.

We have seen the *"blessing of the curse,"* the fact that these social rejects, these dropouts (curse), are the creative hubs of a society's economic advancement (blessing). Looking behind the *"blessing"* of the entrepreneur's creative and productive function, what is the spark that drives him to creative freedom? From whence springs his motivation? What tension gives rise to the entrepreneur's inventiveness, creativity and productivity in his march to become independent and totally free? Some religious leaders say it is the sin nature—the desire to be as God, free of God's law. Some sociologists say it is a lust for power; some economists say it is pure greed. Psychologists give two reasons: (1) It is the fear of authority or the fear of the abuse of authority; (2) It is a sense of unworthiness which inhibits the entrepreneur's ability to give or receive love. Entrepreneurs are terribly competitive. All competition is generated by a need for love. This fear of authority/lack of love complex goes hand-in-hand, for it is in childhood that the entrepreneurial seeds are planted. It is during the vulnerability of early youth that this male child learns that the world is threatening, unloving. During this time, he also associates abusive authority with lack of love. And, whether the small boy was a bastard, an orphan, neglected by his father, or subjected to the discipline and harsh authority of a cold, unloving father, makes no difference. The lack of love and resultant fear of authority is deeply imprinted. This brand on the boy's soul has left its mark. In 60 percent of all cases, the primary influence on the entrepreneur is the father. *"Healthy"* entrepreneurs had exemplary fathers, or good surrogate fathers, or a loving *"heavenly"* Father.

As the result of deep emotional scars, many entrepreneurs go through life building incredibly complex defenses. What a paradox. Tremendous internal turmoil produces vital external fruits which benefit society generally, particularly those who are not too close to the entrepreneur.

Dr. Arthur Janov, in his book, THE PRIMAL SCREAM (Dell Publishing Co., Inc., New York, 1970), shed some important light on this entrepreneurial discussion:

> *"A loved child is one whose natural needs are fulfilled. Love takes his pain away. An unloved child is one who hurts because he is unfulfilled. A loved child has no need for praise because he has*

not been denigrated. He is valued for what he is, not for what he can do to satisfy his parents' needs. . . .

"Unfulfilled needs supersede any other activity in the human until they are met. When needs are met, the child can feel. He can experience his body and his environment. When needs are not met, the child experiences only tension, . . .

"The attempt of the child to please his parents I call the struggle. The struggle begins first with parents and later generalizes to the world. It spreads beyond the family because the person carries his deprived needs with him wherever he goes, and those needs must be acted out. . . .

"The fascination of seeing our names in lights or on the printed page is but one indication of the deprivation in many of us of individual recognition. Those achievements, no matter how real, serve as a symbolic quest for parental love. Pleasing an audience becomes the struggle.

"Struggle is what keeps a child from feeling his hopelessness. It lies in overwork, in slaving for high grades, in being the performer . . ."

In a few paragraphs, Janov has written more than a mouthful, pregnant with implications for today's entrepreneurs, fragmented families, social instability, tension in business, as well as the need for recognition by politicians. We could almost conclude that those who are driven to be politicians, who desperately need to be politicians, shouldn't be. How can they represent us objectively when they are still busy working out their own problems, when their own basic needs are unfulfilled. Should we loan them our money to build empires?

Back to what Janov said concerning entrepreneurs, *"Struggle is what keeps a child from feeling his hopelessness. It lies in overwork, . . ."* And just what were our earlier outlined characteristics of entrepreneurs? Working long hours, fourteen hours a day, seven days a week, and never knowing what time it is. Work for the entrepreneur is *"The Great Escape."* The entrepreneur always has his motor running. He is driven. His productive output is the result of the pressure, tension and conflict of internally unresolved needs! While some find their emotional release in sex, alcohol, performances, lectures, athletics, and outright hostility, the entrepreneur simply works—hard! He runs from the pain of a lack of love to the one thing he does well and is rewarded (loved) for—work!

Arthur M. Louis, in his book, HOW AMERICA'S MOST SUCCESSFUL EXECUTIVES GET TO THE TOP (Simon and Schuster) outlined the characteristics of tycoons/entrepreneurs. They are: (1) Workaholics, with no regard for weak subordinates or their health; (2) Exceptionally energetic; (3) Motivated more by power than money;

(4) Incredibly competitive; (5) Highly inquisitive and intelligent; and (6) Marked by an uneasy ability to bounce back from adversity which would have destroyed most other investors.

How important is love? Scientists have discovered that monkeys, when raised in isolation are socially inept, a characteristic of the entrepreneur. Monkeys, when deprived of their mothers, tend to be apathetic, hyperactive and given to violent outbursts. Again, we find some of the characteristics of the entrepreneurs. (The young in the animal kingdom depend upon mothers, not fathers.) Diet-induced heart disease in rabbits has been reduced by handling and petting, in order words, by love.

The central demand of the body is to be felt, to be loved. The wise Victor Hugo noted that we need affirmation more than bread. The missionary Mother Teresa wrote, *"At the hour of death, when we come face-to-face with God, we are going to be judged on love—not how much we have done, but how much love we have put into our actions."*. . . *"God is love."* (I John 4:8)

Doron P. Levin, a WALL STREET JOURNAL reporter, quoted Fred Rogers of the television program, *"Mr. Rogers' Neighborhood,"* as saying, *"The root of all competition is the need to be loved. We need to know we are lovable and capable of loving."* Fred Rogers went on to add, *"That, by the way, is the bottom line of all labor-management relations."* David Seabury said effectively the same thing in his book, THE ART OF SELFISHNESS, wherein he observed that the two basic principles of human relations are: (1) No ego satisfaction, and (2) Never compromise yourself.

I sum up good human relations in one word—*empathy,* being able to see the problems or viewpoints through the other man's eyes, being able to walk a mile in another man's moccasins. In terms of justice, this empathetic principle is clearly communicated by The Golden Rule: *"Do unto others as you would have them do unto you."* (A verbal rearrangement of Matthew 7:12). The social application of this emphathetic principle is, *"Thou shalt love thy neighbor as thyself."* (Matthew 19:19) We win by giving.

This obsession with work by entrepreneurs has its counterpart among commodity traders who drown themselves in the market. I'd hate to count the number of commodity traders I've known who are always seeking to find some new and creative analytical technique that will provide them with *"the key"* to the market, *"The Holy Grail."* These commodity traders, like entrepreneurs, must always be busy, researching some system. They cannot stop. They dare not stop. They are compulsive and unreal. The truth is, they cannot face the pain of being unloved that comes with idleness.

And what about pride, the tremendous pride which is *"a,"* if not *"the,"* major part of the makeup of many entrepreneurs and commodity traders. Often have I written that for too many commodity traders, it is far more important to be correct than it is to make money. This is pride in action. Regarding pride, Dr. Janov wrote,

> *"Pride is the unreal self succeeding. Pride is a nonfeeling. It is pointing to something, some act, which, often unconsciously, makes 'them' proud. It is the performances for them. Feeling people do not need a performance in order to feel. . . . The need remains constant. What we do as we grow older is spin ever-widening circles of defenses around the need until we are lost in a maze of symbolic activities."*

Entrepreneurs are known for their symbolic idiosyncrasies. Max Gunther in his book, THE VERY, VERY, RICH AND HOW THEY GOT THAT WAY (Playboy Press, Chicago, 1973), made a detailed study of the super rich. Gunther also noted that entepreneurs are misfits, dropouts and social rejects. Gunther quoted Dr. Paul Feldman, a New Jersey school psychologist, who wrote, " *'The most successful adults, at least in terms of our current money-oriented standards of success, are often men and women who, as students, made the least favorable impression on their classmates. These are the classroom's social misfits, the shy and the awkward, the 'oddballs' and the 'weirdos'. . . .' "*

Psychologists, including Sigmund Freud, have noted that the design of the very, very rich to accumulate material things stems from a fear of loss. This need for possessions, and the fear of losing them, springs from their insecurity, lack of love and fear of authority. It leads to exercised tight control by the entrepreneur over his life, business and possessions.

Earlier we observed that the primary influence on the entrepreneur is the father. Gunther remarked, *"It is not a statistical accident that all the very, very rich individuals in this gallery are men."* Regarding child-parent problems, Gunther wrote,

> *"Looking over our gilded gallery, it's remarkable how many of these stupendously successful men lost one or both parents early in life through death or divorce. More than half of them, in fact, went through that wounding experience. . . ."*

These very, very rich entrepreneurs did not enjoy the love and security in early life which comes with a strong family, headed by a caring father. Gunther continued,

> *"Three college professors—David Moore of Cornell, Orvis Collins and Darab Unwalla of Michigan State—went out and interviewed the 'founding entrepreneurs' of 110 companies. 'The*

*theme of parental death crops up repeatedly,' they reported in
their book, THE ENTERPRISING MAN. 'The picture that
comes through from the interviews is one of the lonely child,
grubby fists in tear-filled eyes, accepting the loss and facing a
dangerous future . . . '*

"*Why does the death or going away of a parent make a
youngster start out to become wealthy? The three researchers suggest a couple of possibilities. One is that the bereaved child from
then on has a massive sense of insecurity. He sets out to get so
much money that he can never be left stranded again. Another
possibility is that the loss of a parent makes him more than
usually self-reliant. In trying to heal his emotional wound, he con-
vinces himself that he doesn't really need the parent; he can hack
it on his own . . .*"

Gunther further learned that half of his very, very rich *"supermen"*
were high school dropouts and only a third finished college.

"*In a classic statistical study of 600 millionaires in 1925,
sociologist Pitirim Sorokin found to his surprise that only 11.7
percent had college degrees.*"

This composite of the entrepreneur as a social misfit, a displaced person, holds true down through the generations. It likewise speaks to the
maverick nature of commodity traders today particularly, and in years
gone by. The sins of the fathers apparently are visited upon the sons.

We have seen that entrepreneurs (commodity traders) were unloved
children in many cases. And, as the *"sins of the father are visited
upon the sons,"* so to speak, one would expect these very, very rich
men to, in turn, have great difficulty loving their wives and children.
Such would be consistent with our profile of such an entrepreneur.
Gunther wrote:

"*Pitirim Sorokin was also struck by the fact that, among his
600 millionaires, divorce was statistically twice as common as in
the general U.S. population . . . The rich seemed to have more
marriage and sex problems than other people . . .*

"*The men in our gallery faithfully follow the trend. Half have
been divorced as least once.*

"*. . . self-made rich men often have a peculiar lack of warmth,
an inability to form a close, lasting relationship with man, woman
or child.*"

Dr. Alfred E. Messer, a professor at Emory University in Atlanta,
Georgia, and chief of the Georgia Mental Health Institute's Family
Studies Laboratory has declared:

" *'The man's childhood is likely to have been rough. The
typical story is that of a parent dying or going away or—what
amounts to the same thing—rejecting the child, abandoning him*

emotionally. The child grows up with the understandable feeling that he can't rely on other people; he must prove himself worthy by himself. He seeks to prove it with money . . . .' "

It is apparent now why entrepreneurs often have unsuccessful marriages. It is also obvious that these very, very rich men are, in compensating manner, very, very poor emotionally. In fact, many are unable to enjoy their wealth. So, the very, very rich escape to their work. Gunther wrote:

"For a worship of work, an absolute love of it, is notable among the shared traits of the great self-made rich. . . .

"The rich work—either because they enjoy it or because they feel driven to it. Many of them admit quite frankly that their compulsion to work has destroyed their marriages and hurt their relationships with their children and perhaps damaged other components of their personal lives. They sometimes talk about this in a sad and apologetic way, but they always end with a shrug. There's nothing they can do about it. Work is part of their being. They can no more easily change their work habits than they can change the color of their eyes."

Is there a way to maintain, as David McClelland put it, the *"entrepreneurial motive,"* which provides the progressive spark for society, and yet neutralize many entrepreneur's self-destructive tendency? A perspective on self-destruction is critically important.

Beyond a shadow of a doubt, the greatest tendency I have noticed among commodity traders throughout the years is the tendency to self-destruct. This is the negative side of that entrepreneurial drive and motivation to be independent which, in our society, is a status reserved for the very rich. To understand how we get off this vicious merry-go-round, we must focus on the father, our individual fathers, and ourselves as fathers.

Our society doesn't think much of fathers. In fact, it outright attacks them, despite the fact that men are always the source of upward mobility in any society. It is the men who lead the group from poverty, as George Gilder (WEALTH AND POVERTY) has clearly pointed out. Men in all societies do most of the economic providing. With hope for the future (children), they sacrifice short-term for their families' welfare long-term. This leads to economic progress and stability. Matriarchal societies have never been in the forefront of highly developed civilizations. How can they be when, in a matriarchal society, men fail to exercise their leadership so that women are forced to assume the males' responsibility in addition to their own. Men with the focus of leadership and saddled with the burden of responsibility have deep roots in our country. In our earlier history, only men could own property and only men could vote. The importance of a man as the head of the household is even more deeply rooted in our Christian culture, going back to the patriarchs of the Old Testament of the Bible. How far we have come from this tradition is clearly seen by the fact that many of the *"modernists"* want to take the masculine emphasis *"He"* out of the Bible.

Fathers, though many may not know it, stand as the sentries against the onslaught of atheism, communism and socialism. Communism, when it takes over a country, attacks families. By destroying families, communism destroys authority and thus can establish *"equality"* (mediocrity). When children are raised in families, particularly families headed by fathers, there is inequality. Father rules the roost. Today the attack on fathers comes with the ERA, *"kiddie lib,"* etc.

Sex as liberty rather than as a responsible act within the family is another attack on the father-headed home. At least 40 percent of all U.S. marriages now end in divorce due to sexual pressures, the equal rights movement and inflationary pressures which, in many cases, force the wife and mother out of the home to help make ends meet.

The idea that *"all men are brothers"* is a primary concept used by communists against fathers. If *"all men are brothers,"* then there is no need for distinct father-headed families. And, further, if *"all men are brothers,"* what belongs to one belongs to everyone. So there is no need for property rights either (or marriage, for that matter).

The basic unit of government in our country used to be the husband and father at the head of a united household. A working father and a mother at home with children, once the typical American family, now makes up only 7% of all American families. One of the father's primary responsibilities was education of the children. This role has been gutted by the public school system. Women teachers are thus forced to play the role of men, with the main casualty being the male student who has a poor, or no, masculine example. Boys who are dominated by women tend to become effeminate, and when full-grown, are more interested in approval from those they are leading, rather than in respect for doing the right thing. (Jimmy Carter?) It boils down to character and a long-term view versus a pragmatic, short-term one.

The inheritance tax destroys a family continuity from generation to generation. Property taxes disrupt family roots. The incredible mobility of our society is an added negative in this regard, too. For it takes, on average, three generations for a family's perspective to crystalize. Arthur Kornhaber and Kenneth L. Woodward, in their book, GRANDPARENTS AND GRANDCHILDREN, discussed how the grandparent bond to grandchildren is second only to the parental bond. So called indifference by grandchildren to grandparents has been found, in fact, to be suppressed rage.

Court rulings, particularly on the federal level recently, have effectively castrated the father's authority over his children. Welfare destroys families in that it effectively tells a father that he is unnecessary, that he cannot or does not have the ability to provide for his family. This degradation has destroyed the poor, but previously strong, black families in America's ghettos.

And yet, when we get down to basic reality, unless there is a father, there is no family. The father is biologically the instigator of the family, the life source. From this basic reality stems fatherly responsibility, authority, love and basic family government, which provides family identity, security, protection and provision.

Ever wonder about the increasing homosexuality and suicide among the young in our society? If homosexuality is so *"natural,"* why are there so many more homosexuals today than there were 50 years ago? Psychologist after psychologist has observed that male homosexuals did not have good father images. Some psychologists have gone so far as to state that they have never observed a case of homosexuality where a son had a warm, loving relationship with his father. Also, continually emerging among girls and young women who commit suicide is the fact that they did not have a continuous, consistent relationship with their fathers.

The May 14, 1981, WALL STREET JOURNAL featured *"Losing the Way: Teenage Suicide Toll Points Up the Dangers of Growing Up Rich."* This article discussed how a man's success is detrimental if it comes at the expense of time that should have been spent with his children. Children can tell what their parents think is important. If the children are put on the back burner, they cause heartache down the line. Children put under excessive parental stress to achieve or become successful find a release through sex, alcohol and drugs. Sex and cults are poor substitutes for a lack of intimacy, belonging and structure at home.

One thing we can say for sure about our society is that our fractured families are breeding an overabundance of potential entrepreneurs, for better or for worse. Can we now more fully appreciate the social waves which will be created as these insecure youths move into adulthood and clash head-on with an entrenched bureaucratic, stifling, mediocre establishment? Children who are not trained to respect and obey authority become adults who are practical anarchists. In the final analysis, they cannot even command themselves. This family/father breakdown occurs near the end of a civilization. As I wrote in CYCLES OF WAR (page 103):

"*. . . Toward the end of the Hellenistic Age, there was no greater revolution in Rome than that of women's rights. In the Second Century B.C., they became emancipated in every way, including economically. The United States' declaration that all men are created equal in term of practical ability excluded women. Apparently, the difference in essence was enough. The growing role of women in the United States has led to many changes in public opinion, including the following: the desire for freedom to be replaced by security, the tendency to focus on the child and the youth worship syndrome, the suspicion of individualism, the desire to avoid risk and the emotional personalization of issues. In Rome, the increasing voice of women in formulating public opinion resulted in the establishment of a virile Caesar. Masses of people, such as are found in the cities of the United States today, display the emotionalism collectively that is common to women. They must instinctively look for compensating, masculine leadership which cannot be found in a congress but in a Caesar.*"

Put bluntly, the compensation for effeminate men, for irresponsible fathers who burden women with a double workload, is found ultimately in a virile Caesar who usurps responsibility, and that which is commensurate with responsibility—freedom. A society's freedom rests upon the shoulders of its men. Walk around any park. The statues and monuments are almost always tributes to men.

We have come full cycle to the maturity of our civilization. One sign of its demise is the fragmentation of the classic family and demasculinization of fathers. This has created tremendous insecurity, loneliness and distrust of authority in our love-starved youth. Reaping what we sow, these very entrepreneurial, revolutionary, poetic and artistic youth may vent their anger on our institutions which have not provided for their needs, and whose rigidity will be unable to cope with their creative anger.

What do we do, me and thee? The first step in solving a problem is its recognition. We have recognized the entrepreneurial problem, dissected it, and discussed its many ramifications for our way of life. We now have more comprehensive knowledge. The second thing that we must do, individually, as entrepreneurs and as commodity traders, is overcome it and forgive our fathers—totally. We, individually, must grant each of our personal fathers a blanket pardon for being imperfect, for not loving us enough, for being too harsh, for working all of the time, for having other priorities, for divorcing our mothers, for not spending enough time with us, for dying too soon—for any and all reasons he failed us. We must forgive him for being human. With this forgiveness comes a tremendous release of tension. Forgiveness puts out the fire of internal turmoil and is one of the kindest manifestations of love.

Modern medicine has taught us that tension and internal friction kills. It shortens life. One of the Ten Commandments is, *"Honour thy father and mother: that thy days may be long upon the land which the Lord thy God giveth thee."* (Exodus 20:12) True honour includes the type of respect which leaves no room for the hostility, resentment and bitterness that sons harbor toward their fathers as a result of their weaknesses and failings. We see here the connection between the principle of forgiveness and long life in families. Looking forward to our own sons and daughters, we, as fathers, do not want to repeat the mistakes that our fathers made with us. That we will err in a similar way, in a twisted bit of irony, is highly likely. Fathers often find themselves repeating the same mistakes with their own children that their fathers made with them. It's hard to break that old entrenched pattern. *"The sins of the father are visited upon the sons."* Fathers have incredible influence. They are so important. In looking through STRONG'S EXHAUSTIVE CONCORDANCE OF THE BIBLE, I found almost 1,700 individual references to fathers. And the liberal-types want to take the masculine emphasis out of the Bible?

For those who are unpersuaded by the psychosomatic and religious argument, and fancy themselves as more practical and pragmatic, consider this: In this life, we reap what we sow. Our commodity account teaches us that regularly. Who is going to take care of us in our old age now that the postwar baby boom is behind us and the U.S. population is aging? Who will tend to our needs during the wintertime of our lives with the Social Security System bankrupt? The federal government? How? Or, perhaps more to the point, will there even be a federal government to take care of us when we join the elderly? Is it not logical to recognize that the best investment that any of us can make for our old age is our children. It is also a fair and just swap. We took care of them when they were young. They assume the responsibility for us when we are old. Turnabout is fair play, or should I say, fair trade. Can't have children? Adopt some.

Is it possible to train up secure, loving and caring children who still have the creative energy and innovation to be successful entrepreneurs? Sure. Our great grandfathers did it. The technique was known as apprenticeship. Men were craftsmen. Master craftsmen trained their young apprentices. These young apprentices, in time, matured to be craftsmen in their own right—successful, prosperous, and well-balanced entrepreneurs. They were creative, building upon the heritage which preceded them. Social stability was ensured. Family ties were maintained.

Now, there is no arguing the fact that the *"good old days are gone,"* and that such balance between entrepreneurial creativity and security is difficult to establish in today's world. But, where there is a will, there is a way. Modern technology, computers and satellites are making radical decentralization again possible, whereby the future work unit may again be the family in its home! Providing a loving and instructive environment for our children is a very secure one in which creative thinking and education can be carried out. After all, fathers, it is our responsibility. And we are without excuse. I have often observed that the greatest blessing a son can have is a just, loving and instructive father.

It's tough in this world, with pressures on all sides, to maintain balance in our male roles as husbands, fathers and leaders. Each of us has different weaknesses, different pitfalls, that tend to capture all our time. The tyranny of the urgent is always with us. I tend to fall into a Type-A workaholic pattern. In order to beat it, I build in some controls that bounce me back when I get too far off center. The two best controls I have found personally are embodied in the lyrics of two songs—*"Cat's in the Cradle"* by the late Harry Chapin and *"Absentee Fathers"* by Rock Killough. I hope that the words of these two thoughtful men will be as helpful to you as they have been to me. For, no matter how far afield I go, the lyrics to these two songs always stop me dead in my tracks and bring me home to where the heart is.

"Cat's in the Cradle," by Harry Chapin. "Harry Chapin: Greatest Stories Live" album. (Elektra Records, 962 North La Cienega Blvd., Los Angeles, California 90069, 1976, Story Songs Ltd., New York, NY.)

A child arrived just the other day.
He came to the world in the usual way.
But, there were planes to catch and bills to pay.
He learned to walk while I was away.
And he was talking before I knew it, and as he grew,
He'd say, "I'm going to be like you, Dad.
You know I'm going to be like you."

Chorus
And the cat's in the cradle and a silver spoon
Little Boy Blue and the Man in the Moon.
"When you coming home Dad?" "I don't know when.
But, we'll get together then, Son.
You know we'll have a good time then."

Well, my son turned ten just the other day.
He said, "Thanks for the ball, Dad. Come on let's play.
Can you teach me to throw?" I said, "Not today.

I've got a lot to do." He said, "That's OK."
And he walked away but his smile never thinned and said,
"I'm going to be like him.
You know I'm going to be like him."

Chorus (repeat)

Well he came from college just the other day,
So much like a man I just had to say,
"Son, I'm proud of you. Can you sit for awhile?"
He shook his head, and he said with a smile,
"What I'd really like Dad is to borrow the car keys.
See you later. Can I have them please?"

Chorus

And the cat's in the cradle and a silver spoon
Little Boy Blue and the Man in the Moon.
"When you coming home, Son?" "I don't know when.
But, we'll get together then, Dad.
You know we'll have a good time then."

Well, I've long since retired. My son's moved away.
I called him up just the other day.
I said, "I'd like to see you if you don't mind."
He said, "I'd love to Dad if I could find the time.
You see my new job's a hassle and the kids have the flu.
But, it's sure nice talking to you, Dad.
It's been sure nice talking to you."
And as he hung up the phone, it occurred to me,
He'd grown up just like me.
My boy was just like me . . .

"Absentee Fathers" by Rock Killough, "Killough & Eckley" album.
(Epic Records/CBS, Inc., 51 W. 52nd Street, New York, NY 1977,
Tree Publishing, Nashville, TN)

You absentee fathers
You follow tradition
The fires of ambition will carry you far
Far from the laughing
Far from the crying
Far from knowing your children.

You're living in Eden
The Garden of Eden
Where love springs forth every day
But in your search for power

That poisonous flower
Your sons get left by the way

Chorus
Oh where is the father
The old-fashioned father
The kind who stands by the door
A compassionate sentry
Who guards the main entry
His children are his treasure
His business is his chore.

Your business is calling
Your credibility falling
So you bribe your family once more
As you fight for position
A sinister sedition
Your daughter don't know what fathers are for.

Chorus (repeat)

You absentee fathers
You slaves of tradition
Yes, the fires of ambition will carry you far
Far from the sowing
Far from the growing
And far from knowing your children.

*   *   *

"The successful entrepreneur is driven not so much by greed as by the desire to create. He has more in common with the artist than with the bureaucrat. His principal satisfaction comes not from his bank balance but from the jobs he provides and the benefits he spreads through his products and services. No other economic system so amply furnishes these spiritual rewards and incentives; hence the moral virtues of capitalism, which are intrinsic, greatly outweigh its vices, which are remediable."

Source: THE FREEMAN, 30 South Broadway,
Irvington-on-Hudson, N.Y. 10533

*   *   *

The number of craftsmen diminish proprotionally with the increasing age of a civilization. As a civilization matures, it becomes increasingly short-term oriented. With this short-term perspective, the civilization has no need for craftsmen who are blessed with a long-term perspective. Craftsmen and a long-term view are one and the same. Craftsmen make products that last.

This says a great deal about our society. The short useful life of our manufacturered goods is a reflection of the short-term perspective of our people.

* * *

"Criticism comes easier than craftsmanship."

Zeuxis

* * *

"Unemployed purchasing power means unemployed labor, and unemployed labor means human want in the midst of plenty."

Henry Agard Wallace

* * *

"Life has no meaning except in terms of responsibility."

Reinhold Niebuhr

* * *

"It is worthwhile for anyone to have behind him a few generations of honest, hardworking ancestry."

John Phillips Marquand

A Father's Prayer

Build me a son, O Lord, who will be strong enough to know when he is weak, and brave enough to face himself when he is afraid; one who will be proud and unbending in honest defeat and humble and gentle in victory.

Build me a son whose wishbone will not be where his backbone should be; a son who will know thee and that to know himself is the foundation stone of knowledge.

Lead him I pray, not in the path of ease and comfort, but under the stress and spur of difficulties and challenge. Here let him learn to stand up in the storm; here let him learn compassion for those who fail.

Build me a son whose heart will be clean, whose goal will be high, a son who will master himself before he seeks to master other men; one who will learn to laugh, yet never forget how to weep; one who will reach into the future, yet never forget the past.

And after all these things are his, add, I pray, enough of a sense of humor, so that he may always be serious, yet never take himself too seriously. Give him humility, so that he may always remember the simplicity of true greatness, the open mind of true wisdom, the meekness of true strength.

Then, I, his father, will dare to whisper, "I have not lived in vain."

Anonymous

*　　　*　　　*

The creativity and productivity of the entrepreneur is a tremendous source of blessing for society. The curse of entrepreneurship, however, must be kept in check by the abolition of debt capitalism. Reestablishing free enterprise, whereby entrepreneurs are financed, not by debt, but by partnerships, joint ventures and issues of stock provides for both *"the greatest good for the greatest number"* and the entrepreneur long-term. By this means, *"Wealth for All"* is equitably distributed throughout society, and human checks and balances are maintained.

DEPRESSION REFLECTION

5/21/82

Frustration turned outward is anger. Frustration turned inward is depression. Anger usually precedes depression.

The American public was frustrated by inflation during the 1970s. The masses expressed this frustration in anger as manifested by the torrid pace of economic activity in the 1970s. Everyone, seemingly, angrily competed with everyone else in an attempt to beat inflation. Exhaustion finally set in.

With exhaustion, the frustration changed from outward anger to inward depression. When consumers eventually reach the point that they feel there is *"no hope,"* complete internal depression will trigger an external one, since consumer spending makes up two-thirds of GNP. Depression is the most common psychiatric disorder today.

Consumer credit is economic suicide. It is the primary contributor to the boom/bust cycle. Just like driver's licenses are not issued to children, so should not consumer credit, particularly when it's activated by the multiplier effect through our fractional reserve banking system and use of credit cards, be extended to the general consuming public, who have little or no economic and financial acumen. The general public creates its own misery through the boom/bust cycle of greed and fear, first over borrowing and overspending, then hoarding and overconserving.

A generation is 25 years. The boom/bust cycle takes 50 years, hitting three generations. Sons remember the lessons of their fathers. But grandsons do not learn the lessons that grandfathers taught their sons. Thus, it takes three generations to forget the lessons of a depression and commit the same folly all over again. Therefore, the 50-year, three generation economic cycle from bust to boom to bust exists. The grandsons, whose grandfathers went through the Great Depression, know little of it. The grandsons' economic ignorance is compounded by the fact that we no longer have multigenerational families, where grandfathers teach valuable economic lessons to grandsons.

TIME AND CHANCE

6/4/82

Edward R. Dewey, founder of the Foundation for the Study of Cycles, wrote,

> *"Anyone who starts out in business without knowing what time it is on the economic clock will obviously owe much to luck if he succeeds. And many men who have engaged successfully in business for a long time owe much to their sheer good fortune in having started out when the economic sun was rising."*

Elaborating on Mr. Dewey's controversial statement, I have written,

> *"Most men are successful because they are lucky. (This includes yours truly.) They fall in line with destiny. They catch the primary, rising 'human need tide' and ride that economic trend for all it's worth. Sure, they work hard, beat the competition, pay attention to detail, satisfy human wants and profit. They are, however, by and large, only slightly smarter than the average man. They are just more creative in their field. And they are, in most cases, more narrow intellectually in their perspective. They only know their business, little else. Wisdom is often lacking. This is why intellectuals often despise businessmen. To many intellectuals, businessmen are dumb and don't deserve their elevated economic status. This is one reason why university professors are often 'down' on business."*

I have often discussed how my contact with self-made millionaire businessmen was consistent with Dewey's observation and historical business reality.

It has been brought to my attention that in *Ecclesiastes* (in the Old Testament of the Bible) in Chapter 9, verse 11, the *"Preacher"* wrote,

> *"I returned, and saw under the sun, that the race is not to the swift, nor the battle to the strong, neither yet bread to the wise, nor yet riches to men of understanding, nor yet favor to men of skill; but time and chance happeneth to them all." (KJV)*

Now being thoughtful men and prudent investors, it seems wise that we reflect upon the consistency of my observations, Edward R. Dewey's comments and the words of the writer of *Ecclesiastes*. The distinguishing difference in *Ecclesiastes* is that no cyclical anchor is

230

mentioned. Nevertheless, all of us have said much the same thing in our own words over a wide span of historical time. When what I consider to be one of my more important observations lines up with the likes of Dewey and *Ecclesiastes*, I give some serious thought to the matter. *"Time and chance happeneth to them all."* The swift don't win races. The strong don't triumph in battles. Men of understanding don't get rich. . . . Such alarming statements require us to think through our perceptions of reality and the resultant structuring of our personal and business endeavors.

The writer of *Ecclesiastes* was, of course, referring to *"time and chance"* being superior to the machinations and best laid plans of mice and men. Edward R. Dewey echoed this *"time and chance"* theme somewhat in his discussion on business activity. Dewey's anchor was cycles. I, too, affirmed both *"time and chance"* and cycles based upon my research, observations and experience. In thinking all of this through, in terms of meaningful application for us, I have concluded that I have stumbled upon what seems to be the two touchstones of humanism, *"time and chance."* It is also the essence of evolution, when it is established as basic reality and a sovereign God is dismissed.

Let's take another hard look at *"time."* While *"time"* is inescapably involved in everything we do, and influences our chosen activity dramatically, we seldom contemplate *"time."* We are conscious of *"time"* but not *"time"* aware, at least in a declarative, philosophical sense. We feel the pressure of the concrete limitations of *"time"* in the daily rat race of going to and from work, carrying out our business activities, investing our money and winding up the day at a decent hour. But the critical perspective on where we stand in historical *"time,"* the elements of *"time,"* and the long-term view of *"time"* escape us. We are a society wrapped up and preoccupied with the *"urgent"* while the *"important"* passes us by. It is all part and parcel of the subjectivity which dominates our society, an emotional preoccupation with self which leads to a myopic viewpoint. We, collectively, aggressively resist progress. Governments at all levels, that so dominate our society, fight to maintain the status quo. Governments resist change. The bureaucrats which dominate government and the people which are supportive of big government are risk avoiders. Events in future *"time"* could be different from events in the present or past. This is unknown and frightening territory. It involves risk. Risk is the antithesis of security. Big government's (and big business') first and foremost activity these days is to provide for the security of the future. Thus, government's goals are antagonistic to progressive and risk-filled change in future *"time."* So, governments attempt to stop the clock.

This attempt to stop *"time"* pervades our culture in many ways. Women use cosmetics, have face lifts and color their hair to disguise the aging process. In so doing, they attempt to stop *"time."* Our emphasis on youth and our throwaway society which puts a premium on exercise, diet, new cars, new houses, new clothes and new friends, all are a reflection of the rejection of the old in a desperate attempt to stop *"time."*

Our growing infatuation with Far East religions and the *"Great Circle"* concept is another manifestation of our collective resistance to on-marching *"time."* After all, if life is simply one eternal cycle, one *"Great Circle,"* then effectively there can be no progress. So, we all might as well spend our time under shade trees smoking peace pipes. Life has no meaning. History has no meaning. Any changes we make are temporal at best, since we all come back around to the same starting point in the *"Great Circle."* No wonder societies which embrace the *"Great Circle"* view of *"time"* never progress meaningfully. Progress is, to them, intellectually futile and practically impossible.

A very few members of our culture think a great deal about *"time."* Society-at-large does not embrace the concept of *"time."* Only in the investment community and academic circles do we find a small subculture that considers *"time"* important. Those in the investment arena, who actively think about the philosophical and subsequent applied aspect of *"time"* to investments and society, are only a small microcosm of the investment community. The same is true for academic circles. Regrettably, those who think on *"time"* are an unheard of, and a numerically insignificant, minority in our society. How many people who, in and of themselves, while making history, think consciously of how events occur in *"time?"* How many market analysts and investors are conscious of the *"time"* element of their investment decisions? They contemplate *"price."* By focusing on events and price, and ignoring *"time,"* these folks ignore 50 percent of the parameters which make up the total package of *"time and price"* and *"events in history."* How can decisions be accurately made when 50 percent of the perceptional framework is missing? In fact, this is what our society does when it ignores *"time."* It fumbles around in the half of the room which is lighted, and ignores the other half because it is dark. Why? They don't know where the light switch is, and if they did, they might not turn it on. Men love darkness more than light.

Decisions made under such bleak circumstances, with mental blindness to the importance of *"time,"* result in *"chance"* decisions. Thus, it seems to have ever been, at least to the writer of *Ecclesiastes* that the modus operandi of man is *"time and chance."*

In past times, I have had considerable scorn (I've mellowed) for all the so-called Christian religious experts and the theologians who argue, for example, the critical doctrine of *"salvation"* without even perceptually considering the *"time"* element, not to mention the multiple meanings of the word. The result of their perceptual blindness *("time")* has led to a splintering of the Christian religion into thousands of *"denominations."* And make no mistake about it, homogeneous religion is basic to any society's harmony. Religious presuppositions about the nature of reality give rise to beliefs which give rise to thoughts which result in actions that lead to institutions that run and dominate the culture and society. The abstract, metaphysical, long-term, timeless realm finds its fruition in the concrete, physical, short-term world in which we live. *"Time"* is basic. If 20th century theologians would just go to the trouble to consider the idea that an eternal God speaks from an eternal frame of reference as well as from a *"time'* viewpoint, then all the various doctrines of *"salvation"* would better tumble into place. And when the *"eternity"* and *"time"* niches are established for the frame of reference of the writer, the so-called problems of *"grace versus law,"* *"predestination versus free will"* and *"faith versus works"* disappear and doctrines fall into place, particularly in light of the covenant.

If this light would ever dawn on our religious leaders, they would discern that the men who founded this country were not all that stupid but, in fact, brilliant. They would realize that men are accountable and responsible in *"time."* The subsequent action resulting from such a religious revelation would go a long way toward stemming the cancerous growth of Marxist communism. Marxism, of course, is an *"anti-religious religion."* Clarence B. Carson wrote in his work, WORLD IN THE GRIP OF AN IDEA,

> *"Marxism . . . is an anti-religious religion. It is an earthbound, materialistic, man-centered, cataclysmic, prophetic and dogmatic religion. Dialectical materialism is its revelation. History is its god. Marx is its prophet. Lenin is its incarnation. The revolution is its day of judgment. And communism is its paradise. Its claim to being scientific even satisfies the intellectual's desire to have a rational religion."*

It is no accident that primary religious/social activism in today's world is Marxist. It's consistent with the theology. Social, economic and political action used to be consistent with American Christian theology. We are a far cry from that perspective now. But this is to be expected at the end of a 200-year national life cycle and at the culmination of a 510-year civilization cycle. If all error in *"time"* is ultimately the result of erroneous, timeless religious presuppositions, as logically follows is the case, then we would expect such resultant institutional darkness as we now experience. It was true for Christ at the end/beginning of that 510-year cycle. It was true for Rome in 475 A.D. It was true for John Knox, Martin Luther and John Calvin at 1500 A.D., at the end of that 510-year cycle and the beginning of our present 510-year cycle. It is true for us as we stand at the termination of our 510-year cycle. But don't give up hope. There is a new day dawning. With the end of every 510-year cycle comes a new one. And ours is about to break wide open.

We are locked into the cyclical nature of *"time."* Women experience their fertility cycles. We dress for comfort according to the seasons (cycles) of the year. We structure our day according to our biological rhythms (eating) and our work and rest requirements. And we, too, are chained to how these cycles work out over our linear life spans. All our bodies' cells replace themselves every seven years. Men go through a mid-life crisis at approximately age 40. The linear reality of how they have been spending their cyclical *"time"* hits home as men reevaluate what's really important, and what they are really doing with their lives in terms of family, friends and profession around age 40. This linear time crisis is what Gail Sheehy's book, PASSAGES, is all about.

While we get carried away in the *"urgency"* of our daily lives' cyclical activity, we learn all too soon that long-term linear reality has the final say. For, in fact, we all die. We are born, grow up, mature, age and die. This linear progression is inescapable. Cyclical life harmonics are inescapably subordinate to this linear reality. Thus, it's important that we keep the *"urgent"* things in life subordinate to the *"important"* things. The urgent things are subordinate to the important things, as the cyclical perspective is subordinate to the linear.

At this point in our discussion, it should become obvious why *"chance"* follows *"time."* With so little consideration given to *"time,"* life is a lot more *"chancy."* But even if the *"time"* element is not considered, *"chance"* in decision making is the method preferred by men. Few are the men who are willing to learn and change. Learning, growth and change requires humility and risk. It requires an abandonment of pride and apparent security. Pride and apparent security aren't things that men give up easily or quickly. The future *("time")* is frightening. We resist the unknown. We are reluctant to change. Thus, we stifle growth. A person who is proud cannot or will not listen and thus cannot learn, cannot change, cannot grow, and therefore will not adapt. And yet, change and adaptation are vital to survival and success in an ever changing world.

Have you ever noticed how humble, wise men feel the *"tension of time?''* Ever learning, they are ever impressed with how much more there is to learn and how little they know. They speak of options, choices and probabilities concerning facts, recognizing the reality of their limited minds and limited *"time."* By contrast, have you ever noticed how an illiterate or poorly read individual tends to be *"cocksure,"* have all the answers, dogmatic, eager to offer an opinion, proud as a peacock, and possessed of all the *"time"* in the world? Which of these two is the real slave of *"time and chance?"*

Men collectively prefer to lean on their biases, education, parental training, religious convictions, group values and locked-in self-interest for decision making of all kinds. Men love tradition and habit. Put simply, men reject information, the harmonious combination of principles (long-term) and facts (short-term), in favor of personal preference. Put yet another way, men prefer *"chance"* to abstract and physical informational reality. Men would rather guess, even when the information is available. Men collectively are lazy. And they pay the price for their arrogance (pride) in *"time."* Kurt Vonnegut writing in the August, 1981 PSYCHOLOGY TODAY observed:

". . . Information seems to be getting in the way all the time. Human beings have had to guess about almost everything for the past million years or so. Our most enthralling and sometimes terrifying guessers are the leading characters in our history books. . . .

"The masses of humanity, having no solid information, have had little choice but to believe this guesser or that one. . . .

"Persuasive guessing has been at the core of leadership for so long, for all of human experience so far, that it is wholly unsurprising that most of the leaders on this planet, in spite of all the solid information that is suddenly ours, want the guessing to go on. It is now their turn to guess and guess and be listened to. . . .

"Some of the loudest, most proudly ignorant guessing in the world is going on in Washington, D.C., today. Our leaders are sick of all the solid information that has been dumped on humanity by research and scholarship and investigative reporting. They think that the whole country is sick of it—and they could be right. It isn't the gold standard they want to put us back on. They want something even more basic than that. They want to put us back on the snake-oil standard again. . . .

"What good is an education? The boisterous guessers are still in charge, the haters of information. And the guessers are almost all highly educated people! . . . [23]

Aren't Vonnegut's observations a solid reason for massive decentralization? At least in a decentralized environment, individuals would have the opportunity to assume more responsibility, leading to freedom. Furthermore, the tension of checks and balances and immediate feedback in a properly decentralized system could encourage men to make more decisions based upon facts, rather than *"guess."*

Vonnegut's hero was physician Ignaz Semmelweis. Semmelweis was born in Budapest in 1818. While serving as a physician in a maternity hospital in Vienna, he suggested that doctors wash their hands after finishing dissecting corpses, prior to examining mothers in the maternity ward. Semmelweis' fellow physicians, in a spirit of scorn, agreed to *"wash up."* Mothers in the maternity wards suddenly stopped dying. Did Semmelweis become a hero? No! He was forced to leave the hospital, kicked out of Austria, and finished his career in Hungary. The moral of this story: Society does not like information and progress. It reserves the right to be proud, to guess, and to maintain the status quo. It prefers *"time and chance."* Nuclear war, anyone?

We, you and I, have a tremendous opportunity to be successful in all areas of our lives. Given the collective unwillingness of mankind to consider *"time,"* and the collective pride of humanity that prefers *"chance,"* we now have the perspective, and hopefully the motivation, to move to action in a constructive, organized, effective and efficient manner, to maximize our productivity, success and happiness, and to establish our cyclical priorities in our linear life span on this earth. A man at age 21 can make a decision, for example, that by the time he is 30, he will be thinking like a man 60. This decision boils down to a correct realization of *"time and chance."* For, at age 21, a man can recognize that he has limited *"time"* on this earth. And, though experience is a good school, it is a hard one and not the only one. He can learn from others who are older and wiser than himself in various areas of expertise. It is not necessary that anyone go through life like a ping-pong ball, bouncing randomly from one experience to another, winding up as an old man true to the collective adage, *"Wisdom only comes with age."* Rather, recognizing the limited nature of one's linear life span, a man can establish his priorities—do what is *"important,"* rather than fall prey to the tyranny of the *"urgent."* He can cling to good information, seek out the harmonious union between abstract, metaphysical, long-term concepts with concrete, temporal, short-term facts and intellectually and productively depart from the self-imposed limitations of *"time."* It takes some humility, a willingness to submit to the authority and wisdom of others. It thus involves a rejection of *"chance."*

"Time and chance" is a bloody slave's wheel, around which most men naturally trek. It is a circle of mass misery. Most men are bound by chains of pride, and apparent security, shielded from the light of *"time."* But, there is a more exhilarating and enlightening road. It is a

road marked by the signposts of humility, responsibility, risk assumption, organization and planning based upon information, and backed by correct religious presuppositions. These signposts are enveloped with an accurate understanding of the nature of *"time."* This is the trek of freedom. This is the direction our Founding Fathers laid out for us. It is the way to true prosperity in all areas of life.

WEALTH FOR ALL: A SUMMARY

The economic recipe is composed of only two ingredients—land and labor. Thus, economics is human action involving raw materials and the representative of these commodities, money.

Human action maximized leads to wealth. A fair-play economic system, wherein economic activity is maximized, leads to *"Wealth for All."*

Men who are free, and not subsidized, are the most economically productive, and thus produce the most wealth. Because men are, in a sense, biological machines, they require basic energy input (food and water) to survive. Thus, in order for men to meet their basic food, clothing and shelter needs, if they are not subsidized, they must work. They must be productive. Men who are not subsidized cannot be parasites on society and thus cannot reduce the economic wealth which exists in that social order. Any excess any individual man produces adds to the wealth of the social order, which he may consume while not working, or save.

It follows that free men, who are not subsidized (subsidy being a form of slavery), will creatively work and develop their talents to their own best economic self-interest long-term if the free market is basically left alone and society supports the long-term perspective. Because men have different talents and skills, they will naturally tend to cooperate in the free market—buying, selling and trading goods and services, with each other, each maximizing his own best self-interest, and in the process, meeting the needs of the other party to the transaction. This specialization and division of labor then increases the total wealth in a society. Each man, doing what he does best, creates a good or service more efficiently than another man, to whom he trades his excess production. And so it goes.

This excess production, savings, accumulated capital, can and should be passed down from father to son, from one generation to another as inheritance, thus increasing the starting point of wealth for each subsequent generation, assuming no natural tragedies, wars or revolutions.

To further increase man's economic productivity in the limited time each man has, with his excess productivity, his savings, his accumulated capital, man can create tools (technology), which can and do produce new goods and services or better goods and services. In this way, economic wealth is further increased. Or, a man with capital may wisely invest in the vigor of youth, linking capital and wisdom with human energy, providing continuity between generations and promoting *"Wealth for All."*

The yet uncontrollable variable in the economic equation is land, the natural order, and more specifically, weather. But, men are bringing the land, the natural order, and weather increasingly, under dominion, too. A modern home or office building, with its artificially controlled level of humidity and air conditioning comfort adjustments, shields men from the natural elements and allows them to be more economically productive. In such an environment, weather is effectively subdued. Irrigated farmland, forests that are replanted after forest fires, land which is claimed from the sea, in the case of Holland, or from the desert, in the case of the potato growers along the Columbia River in Oregon—all these are evidences of man's increasing dominion over nature. It is entirely possible that one day man will completely control the weather, that our globe will become one large, beneficially controlled, air conditioned planet. Abundant free energy from solar satellites, along with advanced technology, may allow us to direct and redirect winds, effectively alter the climate of continents, and reclaim deserts by extracting desalinized water from the oceans for watering these arid lands. Vast frozen areas of planet earth may be able to be thawed and made places for pleasant human habitation. Clouds may be redirected to various parts of the earth to produce desired temperature levels and appropriate rainfall. A clear water vapor canopy could be reestablished above the earth, watering our planet at night, and protecting men from harmful radiation during the day. Then, men could again live for 1,000 years.

This is the essence of *"Wealth for All"* economics. When economics is viewed in such a light, it becomes quickly obvious that man and his institutions are presently operating in economic infancy. Stated differently, man is creating his own economic misery. When men are free, when government is simply a moral institution that protects, defends and ensures justice, permitting global free trade and social harmony; when taxes are pegged at a modest level to ensure the fulfillment of only these minimal government functions (a head tax, flat income tax or a national sales tax being the most desirable); when men control their own productivity—commodities and commodity substitutes as real money, as freely determined in the free market; then real human economic advancement, *"Wealth for All,"* will kick in.

Because energy and matter are interchangeable, we get a huge dose of potential real new wealth every day courtesy of the sun. Because this energy, real new wealth, can be converted into commodities, that part of commodity production (fish, timber, livestock, agriculture, crops, etc.) which can be attributed solely to this free real new wealth can then be monetized. In this way can the money supply legitimately be increased without causing inflation. Here, too, allowing the free market to function in determining the value of this free real new wealth, as is transformed from solar energy into commodities which can then be monetized, is the best approach. Only in the free market-place can the price (value) of this effective free real new wealth be determined. (This is best accomplished on the local level to maximize freedom and accuracy of value.)

When viewed from this beautifully simple and logical perspective, it becomes painfully apparent that man has to err in a number of blundering different ways to slip into poverty and economic squalor. The only other explanation for the economic misery which exists globally today is that men, in slave-like fashion, have been taught and educated to act contrary to their own economic best interests long-term, so that the masses continue to live in poverty or on the economic borderline, while the few who dictate the rules of the economic order get filthy rich preying on their fellow man. It seems we have far too much of the latter today. It's time for a change. It is time for *"Wealth for All."*

CONCLUSION

Every analyst and thinker this writer knows, who is worth his salt, schedules some quiet time, some down time to ponder reality. For, it is during these special moments that the subconscious works and integrates wisdom, which eventually percolates up to the surface. For this writer, these times occur during long, slow mountaintop horseback rides, during long runs through the Montana foothills, or while sitting in the grass, admiring the magnificence of Montana's mountain panorama. These special environments are static free, the antithesis of the fast-paced, noisy, grinding and irritating environment of the city. Cities are *"fact"* centers where, it seems, it's difficult to glean wisdom and gain perspective. Those who are able to do so in such a hectic environment, do so at a very high price indeed.

Because approximately 80% of our population live in cities and, thus, tend to be *"fact"* oriented and short-term in perspective, it is unlikely that we will rediscover and apply the long-term, principled wisdom there necessary to painlessly save our civilization. Also, in a one-man, one-vote, democracy, it is difficult for things to be otherwise. I have noted, with particular interest, that during times of national testing, God tends to bring men down from out of the mountains and from out of the wilderness to the cities. So, these observations of mine aren't new or unique.

While the *"whole,"* in a synergistic sense, is greater than the sum of its parts, the quality and productivity of each individual unit, whether human, animal or mechanical, is basic to the productivity of the end product. In terms of both individual and collective welfare long-term, this writer has identified four principles/virtues which, if incorporated on the individual level, maximize desirable social and economic objectives long-term. They are: humility, responsibility, giving and a long-term view. These ethics precede the thoughts and following human actions (economics) which form the basis of all truly great individuals and societies. They, thus, also form the basis of economic prosperity. A quick survey of our social landscape reveals that these wholesome characteristics are in conspicuous absence today. Small wonder we are sinking into poverty and slavery.

241

The basic, traditional family is the most important social and economic unit. The raising and educating of children, the acquisition and management of property, basic welfare needs, the meeting of fundamental, psychological, social and biological needs, and the roots of self and social government are established in a properly constituted, basic family unit. Because, ultimately, physical strength and primary thinking objectivity resides with men, the responsibility for the general health and welfare of the basic family, and thus society-at-large, rests squarely upon the shoulders of the men in all societies (the stretching and distortion of this truth by modern secular anthropologists to the contrary). Where men are irresponsible, the culture inevitably falters.

Because human biological needs are basic, the economic structure of the society is likewise fundamental. There are three characteristics which are necessary for the long-term successful viability of any unregulated free economy. They are: A social norm antagonistic to the use of debt, an operating principle that *"Self-interest is best served by service,"* and letting the free market decide which commodities shall serve as money, with only real new wealth raw materials being monetized on the local level, as they are demanded by the economic system. All booms and busts are the result of the use and abuse of credit/debt, a situation aggravated in a fractional reserve banking system such as ours is today. Economic distortions and resulting over-regulation are the inevitable by-product of violation of the principle, *"Self-interest is best served by service."* Controlled money is the worst tyranny possible. Men must husband their productivity, their money, like they do their wives.

The political system primarily gets itself in trouble when it violates on the collective level the sound individual principle, *"Theft is wrong."* Because it is wrong to steal from an individual the fruits of his productivity, so, too, is it also wrong to steal and redistribute wealth via government on a collective level. The social disharmony we experience today, the continuous political conflict and bickering, the resulting military weakness, and the overwhelming power of special interest groups are all the undesirable result of violation of the principle, *"Theft is wrong."* Government has no legitimate role whatsoever in economics (theft-wealth distribution). None! With the application of this time-tested principle, *"Theft is wrong,"* the problems which plague us would disappear. It is the *"entitlements,"* which make up approximately 48% of the federal budget, that have caused and are causing us the tremendous distress, not only with our federal budget and deficit, but also in the long-term mortgage and bond markets, the fundamental financial markets of our society. Notice that it is the misuse and irresponsibility regarding money, both individually and collectively, that are basic to all our problems.

In terms of structure, *"decentralization"* becomes the desired ruling principle in society. Only with decentralization is individual freedom maximized. Only with maximized individual freedom can a person develop his economic talents (an extension of human rights), and have the opportunity to mature into an humble, responsible, giving adult, possessed with a long-term view. Only individual decision making can result in the humble decision to listen, learn and grow. Only the individual decision to accept responsibility in all areas of life can ward off the delegation of responsibility and rights, which inevitably brings on slavery. Only an individual can make the decision to give, both in the tangible and intangible realms, seeing that his self-interest is best served by so doing. Long-term, then, the individual reaps a bountiful harvest of psychological and material returns. Only the thinking individual can see that all of *"human action,"* if pursued with the long-term view, is not only in his own best self-interest, but also in the best interest of other individuals in society. It is a *"win-win"* compact. It is the essence of harmonious human action.

Finally, fundamental to social and economic prosperity is an honest and practical view of God, law and man. While all the foregoing inevitably chips away at all the social, political, financial, religious and economic misery heaped upon the common man today, due to the slavery of centralized multinational corporation, banking, religious, education, labor, government and media powers, the fundamental shovel necessary to uproot these weeds in the garden of human freedom (which promote unnatural competition rather than natural cooperation) is a correct view of God, law and man. Prosperity is maximized where the individual is viewed as the basic, most important building block in a society, and where a society holds to the perspective that there is only one sovereign, personal God/creator who is simultaneously love and law. Only from such a deity can an individual draw his claim to human rights and following economic rights. Only with this view are all men truly equal and seen as individually imperfect under the sovereign and perfect law of a loving, just God. It quickly follows that the laws decreed and issued by such a God establish the unshakable rules for governing all men and justly operating a society, with the principle of restitution primary. Men become the policemen of the laws rather than the initiators of them. With this view of God and law, the view of the importance of individual man automatically becomes elevated. Tyranny is checkmated. Because thoughts precede actions, and ideas have consequences, the fallout is that centralization schemes, legislated special favors, competition, violation of human and following economic rights, and all other forms of slavery are cleansed from a society that has such a view of God, law and man. Justice and long-term hope become the hallmarks of such a vibrant, dynamic, prosperous and happy culture. In generalistic wisdom, theology, political science, economics and sociology are all fused into a synergistic whole which leads to an explosion of human *"Wealth for All,"* in all areas of life.

Because man has basic biological needs which must be met first and foremost, economics is primary. But economics must not be elevated to the status of a god. Such perverts men into power seeking, lustful, evolutionary animals, and leads to a society-killing sickness, manifested by the slogan, *"The man who dies with the most money and toys wins."*

The great thinkers of Western civilization have thoughtfully observed and documented the fact that Western civilization is in rapid decline. They declare, almost to a man, that it will take a miracle to save us. In this writer's opinion, such a miracle is not a farfetched, unrealistic hope. It simply begins with each individual seeing the logical consistency of the foregoing analysis, then tying it into his own best self-interest long-term, and finally accepting the gift of love and freedom made possible by the life and work of Jesus Christ. Our only other choice, a totally unacceptable one, is to continue as we are now, doing nothing, and self-destruct. As finite men, we must connect to an ultimate source, to an ultimate anchor and provider. Such was the purpose of Jesus Christ's advent in history. Jesus Christ came to give to man, not take from him.

In terms of the 50-year economic cycle, whether one views it from James M. Funk's 50-year human action progression, MIT's capital spending sequence, the expansion and contraction of the debt cycle, the Kondratieff wave, or a variation of the Hebrew's 50-year cycle ending with the year of Jubilee, in any and all cases, Western civilization has just completed its final 50-year economic cycle. Given present debt loads and the accompanying unwieldy burden of compound interest, our only options are a reckless hyperinflation or a sobering deflationary depression, joined by a massive overhaul of our political and economic system.

A hyperinflation will destroy our civilization and freedom as we know it. If this occurs, then we will have fallen prey to the 510-year civilization cycle, calling to termination a frozen Western civilization.

The accelerated destruction of the long-term debt market, beginning in 1977, the inevitable result of a society captured by a pervasive short-term orientation, guaranteed that this 50-year cycle would be the last one, at least in a *"normal"* sense. The crumbling of this long-term debt market is the demise of the foundation upon which our whole social order rests. Only if individual men (in convincing numbers) decide, using their own free will, to again link up with their Spiritual Anchor, will we then be able to derive and generate the internal strength and energy necessary to apply the foregoing principles and solutions in all realms of human action, and, in the process, also rise above and then defeat both the 50-year and the 510-year animalistic cycles. This achievable, glorious victory will then move us into the golden age of *"Wealth for All."*

APPENDIX A
ECONOMICS: CHRISTIANITY'S FINAL HURDLE
(THE CHRISTIAN LIFE: A GRAPHIC PRESENTATION)

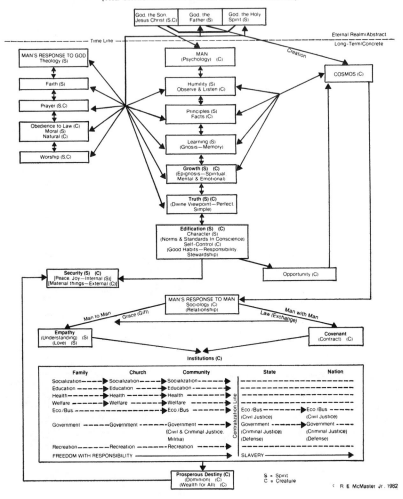

APPENDIX A

Economics: Christianity's Final Hurdle

Any unknown area of human action can seem invincible and insurmountable until attacked. So it is with the area of economics and finance for the average American. However, once this fortress is assaulted, its vulnerability becomes quickly evident. The attack begins with each individual controlling his own productivity, his money, on a local level, and then collectively (through individuals voluntarily joining together) dictating to the establishment order, particularly the political order, exactly how, and how much, taxes shall be levied, how those dollars will be spent, and that a free market in money shall be established. The individual American is the most powerful latent force on this earth. All he needs to do is flex his muscle to break society's financial and political institutions to his will. It's time that Americans, slumbering giants they are, wake up.

The Christian community should rightfully be in the forefront of financial and economic reform which, in turn, reforms all of our other institutions. Once Christians get their Bible economics and finance straight, they will be able to rapidly correct the problems and evils they see existing in today's world. For, an economic and financial base underlies them all. Furthermore, the American population should be supportive. Some 92% of all Americans believe God exists. Approximately 80% believe Jesus Christ is the Son of God. About 40% believe the Bible is the inerrant word of God. These are incredibly high percentages, given the degree to which we have been bombarded with evolutionary humanism over the last half century. These percentages are encouraging. They speak clearly to man's natural orientation toward truth, regardless of the intensity of the propaganda presented.

For years and years, Bible believing Christians stumbled around like blind men, attacking this feign or that shadow of Satan. Then men like Francis A. Schaeffer and R. J. Rushdoony appeared upon the scene and pointed out that the roots of the spiritual/philosophical/historical/mental conflict were all wound up in the word *"humanism."* Once Christians saw that humanism is the abstract source from which all satanic intellectual systems spring, they were able to identify

247

humanism wherever it appeared, and then combat it.

In terms of the spiritual battle in the physical world where humanism is overtly manifest, Christians must recognize that economics/finance is the fuel which feeds this humanistic fire. So, while Christians' philosophical attack must be on humanism, their focused assault must be on the economic gates of hell in the real world in order to snuff out the humanistic fire. Once economics and finance come under Christian dominion and occupation, humanism effectively dies as a force to be reckoned with in society-at-large. The humanistic parasite, which feeds upon society generally, will have been eliminated. The battle against humanism then will only continue to be primarily fought in the hearts and character of men, where it is a never-ending struggle due to man's sin nature and desire to be as God (determining for himself good and evil).

Men are either free and seek economic dominion over the earth, or they seek dominion over other men in humanistic slave empires. It is no accident that there have been no world empires since Jesus Christ walked on the face of the earth. He set men free. In slave empires, when people are tied down with debt, continuous labor, poverty and/or ignorance, the evolutionary/humanistic ruling class can live in sumptuous splendor, literally like gods. Such a ruling hierarchy is repugnant to both the nature and history of America. Perhaps we can now see more clearly why economics is Christianity's final hurdle. The economic extravagant methodology of the empire builders must be smashed.

The essence of this economic battle for freedom and *"Wealth for All"* is a consistent thread running through the first book in this series, WEALTH FOR ALL: RELIGION, POLITICS AND WAR. Just like with humanism, because economics is basic to all our institutions, corrective Christian surgery in the economic and financial realm must occur in all areas of human action. Economic perspective in the Christian arena alone is needed to facilitate understanding of the Gospel, eternal life, dispensationalism, covenant, the law of God, the rapture, the character of Christian believers, stewardship/responsibility, cultural heresies, Christian seminaries' perspectives, communist activity in the religious realm, the natural mind-set of religious leaders, the millennium, what the Bible has to say with regard to practicality, the exploration and explanation of verses which are problematic economically, and statements of discernment concerning the principle of unity amid diversity.

The starting point for the attack against economic humanism begins with I Timothy 6:10: *"For the love of money is the root of all evil: . . ."* Practically speaking, the free real new wealth concept is laid out in Mark 4:28: *"For the earth bringeth forth fruit of herself; first the blade, then the ear, after that the full corn in the ear."* The long-term Christian perspective is epitomized by Jesus' words, *"It is more blessed to give than to receive." ("Self-interest is best served by service.")* This is in radical contrast to the humanistic, evolutionary, short-term debt and welfare Keynesian economics which dominate us today, which are exemplified by Lord Keynes' quip, *"In the long run, we are all dead."* The bankruptcy of Keynes' statement is directly traceable to the bankruptcy of the world economy today.

Christians today, almost across the spectrum, are somewhat hostile, antagonistic and resentful of the great wealth obtained through humanistic and evolutionary means. And rightfully they should be. Since social Darwinism became acceptable in the late 1800s, financial evolutionary humanists have bulldozed over any and everything in the path, including the environment and the common man, all the while using the common man's money, through OPM debt capitalism, and government sanctioned monopolies, to claw to the top of the evolutionary spiral. Money is the god, the ultimate source of pride and security for these evolutionary and humanistic animals who have walked all over the rest of us. No wonder they are resented. No wonder they are condemned Biblically by such passages as Matthew 19:21-24, I John 2:15-16 and Mark 8:36. But, Christians have erred egregiously while, in noting this devilish financial evil, they have turned their backs on it, somehow foolishly believing it would go away and not consume them. Such folly! Such inaction is a throw-back to the pagan Greeks who effectively saw the spiritual realm as uplifting and the material realm of money as base. The Church has always tended to adopt the cultural heresies of its time. Such it has done today in the areas of economics and finance.

Our forefathers saw that individual stewardship and responsibility, particularly in areas regarding money, led directly to freedom and *"Wealth for All."* This is what *"The Christian Life: A Graphic Presentation"* is all about. Too many Christians today spend all of their time in pursuit of *"Man's response to God."* Though an important part of the Christian way of life, it is only a piece of Christian responsibility. Man's development of his character, leading to edification and internal security, his edification then leading to opportunity in the real world, where he interacts meaningfully with other men in terms of both covenant and empathy, which in turn formulates the institutions that allow him to be free with responsibility, leading then to a prosperous destiny (*"Wealth for All"*), and thus material security combined with internal peace and joy—all are equally important parts, making up the complete Christian way of life.

The Bible does not declare that money is evil. The Bible declares that *"the love of money"* is evil. Love and sex in marriage are sanctioned by God. Fornication and adultery are condemned. When money is elevated to the status of a god, when money is loved, it is condemned Biblically because such is idolatry. Matthew 7:11 and John 10:10 at least imply economic prosperity for Christians. Throughout Scripture the men that God chose to do His will were not poor. To list a few prosperous saints (in no particular order) who were of economic means include Adam, Noah, Abraham, Joseph, Moses, Job, David, Solomon, many of Jesus' disciples—James, John, Matthew, Luke and Joseph of Arimathaea.

The Bible clearly commands free enterprise, individual economic stewardship and responsibility, and the development of individual talent through work. (Mark 4:25, Galatians 6:4-5, 7, Matthew 25:14-30, Romans 14:12, II Thessalonians 3:10, I Timothy 5:8, Ephesians 4:1, 28.) Dr. Harold Lindsell's 1982 book, FREE ENTERPRISE: A JUDEO-CHRISTIAN DEFENSE, clearly shows that there is no Biblical justification for the link-up between Christianity and socialism/communism. Think about it. Unless there was excess wealth, money and material goods, how could men tithe to support the local church, provide charity for the needy, elderly, underprivileged, sick and afflicted, or provide funds for evangelism? It is wealth, the excess over that which is needed for basic subsistence, which provides the resource which can be used for medical research, technological advancement, environmental protection and all the other important activities which are vital to a Christian society. Utilizing wealth is just like any other human action. When harnessed with the long-term Christian perspective, it is a blessing; when not, it is a curse. Wealth is a tremendous blessing or a horrible curse because economics is basic. Unless our food, clothing and shelter needs are first met, all other human activity falls by the wayside. Wealth, thus, entails tremendous Christian responsibility. Luke 6:38 reads: *"Give and it shall be given unto you; . . . "* Luke 12:48 declares: *"For unto whomsoever much is given, of him shall be much required: and to whom men have committed much, of him they will ask the more."* Ephesians 4:28 states: *"Let him that stole steal no more: but rather let him labour, working with his hands the thing which is good, that he may have to give to him that needeth."*

Have we seen instances of this Christian charitable system working effectively in society in history? Of course. W. K. Jordan in his 1959 book, PHILANTHROPY IN ENGLAND 1483-1660, documented how the Puritan merchants of London, by their generous gifts to independent charities, literally reshaped their society. The Puritans in the early history of this country followed the same generous program. As we saw in *"Pedigree,"* rich men desire love, attention and approval. What better way to get it than by giving locally.

The indisputable, unshakable truth for a rich man is that he will maintain more of his wealth long-term when he tithes to his church, supports local charities, and sees that the health, education and welfare needs of his local community are met through his offerings. If, instead, he takes a short-term selfish perspective and hoards his wealth, government will fill the vacuum of his irresponsibility. Then, the health, education and welfare needs of the people will be met inefficiently by government through its bureaucracy at a much higher cost, at least four times higher, and possibly to the point of total wealth confiscation if a communist or socialist government is established. So, rich men have a choice. They can either pay a little now, or literally have hell to pay later.

APPENDIX B

Conspiracies: A Christian Perspective

Supporters of conspiracy theories have long been ridiculed by the media and educational establishment as kooks. However, when we think of conspiracies as coordinated plans made by powerful men to better their own financial/political self-interests short-term, at the expense of other men, such conspiracy theories become both more plausible and more acceptable. It should be remembered that it was the father of free market economics, Adam Smith, who warned that businessmen tend to get together in private and conspire to set prices. Such men love darkness more than light. This is why it is important that all men control their own productivity, money, rather than lend it out. It also follows that when society-at-large becomes irresponsible, as is the case today, the greed and lusts of such men can run rampant, bringing to surface the truth, *"the love of money is the root of all evil."* Money is then viewed as ultimate security. God is dismissed.

If, as under Christian cosmology, Satan, by his separation from God, is the source of all evil, and it is also true that *"the love of money is the root of all evil,"* then we would logically expect a very strong (and wrongful) link up between Satan and money (economics). If Christian cosmology is correct, we would logically also expect to see an occult link up of economics with political conspiracies. And, this is exactly what we find, as Rhodes scholar and Harvard professor, Dr. James H. Billington, documented in his book, FIRE IN THE MINDS OF MEN: ORIGINS OF THE REVOLUTIONARY FAITH.

Conspiracies for money and power among these occult, humanistic evolutionists, we would expect to find centered in the *"jungle"* where these conspirators, the *"survival of the fittest,"* reign supreme. And, this is exactly where they occur, in today's *"jungles,"* the cities. Today's cities are evolutionary *"jungles"* where the *"animals"* operate under the *"law of the jungle."* These city *"jungles"* are, as expected, atheistic and hostile to the Christian spiritual principles which built America. (Early Christian America was definitively rural.) Furthermore, as banking and business are money oriented, and since money is power and politics is power, and *"the love of money is the root of all evil,"* it should come as no surprise to find that these satanically directed, animalistic, short-term oriented, rapacious schemers are operating out of the likes of New York City and Washington, D.C. Simple, logical reasoning, in keeping with Christian cosmology, leads us to this inevitable conclusion. The Trilateral Commission, The Council on Foreign Relations, the federal government, multinational banks and corporations, big religion, education, media and labor are all located in the big city *"jungles."* Perhaps it can be more easily seen now why the sovereign, loving, personal God of the Bible favors decentralization. There, individual and subsequent group needs are more harmoniously and honestly met.

Big government, along with big financial institutions, big business and big religion are the foremost economic enemies of the common man. All move inexorably toward humanistic, evolutionary, slave-oriented empires, manned by bureaucracy-managing empire builders. It is the burden of debt and compound interest, fomented in the city *"jungles,"* which has enslaved and made miserably poor the common man today. Debt and compound interest are the life's blood of major, centralized financial institutions and corporations (big banks and the like). A sovereign, loving, personal God, by contrast, warned man to avoid debt and usury (Leviticus 25:36), for his own good. This same God warned man that big government was a curse in the Old Testament of the Bible. (I Samuel 8) It was big government that, along with organized, centralized religion, saw to it that God's Son, Jesus Christ, was crucified on the cross. How better could big government and organized, centralized religion be seen as anything other than a tool of Satan? Jesus Christ's very words in Matthew Chapter 23 of the New Testament makes it clear in no uncertain terms that organized, centralized religion is a burden for mankind that comes straight from hell. Jesus effectively called such a satanic conspiracy.

Isn't it interesting that big government, big banks, big business and big religion are all so materialistic, possessed with an all-consuming greed, pride and lust for power, which are founded first in a lust for money. *"The love of money is the root of all evil."* The plans and schemes (conspiracies) of the ruling elite in these *"big"* organizations must be kept secret. How could it be otherwise? If the truth of their conspiracies came to light, they would be ripped apart by the outraged common man. Unfair advantage is always subject to censor by honest and just men, which the common people tend to be, having to live, deal and contract in the real world of honest mutual exchange.

Is Satan the author of deceit and lies, the father of such conspiracy? The Bible declares him to be. (John 8:44) One thing becomes startlingly evident from being around these power brokers. They are simply not that smart. Nor are they quick. Nor do they anticipate the future accurately. And those who have carefully studied the self-seeking interests of big government, finance, business and religion (Billington) have remarked that there seems to be an *"unseen hand"* coordinating the whole conspiracy show, unknown to the various self-seeking parties. The hand of Satan? The prince of this world?

Evolutionary and humanistic leaders at the top of the big government, banking, business and religious evolutionary/humanistic spiral do not see their conspiratorial actions as evil. They have simply acted in their own best self-interest, short-term. What they have failed to see is that through their short-term actions, *"the greatest misery for the greatest number"* has been maximized, a poor short-term trade-off for their personal indulgences.

These elite *"survival of the fittest"* are about to reap the miserable fruits of the ruthless whirlwind they have sowed. They are about to be held accountable by mankind. Big government, the federal government, is collapsing under the weight of moral corruption and a no longer serviceable debt which is compounding exponentially. Big government is now a victim of its created welfare programs it can no longer fund. Such are disintegrating in a crisis of confidence. Big business is losing its economic slaves as the exit from the city to the country accelerates. The corporate multinationals and the military/industrial complex no longer have the confidence of the American people. The common man no longer believes that these mammoths' first and general concern is to serve the general public. They instead serve the elite. Big banking, which is the heart of this satanic, evolutionary, humanistic, occult, conspiratorial system, is seeing its foundation rapidly crumble as equity-to-asset ratios fall dangerously below 5% and banks fail worldwide. Arrogant and stupid loans of depositors' funds made to Third World developing countries, communists, and sloppy big business are being defaulted on, or being rescheduled. Big religion, too, which has deceived man into believing that it (big religion) could save man eternally (focusing the easily beguiled common man's attention on the eternal realm, while bleeding his pocketbook in the temporal realm), is falling by the wayside. Americans are rightfully cynical about big, centralized, organized religion. They see it as a sham, which first and foremost serves its own interest, as all bureaucracies do. Ritual and tradition are poor substitutes for reality. Thousands have dropped out of religion. The same cynicism permeates the general public in the areas of organized labor, education and the news media which, are crumbling, too. The hard truth is becoming crystal clear. The financial base, which has supported big religion, is dying, just as big government, big business, big labor, big education, big media and big banking are all dying as the economy dies. The conspiracy of debt capitalism, which has raped the free world, the Third World and established communism, is failing.

The heart of Satan's conspiracy system in the abstract realm is humanism. The core of Satan's system in the physical/material realm of the real world is economics. It is economics (money) which feeds the humanistic/evolutionary empires of big banking, business, labor, government, media, education and religion. Thus, Christians must attack the root of the satanic humanistic/evolutionary system—economics—if they are to win the battle for this earth, exercise dominion and occupy until Christ comes. Christians need to do to the moneychangers what Christ did in John 2:14-15, when he made a whip and drove them out of the temple. How many more successful Christian battles can be fought for Christian education, worldwide evangelism, political equity and social justice, individual talent development, environmental conservation and charity for the poor and needy if Christians established a Biblical *"Wealth for All"* economy? As long as Christians have limited time and money, which certainly is the case under the present satanic economic system, none of these battles can be fought as successfully. Christians, thus, must attack Satan's base camp—economics. Wealth is a tool, sanctioned by God, to achieve Christian victory. (Isaiah 65:13-16, Psalm 23, Proverbs 13:22, Ecclesiastes 2:26, Psalm 105:43-45, Deuteronomy 28:11-12, Genesis 26:12-14, Matthew 6:32-33, Matthew 19:29.) *"Wealth for All"* is God's economic plan to defeat Satan on earth. The poor who we always have with us either don't follow this plan, are under judgement, or are here to test our grace and charity.

Success and prosperity are naturally following byproducts of the Christian economic system, which is grounded in humility (allowing man to respond to the changing facts in his environment), responsibility (whereby each man works productively and husbands all areas under him, providing human checks and balances), giving (where self-interest is served by service) and a long-term view (promoting win-win transactions). Economic poverty, individually and collectively, is the result of the violation of God's economic laws. Economic subsidies to heathen persons and cultures, when not tied to evangelism, promotes Satan's economic system.

APPENDIX C

The Great Satan

The battles fought over all secular and religious issues ultimately involve, and revolve around, the economic realm. Economics is, by definition, human action, and usually involves money. All human action is based in religious presuppositions about the nature of reality.

How fundamental this economic issue is to classic American Christian religion can be easily seen from the fact that the first temptation Satan offered to Jesus Christ, after Christ had fasted for 40 days and 40 nights, was to *"command that these stones be made bread."* (Matthew 4:3) This was an economic temptation. This basic economic/biological issue is also found established in the Old Testament when David, a man after God's own heart, on an occasion when he was hungry, ate the *"shewbread"* in the house of God. (Mark 2:25-26)

On a broader plane, the war between the forces of evil commanded by Satan, and the forces of God (good) commanded by Christ, are fought on the economic battleground, here on earth, in time. The Bible clearly declares: *"The earth is the Lord's, and the fulness thereof; the world, and they that dwell therein."* (Psalm 24:1) We also know, by contrast, that Satan is the ruler of the kingdoms of this world (tying Satan in with government) (Matthew 4:8-9), and also the prince of this world. (John 12:31) Satan must be an illegitimate ruler. Satan steals his power. So, the issue for Christian nations, such as the United States—the New Israel as early Americans saw it—is the same as it was for Israel of the Old Testament. To put on the whole armor of God and move onward as Christian soldiers, reclaiming the earth for the Lord (the rightful ruler) from Satan (the illegitimate ruler) is both the duty and destiny of Christians. This is why we were put on earth. (II Timothy 2:3, Hebrews 10:13, Mark 12:36)

The age-old issue, which plagued Moses during the exodus of the Hebrews from the Egyptian Empire, is with us again today. It is the issue of slaves versus free men. Too many men love to be slaves. God's ambassadors in time, elected before the foundation of the world to eternal life, are free men on earth. *(If the Son therefore shall make you free, ye shall be free indeed."* John 8:36) Christ's work purchased us from the slave market of sin (Satan's realm) and set us free from the judgment of the law of sin and death. We are now free under the law. (James 1:25, I Timothy 1:8-9, Galatians 6:2, Galatians 5:14, Galatians 3:24) Free men are inescapably and inevitably found in God's Christian realm, while slaves are the evidence of Satan's domain. Thus, Satan's domain is not only apparent today in the atheistic slave-filled communist empires, but also in this country where 50% of a man's income must be paid to government, and 56% live on the government dole. Slavery is inevitably economic in nature, since lack of stewardship/irresponsibility leads to slavery, and slaves own nothing.

Slaves can never rule. Thus, Christian free men are commanded to use God's Spirit, commandments and law to subdue the earth, exercise dominion, and occupy until Christ comes again. (Revelation 22:14) Christians are called at the same time to be possessed of a mental attitude of *"waiting on the Lord."* Faith, patience and works all work together. (Isaiah 40:31)

The purpose of evangelism in the world is for missionaries to call God's elect to repentance, inform them of the reality of their eternal salvation, so that they, too, may be free, in service to Christ in time (for their own good long-term, too). With an humble, giving, responsible and long-term view, Christians should be whipping the socks off of the slaves belonging to the forces of evil in every area of human action. It is the essence of stewardship and the proper use of talents. Wealth for Christians is sanctioned by God. (Ecclesiastes 5:19)

From a legal perspective, Adam's sin (fall) in the first economic garden (the Garden of Eden) triggered man's sin/animal nature and identified mankind with Satan. It was Christ's atoning and substitutionary work on the cross that paid the price of freedom for man and freed him from the shackles and slavery of Satan's perverse, wicked, evil and miserable kingdom. (Romans 5:11) But, Satan keeps trying to duplicate his slave empires here on earth. And economics/money is his prime tool in the material realm. (Mark 10:23) (Humanism is Satan's primary tool in the abstract realm.)

The foregoing perspective is rooted in the finest American Christian tradition, for this is precisely what the Founding Fathers believed. Beliefs produce thoughts, and thoughts have consequences in time. It is, thus, no accident that this true theological base, given to us by our Founding Fathers, has produced the greatest and most prosperous free economic nation on the face of this earth. Jesus declared: *"Render therefore unto Caesar the things which are Caesar's, and unto God the things which be God's."* (Luke 20:25) Our Founding Fathers set up this country in a way so there would be no Caesar (humanistic god). The United States was established as a government *"of the people."* In a sense, then, each and every responsible American is a Caesar in service to the Lord, and the government has no right to our economic production. This theological perspective was the basis for the Declaration of Independence and the U.S. Constitution which every American should read and reread. The U.S. Constitution is our contract with the government. The economic issue for our Founding Fathers was a basic one in the American War for Independence. In a very real sense, the American War for Independence was an economic war of free Christian men against an English government doing Satan's economic bidding. The American Colonies were becoming abundantly prosperous in no time at all by using real commodities as money, or equivalent warehouse receipts. The mother country, England, began exploiting the American Colonies' raw materials and delivering manufactured goods at an unfair price differential. The Colonies revolted at this and also against unfair taxation, *"taxation without representation."* When the Bank of England's money was also going to be imposed upon the Colonies, this was the final straw.

Banking hasn't changed much, has it? The slavery of debt, created by banks, still impoverishes the masses. Control of a man's economic livelihood is control of his will. Debt and taxation are our chains today. This fundamental economic issue cannot be avoided. We even effectively rent all of our real estate from the government these days when we pay *"property taxes."*

Now, perhaps we can better see why, according to Christian cosmology, if Satan is the source of all evil, and *"the love of money is the root of all evil,"* a very close link exists between the religion and operations of Satan and money. We immediately recall that Jesus Christ *"overthrew the tables of the moneychangers"* in the temple of God which, at that time, had already been captured by the forces of Satan. (John 2:14-15) Christ told the Jewish religious leaders: *"Ye are of your father the devil, and the lusts of your father ye will do. He was a murderer from the beginning, and abode not in the truth, because there is no truth in him. When he speaketh a lie, he speaketh of his own: For he is a liar, and the father of it."* (John 8:44) It's an understatement to say that Jesus Christ did not think much of centralized, organized, bureaucratic, occult religion which does the will of Satan. And here we see that the means of economic communication, money, has an undeniably close link with organized, government-sanctioned religion. The IRS sanctions churches today.

To the extent there is a decline in a Christian culture and civilization, the Satanic realm fills this void and slavery inevitably results. Again, Satan and slavery go hand in hand. Satan's realm and slavery are one and the same, with money the driving force behind such a modus operandi. This is obvious with atheistic communism, more subtle in this country. Formerly useful, decentralized, limited in scope Christian institutions, such as government, denominational religions, educational institutions, banks and businesses have become transformed into the institutions of Satan for the purpose of enslaving and destroying the human race. This occurs over time, with age, in much the same way that good water, once it becomes stagnant over a period of time, becomes poisonous. This is what happened to the Jews. Over time, they fell under the influence of Satan, and crucified their very Messiah, Jesus Christ!

In the human realm, when governments, corporations, the media, banks, labor, education and religion all begin building empires which by their very nature enslave men through bureaucracy, then clearly the hand of Satan is upon them. Also, in all empires, money not only *"talks,"* but is a, if not the, central issue.

It should be obvious now why in this critical economic struggle, Christians should avoid debt and *"owe no man any thing . . ."* (Romans 13:8) Debt is fundamental economic slavery. It has been clearly established through economic research that, long-term, debt is detrimental to any human activity. All panics and crashes and following depressions in history have resulted from the excessive expansion of credit, stemming from a love of money/greed. This credit money was used to finance speculative manias. The lending was based upon poor collateral. People mortgaged their past and borrowed from their future, based upon groundless hopes and wishes. Debt takes the wealth of many and transfers it to a few, creating class warfare, and setting the stage for the slavery of dictatorships which follow revolutions.

There are, however, legitimate circumstances which warrant, and reasons for, short-term debt of less than seven years. Debt should only be used for productive purposes in the economic realm, never consumption. Otherwise, debt should be basically charitable, and without profit motivation.

If Christians are defeated in the economic arena, then all other forms of slavery quickly follow. How many Americans today are slaves to a government which provides for their economic welfare? 56%. But this governmental economic provision is a lie, because we have already seen that government is an economic parasite that can only, through legalized theft, redistribute economic wealth. Theft on an individual or a collective basis is a violation of one of the Ten Commandments: *"Thou shalt not steal."* (Exodus 20:15) Thus, whenever we see government involved in the economic arena, we clearly know that it has become the instrument of Satan, for it is acting contrary to the law and commandments of God. What does this say about how honoring to the Lord is the U.S. government today?

Governments practice confiscatory economics through taxation and perform insidious economic theft through inflation. Inflation is, by definition, an increase in the supply of money. Government, a satanic entity when it inflates the currency, is playing the role of God, creating something, called money, out of nothing.

In the trading stock and commodity markets of this world, it is easy to see how the communication media of economic human action, money, is loved and is, accordingly, the root of all evil. The majority who are attracted to these trading markets are attracted by greed, a lust for money, a love of money. Too many of these men live by the creed, *"The man who dies with the most money and the most toys that money can buy, wins."* With their love of money, many are quickly drawn into the occult, satanic realm, seeking to know the monetary future. Thus, astrology is a popular methodology in discerning the future direction of markets. In many cases, astrology is quite accurate. We also note, not by accident, that the world's political empires, slave states of old, also used key astrological consultants. The Bible rightfully condemns astrology because of its link with satanic empires historically, and its use in the quest for money. (Leviticus 20:6) Both are deeply embedded in the satanic realm of influence.

The political epitome of Satan's system is an evolutionary, humanistic slave empire, where the ruler becomes a *"god."* But, this epitome of an evolved *"animal"* is still subject to nature. Now, in pagan, non-Christian religions, the epitome of nature is often the sun, the planets, and the stars. Thus, through astrology, the movements of these heavenly bodies, and their influence on man, become the determinant of man's destiny, not a sovereign, personal, loving God. Under this astrological system, man is still a slave to nature. But, nature is fallen, too, and has been cursed since the Garden of Eden. When man subjects himself exclusively to the laws of a fallen and cursed natural order, he quickly falls under the rulership of the dictator of the fallen order—Satan.

Hopefully, it is more clear now why Christian dominion is so fundamental to God's purpose for man and the Christian way of life. It is necessary to re-establish Christ's rightful kingship and control over the earth, including the restoration of the natural order. It is also necessary for *"Wealth for All."* Perhaps now, it is also apparent why extreme ecologists line up with evolutionary humanists. Nature is their god. (To avoid confusion on this point, conservation, grooming and preservation of the earth is clearly called for in Scripture.)

When Christians establish dominion over economics and money, they have effectively conquered the heart of Satan's system, and cut off humanism's umbilical cord. It therefore follows that the *"Wealth for All"* perspective demands that we take a close and discerning look at all of the institutions which are integrally involved with money today. One would suspect, in our post-Christian era, at the end of our 510-year civilization cycle, that most of our institutions are satanic to the core.

In terms of evil, it's important to recognize that evil seldom appears on the scene wearing a black hat. Even *"Satan himself is transformed into an angel of light."* (II Corinthians 11:14) On an individual level, evil is usually manifested by a person seeking to satisfy what he perceives as his own best self-interest, short-term. In other words, he is exercising his *"animalistic"* instincts. On a collective level, evil is also usually manifested by a short-term orientation, using bureaucracies which are common to all empires, whether of government, banking, business, media, labor, education and/or religion. In all bureaucracies, which are by their very nature empirical, individual, personal, moral accountability and responsibility can be too easily eliminated, avoided, or passed on up the line of authority. Of course, at the very top of the line ultimately sits Satan. In bureaucracies, all bureaucracies, people simply *"do what they are told."* So, men can perform incredibly evil deeds with no sense of guilt. This was the basis of Hitler's horrible persecution of the Jews in Germany and the Gestapo-like actions of the IRS in this country today. Honesty and integrity only tend to govern transactions between individuals, certainly not collective bureaucracies. In bureaucracies, there is no moral accountability. Neither is there moral accountability in evolutionary humanism.

Today, Iran likes to refer to the United States as the *"Great Satan."* While, without question, the Iranian revolution under the Ayatolah Khomeini has all the hallmarks of a satanic, occult, religious revolution, marked by one man playing the role of a god, with a ruling empirical bureaucracy calling for the blood sacrifice of other men, we still have to question whether their reference to us as the *"Great Satan"* has any merit. The United States, and particularly New York City, is the money center of the world today. The love of money is at the root of Satan's world system. Any honest historian who has studied the economic relationship between the United States and Iran, particularly since the time of the Shah of Iran forward, has concluded that the U.S., with regard to Iran, has practiced *"dollar imperialism,"* which is, by its very nature, satanic. Is it any less true regarding our financing of communist bloc countries and the Third World? Has the country which once stood out as the world's beacon of liberty and Christian economics, in fact, become the *"Great Satan,"* much like the

Jews were to Christ, who came as their Messiah, and who was treated as their worst enemy? It's possible. We're at the end of a 510-year civilization cycle for Western civilization, just as in Jesus' day.

It is of more than passing interest that the use of bank credit as money began at least 500 years ago. If the United States has been hideously transformed into the *"Great Satan,"* then the blame for this horrible heresy rests squarely on the shoulders of irresponsible Christians who have ignored their primary responsibility and stewardship in the realm of economics. As the great economist, Elgin Groseclose, wrote, *"The essence of the money problem is moral more than technical—that as money is the standard of economic value and measure of commerce, the manipulation of money is evil . . . "*

Former World Bank president, Robert McNamara, has called for a World Central Bank to step in if loan defaults began to spread beyond the control of the banks in individual countries. If this comes to pass, as nations crumble, then Satan will have his best shot ever at establishing his One World Empire. Will we allow it? Will we become pathetic slaves? No so-called self-sufficient evolved human *"animal"* can survive in such an environment, much less a Christian free man.

What should be our source of money in a Christian, ethical, fair-play, economic sense? Those who argue for free market money and/or a gold standard are effectively arguing for money free from centralized control, and preventing government from determining what serves as money. Economic reality is that the exchange of goods and services is nothing more than barter. Thus, in terms of economically honest money, money is, or represents, a commodity—some existing reality. How, then, can government increase the money supply when honest money is, or represents, a commodity, some *"matter?"* We can't, in good conscience, let the Federal Reserve banking empire do it. Not only has the Fed been ineffective in preventing economic booms and busts; it has, in fact, caused them, the most notable being the Crash of 1929 and the economic debacle of 1980-82.

It is a sham when government or government institutions create money because government does not produce any new goods. Government does not produce any new commodities and, therefore, cannot legitimately create money. Governments can only inflate the existing money supply. When you boil it all down, there is only one source of free, new energy, which automatically creates free, new matter/money/commodities, and that is the sun. The free new matter/commodities/money produced by the sun's energy—agricultural products, timber, fish, etc.—are all commodities that can be effectively monetized when they are brought into the economic mainstream. In this way, and only this way, can the supply of money be increased commensurate with the increase in real new wealth. To the extent there is excess real new production, a situation which certainly exists with a steady state, spiritual, productive population, lack of disasters, and good climatic conditions, prices should generally fall over time rather than rise, as excess goods accumulate.

Our economic/monetary system today is presently insane. It is satanic. Separation from God's reality is the definition of insanity. Not only are we becoming increasingly impoverished through the burden of debt and compound interest, not only have we subjected ourselves to the boom/bust economic cycle through the creation, use and abuse of credit, but we are also plowing under our real new wealth, which could be monetized, which is the equivalent of burning money. The July 29, 1982 WALL STREET JOURNAL declared, *"One Illinois farmer plowed under 250 acres of corn, worth roughly $60,000, to qualify at the last minute for price support programs. He calculated that supports would yield him $115,000 more in total income than selling the 250 acres of grain."* So, in this case, not only was $60,000 in real new wealth destroyed, but also $115,000 from the present economic order was consumed needlessly and uselessly, further impoverishing mankind.

Remember the traditional American Thanksgiving celebration? Its purpose used to be to celebrate a bountiful harvest which represented increased *"Wealth for All."* How far have we strayed from that fine American, Christian tradition?

The economic distress which has and is capturing our society is a direct result of the economic and following political insanity filling the vacuum formerly occupied by responsible Christians who exercised economic stewardship and obedience to God's commandments and laws as they apply to the basic economic realm. Economic rights are human rights because human conditions can only be bettered when the Christian economic answer is understood and implemented throughout a society.

What must we do? Each one of us must maintain control and exercise responsibility over our individual economic productivity (money) directly. We must not delegate or rent the use of it to some third party (such as a bank). Letting go of our productivity for a little usury (compound interest) has made possible most of the evils which exist in our social order today. To stop evil, we must cut it down at its roots, its economic roots. The effective satanic financial institutions' control today over other people's money (OPM) has resulted in wanton waste, corruption, the financing of communism and its slave labor, inflation, the establishment of factories abroad which have thrown Americans out of work, the rape of the environment, the plundering of Third

World countries, and the financing of wars, just for a start. Is this not the work of Satan? Usury (compound interest) is so dangerous because it encourages financial irresponsibility. We don't lend out our wives for prostitution. Why our money? Banks should simply warehouse our wealth and serve as community business centers.

Selling out for a little compound interest which is taxed to high heaven and inflated away anyway, and so really is not worth the bother, has resulted in men in massive numbers giving up control of the fruits of their labor for evil uses. Honest men should avoid debt and use cash if necessary to avoid the fractional reserve banking and debt system, until an honest Christian money, economic and tax order can be restored.

APPENDIX D

What You Must Do To Be Responsible, Free and Prosperous

Maintain responsibility and control over all of your money and financial assets. Keep an emergency supply of cash and gold and silver coins in a safe deposit box. Use banks for the purpose for which they were originally intended in the free market—for storage of valuables—warehouses, as centers where men get together and structure business ventures. Keep only enough funds in a checking account to pay immediate bills. If credit cards are used, pay them off monthly and use them only as a convenient form of record keeping. Do not use credit of any type and work to pay off all debt. Investments should be in youth who have the potential, drive and character in their area of developing talent. This way old capital combines with the vigor of youth, which produces not only needed goods and services, but also maintains harmony between generations. Other investments in businesses, property and the like should be primarily, if not exclusively, in the local area. Money should not be lent out on interest to a third party (financial institution) who can then lend it out to someone else. This destroys the principle of decentralization, the feedback loop, and accountability. Local partnerships, joint ventures and corporations should provide excellent investment opportunities. Any investments made out of the local area should be monitored very carefully with regard to purpose and management policy. Any *"interest"* earned on any investment project should be limited to the percentage of return generated by that project itself, and not extend beyond it. This is in keeping with the principle of decentralization where, if a bad investment or business venture is made, the *"compounding"* effect of interest is cut off with the termination of that project. Thus, there are no guarantees beyond the specific venture itself. This prevents subsequent generations from paying the unfair price of foolish actions taken by their forefathers. Debt should be less than seven years and should be primarily charitable, extracting no interest in cases of charity.

Move to a medium-size rural community. What you are looking for is a community and neighborhood where people have some space to live, interact with each other, raise gardens and animals, and combine the best of intellectual and rural life. Learn, develop and use a trade that is valuable and contributes to the welfare of the local community. Do your best at your trade in keeping with the principle, *"Self-interest is best served by service."* To the maximum extent possible, buy locally-produced goods and services, particularly whenever the cost is competitive or closely competitive. This will enhance getting to know your neighbors and facilitate the discussing of important social, religious, political and economic issues. It will also enhance the swapping of skills, which is part of being neighborly. Help organize and develop a neighborhood security protection organization, a *"crime stoppers"* and *"home watchers"* organization. This will enhance the security and peace of mind of all the neighborhood. Work for a locally-owned and controlled newspaper, radio station and television station. This facilitates free flowing, accurate communication, civic interest and local harmony. Attend all local government meetings, city and county. Let these local officials know your views and hold them accountable for their actions. Rather than listen to what these politicians say, watch what they do. Monitor their budgets, and how they spend your money. Work to see that the local police, fire, sanitation and medical facilities and organizations are adequate in case of emergencies. Work to see that as many government services as possible are transferred back to the private sector of the economy (police and law enforcement excepted). Become civic minded and attend local civic functions and important local meetings. Work for the establishment of a local militia, the ultimate and best protection for any group of people. See that local conservation efforts and local parks are established. In all cases, work to see that your local community has instilled a long-term view which promotes a *"win-win"* situation for all parties to the neighborhood community. Work to ensure that your community has adequate emergency supplies of food, clothing, shelter, water, fuel and fallout shelters in case of natural or man-made emergencies. Attend local school board meetings. Monitor the school budget. Attend and sit in on school classes. Ensure that teachers instill the importance of personal responsibility, character development and accountability in each student. Investigate the background, philosophy, teaching methods and textbooks used by instructors. Investigate and critique the role of school administrators. Insist upon totally independent local schools and a free market in education. Work for local autonomy in all areas of life with the exception of national defense, where the militia and state military units are to be more powerful than the federal military structure. Work to bring industry and culture (the city) into your rural community.

Men, as head of the household, assume responsibility for any and all of your actions, both positive and negative. These affect your local and extended family as well as your community. The buck stops at your desk, men. Mature men blame no one but themselves for anything that goes wrong. This means taking responsibility first and foremost for all aspects of the health, education, spiritual, economic, welfare and recreational needs of your family. Setting aside family time for Bible study, recreation and general family discussions is important. Involving the family in the raising of a garden and animals is long-term beneficial to family members. Such teaches basic economics, responsibility, cooperation, economic independence and thrift. Effectively unplugging the family TV, and only watching television when there are worthwhile educational programs, will free up a tremendous amount of time. The average American family (zombies) watches over seven hours of television daily. Take your family to church regularly and worship together. Educate the minister. Very few ministers have the foggiest idea what the real world of economics and earning a living is all about. Unfortunately, far too many ministers are as naive and ignorant about the relationship between Christian economics and the Christian walk as were the scribes, Pharisees and Sadducees of Jesus' day. Help develop the local church into a community action center that looks after the welfare needs of its members and the community-at-large. Tithe 10% of your income to your local church. Women in the church should be made responsible for charity, missions of mercy, health care and the education of the young. The elderly should teach vital skills and life-learned insights to those who are younger in age. Providing for the education of the young and charity assistance for the needy and the elderly is a primary responsibility of the local church. Your family, your church and your local community are your best investments long-term. Work to support primarily local, decentralized organizations.

The man of the household has tremendous personal responsibilities which, if assumed and carried out, result in blessings and *"Wealth for All"* throughout society. The ability to interact, contract and covenant with other men begins first and foremost with the development of the character of the individual man. A man should find some quiet time to read his Bible daily and pray. Proper rest, exercise and a balanced diet are critical for a man to function efficiently in all areas of life. The reading and rereading of the Declaration of Independence and the U.S. Constitution, your contract with the government, is a must. Read the books in the recommended reading list at the back of this book. Learn how to use a firearm for defense. A nation where individuals are armed, and are willing to use their firearms for defense, cannot be toppled from within or without. A man must remember that his word, both written and verbal, is his bond. It is the measure of his character, by which other men judge his manliness. Following the long-term perspective, rather than the short-term one, seeing that self-interest is best served by service (giving), acting responsibly and with humility, will serve a man well throughout his lifetime. Wives must submit to their husbands and help them in line with Proverbs 31:10-31.

In terms of extended and other responsibilities, work to have all non-elected officials removed from office or made accountable directly to the people. Work for local autonomy in all areas except national defense (a militia is most desirable), and a just court system where judges are elected and all trials are by jury of a man's peers. Work to establish Biblical law, as exemplified in the Ten Commandments, as the basis of the U.S. legal system. In trials where juries judge the facts of a case and apply the principle of Biblical law to these particulars, work to see that justice is tempered with mercy. Work to elect state officials who will stand up for state's rights against the federal government. Work to remove from state office all non-elected officials or have them made accountable directly (elected) to the voting public. Work to have all state programs abolished which are economic in nature. Work to maintain only those state government programs which are involved in the maintenance of peace, protection of property, and ensuring justice. Work to see that voting at all levels is a responsibility and a privilege, not a right. Allow only U.S. born citizens to vote. Insist that only those citizens who pay taxes, own property and can pass a minimum reading and writing test vote. Work to raise the voting age again to 21. Work to prohibit government employees and beneficiaries from voting. Their economic self-interest is at stake when they vote. Monitor and critique the voting records of all elected officials. Work for the principle of restitution for crime rather than imprisonment, in keeping with Biblical law. Work to open all professions and occupations to all people, with unrestricted entry—the economic marketplace alone to decide competence in any profession, thereby also forcing people to grow up and investigate all so-called sacred cow professionals. Government sanctioned monopolies never work for the good of the public interest long-term. Investigate the background, character, family life and personal habits of all men who run for political office. Work to elect solid, reliable, responsible and humble constitutionally-oriented Christian men.

Work for the abolition of all property taxes, all inheritance taxes, the graduated income tax, the IRS, and all the government agencies which make bureaucratic entries into the Federal Register. Work for the abolition of the Federal Reserve, the fractional reserve banking system, the 16th and 17th Amendments to the U.S. Constitution that provided for the federal income tax and the direct election of U.S. Senators, which destroyed the principle of checks and balances in this country. Work for the establishment of a head tax, a national sales tax, or a flat income tax for all people—one of the three, not all three. Any other taxes should be user only taxes. See that all Executive Orders and the Federal Register are abolished.

Work to abolish all military academies and all secret intelligence agencies. A professional military has always been a tremendous threat, not only to its nation's citizens, but also as an incentive for imperialistic wars where young men shed their blood on foreign soil. Often, professional militaries end up ruling a country. Work for the abolition of the draft. Work for the establishment of a strong military with emphasis on local militias, trained in the used of sophisticated weaponry, backed up by a strong civil defense. Work to have outlawed any military ventures on foreign soils that are fought with anything other than volunteer troops.

Work to have all foreign treaties abolished and to void all foreign entanglements. Individuals and businesses can covenant and contract with individuals and other nations; it should be beyond the power of the politicians to contract on the behalf of the people with a foreign power or powers. In this vein, bring all ambassadors home. Abolish the United Nations. Have all United Nations officials and their staffs, including their extensive spy networks, sent home immediately. Monitor and critique carefully the voting record of all elected officials on the federal level, where geographic distance provides less accountability and thus promotes corruption. Work for the elimination of all federal revenue sharing which is nothing more than giving back to the people their own money after siphoning it off wastefully through the bureaucracy. Make use of grand jury and jury power.

Work for the termination of all federal involvement in education. Work for apprenticeship as the means of teaching young men and women economic skills, once the basic educational subjects of reading, writing, arithmetic, English, American history, science, civics, ethics and the Bible are competently acquired. Work to abolish political parties which were hated by the Founding Fathers of this country. Political parties are special interest corporations. Work for the abolition of all other federal government agencies which have any involvement in health, education, welfare or economic activities. Work for the elimination of all appointed federal office holders, either eliminating the office or making them directly accountable through the voting process to the general public. Work to eliminate all monopolies or government-approved organizations which limit and/or restrict competition, set regulations or requirements, and are involved in any and all other activities which do not have to do directly with ensuring justice and protecting people against all enemies, foreign and domestic. Demand a mandatory balanced federal budget, the election of federal judges, free market money where the people choose whatever medium they want to serve as money, with Congress only having the ability to coin gold and silver money. Abolish the Postal Service. Open up mail delivery to the free market. Insist that all taxes be collected locally. Work for the establishment of laws which grant men and women maximum freedom in line with Biblical law and a long-term, humble, giving and responsible perspective. These laws should encourage individuals to develop their talents so that their productivity is harmoniously tied into the best interests of themselves and their fellow man consistent with the long-term view. Once these things are done, we will have a happy, prosperous, free and secure society, well on the road to *"Wealth for All."*

NOTES

1. ACRES, U.S.A., P. O. Box 9547, Raytown, Missouri.

2. Associated Press, 50 Rockefeller Plaza, New York, NY.

3. Reprinted by permission of THE WALL STREET JOURNAL, copyright Dow Jones & Company, Inc., 1982. All Rights Reserved.

4. *Ibid.*

5. *Ibid.*, 1981.

6. ACRES, U.S.A., Vince Rossiter, *op. cit.*

7. The WALL STREET JOURNAL, 1982, *op. cit.*

8. Copyright 1976 by Simoha Productions, Inc., Reprinted by permission of Pocket Books, a Simon & Schuster division of Gulf & Western Corporation.

9. THE WALL STREET JOURNAL, 1981, *op. cit.*

10. *Ibid.*

11. Reprinted from U.S. NEWS & WORLD REPORT, Copyright 1981, U.S. NEWS & WORLD REPORT, Inc.

12. *Ibid.*

13. Colin M. Turnbull, THE MOUNTAIN PEOPLE, Simon & Schuster, Inc., New York, NY.

14. THE WALL STREET JOURNAL, *op. cit.*

15. From "Calendar" in ENCYCLOPAEDIA BRITANNICA, 14th edition (1961), 4:575-6.

16. THE WALL STREET JOURNAL, 1982, *op. cit.*

17. *Ibid.*

18. Reprinted from PSYCHOLOGY TODAY MAGAZINE, Copyright 1977, Ziff Davis Publishing Co.

19. *Ibid.*

20. *Ibid.*, 1975.

21. *Ibid.*

22. *Ibid.*

23. *Ibid.*, 1981.

SELECTED BIBLIOGRAPHY
AND RECOMMENDED
READING LIST

God and His Bible

Bahnsen, Greg L., THEONOMY, Nutley, NJ: The Craig Press, 1977.

Lewis, C. S., MERE CHRISTIANITY, New York: MacMillan Publishing Co., 1943.

Rushdoony, Rousas John, INFALLIBILITY: AN INESCAPABLE CONCEPT, Vallecito, CA: Ross House Books, 1978.

_____. THE NECESSITY FOR SYSTEMATIC THEOLOGY, Vallecito, CA: Ross House Books, 1979.

Schaeffer, Francis A., HE IS THERE AND HE IS NOT SILENT, Wheaton, IL: Tyndale House Publishers, 1972.

_____. THE GOD WHO IS THERE, Downers Grove, IL: Inter-Varsity Press, 1968.

Law and Christianity

Ingram, T. Robert, THE WORLD UNDER GOD'S LAW, Houston: St. Thomas Press, 1962.

Rushdoony, Rousas John, LAW AND LIBERTY, Fairfax, VA: Thoburn Press, 1977.

_____. LAW AND SOCIETY, Vallecito, CA: Ross House Books, 1982.

_____. THE INSTITUTES OF BIBLICAL LAW, Nutley, NJ: Presbyterian and Reformed Publishing Co., 1973.

American History and Christianity

Hall, Verna M., THE CHRISTIAN HISTORY OF THE CONSTITUTION OF THE UNITED STATES OF AMERICA, San Francisco: The Foundation for American Christian Education, 1966.

Manuel, David and Marshall, Peter, THE LIGHT AND THE GLORY, Old Tappan, NJ: Power Books, 1977.

The Christian World View: General Philosophy

Campbell, Roderick, ISRAEL AND THE NEW COVENANT, Nutley, NJ: Presbyterian and Reformed Publishing Co., 1954.

Ellul, Jacques, THE ETHICS OF FREEDOM, Grand Rapids: Wm. B. Eerdman's Publishing Co., 1976.

————. TO WILL & TO DO, Philadelphia: Pilgrim Press, 1969.

Lewis, C. S., THE ABOLITION OF MAN, MacMillan Publishing Co., 1947.

————. THE WORLD'S LAST NIGHT, New York: Harcourt, Brace, Jovanovich, Inc., 1952.

Machen, J. Gresham, CHRISTIANITY AND LIBERALISM, Grand Rapids: Wm. B. Eerdman's Publishing Co., 1977.

North, Gary, THE DOMINION COVENANT: GENESIS, Tyler, TX: The Institute for Christian Economics, 1982.

Rushdoony, Rousas John, THE FOUNDATIONS OF SOCIAL ORDER, Fairfax, VA: Thoburn Press, 1978.

————. THE ONE AND THE MANY, Fairfax, VA: Thoburn Press, 1978.

Schaeffer, Francis A., ESCAPE FROM REASON, Downers Grove, IL: Inter-Varsity Press, 1968.

————. HOW SHOULD WE THEN LIVE?, Old Tappan, NJ: Revell, 1976.

————. THE CHURCH AT THE END OF THE 20TH CENTURY, Downers Grove, IL: Inter-Varsity Press, 1977.

Education and Christianity

Blumenfeld, Samuel L., IS PUBLIC EDUCATION NECESSARY?, Old Greenwich, CT: The Devin-Adair Co., 1981.

Fortkamp, Dr. Frank E., THE CASE AGAINST GOVERNMENT SCHOOLS, American Media, P. O. Box 4646, Westlake Village, CA 91355, $8.95, 149pp.

North, Gary, FOUNDATIONS OF CHRISTIAN SCHOLARSHIP, Vallecito, CA: Ross House Books, 1976.

Rushdoony, Rousas John, THE PHILOSOPHY OF THE CHRISTIAN CURRICULUM, Vallecito, CA: Ross House Books, 1981.

Science, Archeology and Christianity

Gish, Duane T., EVOLUTION: THE FOSSILS SAY NO!, San

Diego: Creation-Life Publishers, 1973.

Kang, C. H., and Nelson, Ethel R., THE DISCOVERY OF GENESIS, St. Louis: Concordia, 1979.

McDowell, Josh, EVIDENCE THAT DEMANDS A VERDICT, San Bernardino, CA: Campus Crusade for Christ, Inc., 1972.

Morris, Henry M., MANY INFALLIBLE PROOFS, San Diego: Creation-Life Publishers, 1974.

Wysong, R. L., THE CREATION-EVOLUTION CONTROVERSY, Midland, MI: Inquiry Press, 1976.

Anthropology, Evangelism and Christianity

Richardson, Don, ETERNITY IN THEIR HEARTS, Ventura, CA: Regal Books, 1981.

Turnbull, Colin M., THE MOUNTAIN PEOPLE, New York: Simon & Schuster, 1972.

The Christian World View: Specific Issues

Bahnsen, Greg L., HOMOSEXUALITY: A BIBLICAL VIEW, Grand Rapids: Baker Book House, 1978.

Chilton, David, PRODUCTIVE CHRISTIANS IN AN AGE OF GUILT MANIPULATORS, Tyler, TX: The Institute for Christian Economics, 1981.

Ellul, Jacques, PROPAGANDA, New York: Vintage, 1973.

_____. THE BETRAYAL OF THE WEST, New York: The Seabury Press, 1978.

_____. THE MEANING OF THE CITY, Grand Rapids: Wm. B. Eerdman's Publishing Co., 1970.

_____. THE NEW DEMONS, Oxford: The Seabury Press,Inc., 1975.

_____. THE POLITICS OF GOD, AND THE POLITICS OF MAN, Grand Rapids: Wm. B. Eerdmans Publishing Co., 1972.

_____. THE TECHNOLOGICAL SOCIETY, New York: Alfred A. Knopf, Inc., 1964.

Lewis, C. S., MIRACLES, New York: MacMillan Publishing Co., 1947.

_____. SURPRISED BY JOY, New York: Harcourt, Brace & World, Inc., 1955.

_____. THE FOUR LOVES, New York: Harcourt, Brace, Jovanovich, Inc., 1960.

————. THE PROBLEM OF PAIN, New York: MacMillan Publishing Co., 1962.

MacDonald, Gordon, THE EFFECTIVE FATHER, Wheaton, IL: Tyndale House Publishers, Inc., 1977.

MacPherson, Dave, THE INCREDIBLE COVER-UP, Medford, OR: Alpha Omega Publishing Co., 1975.

North, Gary, THE JOURNAL OF CHRISTIAN RECONSTRUCTION, Fairfax Christian Bookstore, 11121 Pope's Head Road, Fairfax, VA 22030.

Rushdoony, Rousas John, THE ROOTS OF INFLATION, Vallecito, CA: Ross House Books, 1982.

Thieme, Jr., R. B., EDIFICATION COMPLEX OF THE SOUL, Houston: Berachah Tapes and Publications, 1972.

Freedom and Economic Prosperity: The Link Up

Ballvé, Faustina, ESSENTIALS OF ECONOMICS, Irvington-on-Hudson, NY: Foundation for Economic Education, 1963.

Friedman, Milton and Rose D., FREE TO CHOOSE, New York: Harcourt, Brace, Jovanovich, 1979.

Hazlitt, Henry, ECONOMICS IN ONE LESSON, New York: Manor Books, Inc., 1962.

North, Gary, AN INTRODUCTION TO CHRISTIAN ECONOMICS, Nutley, NJ: The Craig Press, 1974.

Rand, Ayn, CAPITALISM: THE UNKNOWN IDEAL, New York: Signet, 1967.

Roepke, Wilhelm, A HUMANE ECONOMY, Chicago: Henry Regnery Co., 1960.

————. ECONOMICS OF THE FREE SOCIETY, Chicago: Henry Regnery Co., 1963.

————. INTERNATIONAL ORDER AND ECONOMIC INTEGRATION, Dordrecht, Holland: D. Reidel Publishing Co., 1959.

Rothbard, Murray N., MAN, ECONOMY, STATE, Los Angeles: Nash Publishing, 1970.

Saussy, F. Tupper, THE MIRACLE ON MAIN STREET, Sewanee, TN: Spencer Judd, 1980.

Smith, Adam, THE WEALTH OF NATIONS, New York: E. P. Dutton & Co., 1971 (reprint).

Von Mises, Ludwig, HUMAN ACTION, Chicago: Henry Regnery Co., 1963.

Weaver, Henry Grady, THE MAINSPRING OF HUMAN PROGRESS, Irvington-on-Hudson, New York: The Foundation for Economic Education, 1953.

The Cults and Christianity

Lewis, Gordon R., CONFRONTING THE CULTS, Nutley, NJ: Presbyterian and Reformed Publishing Co., 1966.

Martin, Walter R., THE KINGDOM OF THE CULTS, Minneapolis: Bethany Fellowship, Inc., 1965.

The Occult and Christianity

Koch, Kurt, BETWEEN CHRIST AND SATAN, Grand Rapids: Kregel Publications, 1962.

_____. THE DEVIL'S ALPHABET, Grand Rapids: Kregel Publications, 1969.

North, Gary, NONE DARE CALL IT WITCHCRAFT, New Rochelle, NY: Arlington House, 1977.

The Occult, Conspiracy, Political and Financial Connection

Angebert, Jean-Michel, THE OCCULT AND THE THIRD REICH, New York: McGraw-Hill, 1975.

Billington, James H., FIRE IN THE MINDS OF MEN, New York: Basic Books, 1980.

Gunther, Max, WALL STREET AND WITCHCRAFT, New York: Bernard Geis Associates, 1971.

Multinational Debt Capitalism—Finance and Business (General)

Allen, Gary, NONE DARE CALL IT CONSPIRACY, Rossmoor, CA: Concord Press, 1971.

_____. THE ROCKEFELLER FILE, Seal Beach, CA: '76 Press, 1976.

Cohen, Jerry S. and Mintz, Morton, AMERICA, INC., New York: Dell Publishing Co., 1971.

Dinsmore, Herman H., THE BLEEDING OF AMERICA, Belmont, MA: Western Islands, 1974.

Griffin, Des, FOURTH REICH OF THE RICH, South Pasadena, CA: Emissary Publications, 1976.

Groseclose, Elgin, AMERICA'S MONEY MACHINE: THE STORY OF THE FEDERAL RESERVE, Westport, CT: Arlington House Publishers, 1966.

Gunther, Max, THE VERY, VERY RICH AND HOW THEY GOT THAT WAY, Chicago: Playboy Press, 1972.

Katz, David M., BANK CONTROL OF LARGE CORPORATIONS IN THE UNITED STATES, Berkeley: University of California Press, 1978.

Labor Party, U.S., DOPE, INC., New York: The New Benjamin Franklin House, 1978.

Morgan, Dan, MERCHANTS OF GRAIN, New York: The Viking Press, 1979.

Ney, Richard, THE WALL STREET JUNGLE, New York: Grove Press, Inc., 1970.

Sampson, Anthony, THE MONEY LENDERS, New York: The Viking Press, 1981.

Sutton, Antony C., THE WAR ON GOLD, Seal Beach, CA: '76 Press, 1977.

Tolf, Robert W., THE RUSSIAN ROCKEFELLERS, Stanford: Hoover Institution Press, 1976.

Multinational Debt Capitalism—Support of Communism

Sutton, Antony C., NATIONAL SUICIDE, New Rochelle, NY: Arlington House, 1973.

————. TECHNOLOGICAL TREASON, Phoenix: Research Publications, P. O. Box 39026, Phoenix, AZ, 85069, 1982.

The Military/Industrial Complex

Herbert, Anthony B., SOLDIER, New York: Holt, Rinehart and Winston, 1973.

Katz, Howard S., THE WARMONGERS, New York: Books in Focus, 1979.

Sampson, Anthony, THE ARMS BAZAAR, New York: Bantam Books, 1978.

Theobald, Robert A., THE FINAL SECRET OF PEARL HARBOR, Old Greenwich, CT: The Devin-Adair Co., 1954.

Multinational Oil

Blair, John M., THE CONTROL OF OIL, New York: Vintage Books, 1978.

Sampson, Anthony, THE SEVEN SISTERS, Des Plaines, IL: Bantam Books, Inc., 1976.

Stork, Joe, MIDDLE EAST OIL AND THE ENERGY CRISIS, New York: Monthly Review Press, 1975.

Sutton, Antony C., ENERGY: THE CREATED CRISIS, New York: Books in Focus, 1979.

Multinational Debt Capitalism—Political Intrigue and a One-World Empire

Griffin, Des, DESCENT INTO SLAVERY, South Pasadena, CA: Emissary Publications, 1980.

Hayek, Friedrick A., THE ROAD TO SERFDOM, Chicago: University of Chicago Press, 1944.

Knupffer, George, THE STRUGGLE FOR WORLD POWER, London: The Plain-Speaker Publishing Co., 1971.

Piekoff, Leonard, THE OMINOUS PARALLELS, New York: Stein and Day, 1982.

Quigley, Carroll, THE ANGLO-AMERICAN ESTABLISHMENT, New York: Books in Focus, 1981.

_____. TRAGEDY AND HOPE, Hollywood: Angriff Press, 1966.

Reisman, George, THE GOVERNMENT AGAINST THE ECONOMY, Ottawa, IL and Thornwood, NY: Caroline House Publishers, Inc., 1979.

Solzhenitsyn, Aleksandr I., THE GULAG ARCHIPELAGO, NY: Harper & Row, 1975.

Somoza, Anastasio, NICARAGUA BETRAYED, Belmont, MA: Western Islands, 1980.

Sutton, Antony C. and Wood, Patrick M., TRILATERALS OVER WASHINGTON, Scottsdale, AZ: The August Corporation, 1978.

_____. WALL STREET AND THE RISE OF HITLER, Seal Beach, CA: '76 Press, 1976.

The Media Whitewash

Cirino, Robert, DON'T BLAME THE PEOPLE, New York: Vintage Books, 1971.

Chayefsky, Paddy, NETWORK, New York: Pocket Books, 1976.

Fishman, Mark, MANUFACTURING THE NEWS, Austin: University of Texas Press, 1980.

Social Control and Society

Huntford, Roland, THE NEW TOTALITARIANS, New York: Stein and Day, 1972.

Rand, Ayn, ATLAS SHRUGGED, New York: Signet, 1957.

Sargant, William, BATTLE FOR THE MIND, New York: Harper & Row, 1957.

Schoeck, Helmut, ENVY, New York: Harcourt, Brace & World, 1966.

Weber, James A., GROW OR DIE!, New Rochelle: Arlington House, 1977.

Agriculture and Climate

Browning, Iben and Winkless, III, Nels, CLIMATE AND THE AFFAIRS OF MEN, New York: Harper's Magazine Press, 1975.

Carter, Vernon Gill and Dale, Tom, TOPSOIL & CIVILIZATION, Norman, OK: University of Oklahoma Press, 1982.

Walters, Jr., Charles, UNFORGIVEN, Raytown, MO: ACRES, U.S.A., Economics Library, 10008 E. 60th Terrace, 1971.

Time and Cyclical Perspectives

Dewey, Edward R., CYCLES, Pittsburgh: Foundation for the Study of Cycles, 1973.

Goodfield, June and Toulmin, Stephen, THE DISCOVERY OF TIME, Chicago: The University of Chicago Press, 1975.

McMaster, Jr., R. E., CYCLES OF WAR, Kalispell, MT: War Cycles Institute, 1977.

Steiger, Brad, A ROADMAP OF TIME, Englewood Cliffs, NJ: Prentice-Hall, Inc., 1975.

Spengler, Oswald, THE DECLINE OF THE WEST, New York: Alfred A. Knopf, 1926.

Technology and Future Potential

Bova, Ben, THE HIGH ROAD, Boston: Houghton Mifflin Co., 1981.

Carter, Joseph H., AWESOME FORCE, Cadake Industries, P. O. Box 9478, Winter Haven, Florida 33880, $14.95, 400pp.

Kahn, Herman, THE NEXT 200 YEARS, New York: Wm. Morrow and Co., 1976.

Norman, Colin, THE GOD THAT LIMPS, New York: W. W. Norton & Co., 1981.

Thompson, William Irwin, DARKNESS AND SCATTERED LIGHT, Garden City, New York: Anchor Press/Doubleday, 1978.

Toffler, Alvin, FUTURE SHOCK, New York: Bantam Books, Inc., 1971.

_____. THE ECO-SPASM REPORT, New York: Bantam Books, Inc., 1975.

Practical Interpersonal Perspectives

Gall, John, SYSTEMANTICS, New York: Pocket Books, 1978.

Hull, Raymond and Peter, Dr. Laurence J., THE PETER PRINCIPLE, New York: Wm. Morrow and Co., 1969.

Peter, Dr. Laurence J., THE PETER PLAN, New York: Wm. Morrow and Co., 1976.

_____. THE PETER PRESCRIPTION, New York: Bantam Books, 1972.

Schumacher, E. F., SMALL IS BEAUTIFUL, New York: Harper & Row, 1973.

Seabury, David, THE ART OF SELFISHNESS, New York: Pocket Books, 1974.

R. E. McMaster edits a weekly newsletter entitled "THE REAPER." For more information, please contact:

THE REAPER
P. O. Box 39026
Phoenix, AZ 85069

or call toll-free 1-800-528-0559.